MARK TWAIN IN ENGLAND

MARK TWAIN

ANDREW CHATTO

MARK TWAIN
IN
ENGLAND

By

Sydney Reginald

DENNIS WELLAND

HUMANITIES PRESS

Atlantic Highlands, N.J.

Published in Great Britain by
Chatto & Windus Ltd, London

*

Published in the U.S.A. by
Humanities Press, Inc. New Jersey

*

Published in Canada by
Clarke, Irwin & Co. Ltd, Toronto

Library of Congress Cataloging in Publication Data

Welland, Dennis Sydney Reginald.
  Mark Twain in England.
  Bibliography: p.
  Includes index.
  1. Clemens, Samuel Langhorne, 1835-1910 – Apprecia-
tion – England. 2. Authors and publishers – England.
3. Authors, American – 19th century – Biography.
I. Title.
PS1333.W4   1978   818'.4'09   77-17348
ISBN 0-391-00553-7

Printed and bound in Great Britain by
REDWOOD BURN LIMITED
Trowbridge & Esher

CONTENTS

ACKNOWLEDGEMENTS

This study has been based to a very considerable extent on correspondence between Mark Twain, his English publishers, and his English friends. The greater part of this correspondence is owned by the Mark Twain Papers in the University of California at Berkeley and by Messrs Chatto & Windus of London. Their generosity in allowing me unrestricted access to their holdings has alone made this book possible, and it is a pleasure to be able here to express my thanks to them. The other letters and manuscripts on which I have relied are the property of numerous libraries and a few private owners in Britain and the United States. At Appendix II I have calendared all the letters by Mark Twain and members of his family of which I have made use, identifying as accurately as possible their present owners. In view of this, I hope that those owners will not regard it as discourteous if, for convenience, I record my gratitude to them collectively at this point for allowing me to consult the material in their possession and to quote from it as necessary.

A high proportion of the letters discussed have not, to the best of my knowledge, previously appeared in print and they are therefore still protected by copyright. To avoid excessive and tedious footnoting, every letter cited in the text is followed in square brackets by the serial number allotted to it in Appendix II; when I know or believe that the letter or an extract from it is being reproduced for the first time that serial number is followed by an asterisk. Whenever an asterisk is used in the text of this book, therefore, the symbol indicates that the quotation immediately preceding it consists of previously unpublished words of Mark Twain which are copyright 1978 by Thomas G. Chamberlain and Manufacturers Hanover Trust Company as trustees u/w/o Clara Clemens Samossoud. I am grateful to Mr Chamberlain for permission to publish this material and for other help to me.

The collecting and assembling of this data has extended over many years and has brought me into contact with many Mark Twain scholars, amateur as well as professional. To try to identify them all or to acknowledge in detail their several contributions to the work would be impossible, but I am as grateful for their help and advice as I am for the pleasure their acquaintance has given me. The desirability of making two exceptions to this will be readily understood. No student of Mark

Twain in recent years can fail to have been influenced by the writings of Henry Nash Smith, but my debt to him is more personal: it was his seminar at the University of Minnesota in 1952 that first stimulated my interest in Mark Twain and on many occasions since then I have benefited from his knowledge, his suggestions, his encouragement and his friendship. His successor in charge of the Mark Twain Papers, Frederick Anderson, has also maintained a kindly and helpful interest in the progress of my work since its inception.

Some parts of this book are, in varying degrees, related to articles that I have published previously in the *Chicago Review*, the *Bulletin of the New York Public Library*, the *Journal of American Studies*, and *Art and Error* (1970) edited by Ronald Gottesman and Scott Bennett. Full references to these are given in the Notes, and I thank the editors concerned for permission to draw on these again.

My researches have been aided financially by grants from the Rockefeller Foundation of New York and from the University of Manchester, for which I am most grateful.

My final acknowledgements, if familiar, are certainly not perfunctory. Miss Sheila Pollock's cheerful patience at the typewriter went far beyond the bounds of duty on this, as on so many other pieces of work. My wife, with equal fortitude, has willingly undertaken all those irritating tasks that fall to the partners of academics — providing a critical audience for ideas and theories in embryo, removing from successive drafts obscurities and infelicities, reading proofs, and, most crucial of all, giving in so many ways help and encouragement when both were most needed.

INTRODUCTION

Scope, Aims and Documentation

The title of this book is deliberately ambivalent: my concern is less with biography than with the publishing and reception of Mark Twain's works in England, but his visits to and connections with Britain necessarily form part of the story. Its starting point is the recognition of a special relationship between Mark Twain and his British readers: they did not always read him in the same texts as his fellow-countrymen did; they evaluated his work differently; and his regard for them was neither negligible nor exclusively commercial. To the extent that these topics have been hitherto discussed at all, the discussion has been based on incomplete and not always reliable evidence, impressions, and, at times, misunderstandings.

In attempting to correct the perspective I have drawn on a large body of material, much of which has not been utilized before, and large parts of which are geographically dispersed through Britain and the United States. There may well be some items that I have missed; there are certainly many that have disappeared. What has survived, however, has not only taken time to locate and correlate but has, in its abundance, presented sizeable problems of organization and many alluring distractions into attractive by-ways of research. The subject remains, however, too big to be treated exhaustively in this compass: a full account, for example, of the publishing history of every one of Mark Twain's books in Britain would be of limited interest to all but the specialist bibliographer or editor and could have been provided only at the cost of excluding the narrative and biographical elements that seem to me so relevant to the topic.

Several books that have appeared while I have been working on this subject have in some ways made my task easier. Howard Baetzhold's *Mark Twain and John Bull*, for example, by its discussion of Clemens's contacts with and changing views of Britain, enables me to cover this ground more selectively than would otherwise have been necessary; his treatment of Clemens's familiarity with and debts to English literature is particularly valuable. Baetzhold's scholarship has allowed me to develop more fully the relationship between Mark Twain and his British publishers that lies at the centre of my interest. Hamlin Hill's *Mark Twain's Letters to His Publishers 1867-1894* deals very thoroughly with the American side of the subject and in that respect complements my own work (which in turn corrects Hill on some British aspects). Cross-reference to letters published by Hill, and by Lewis Leary in *Mark Twain's Correspondence with Henry Huttleston Rogers 1893-1909* (also in the invaluable 'Mark Twain Papers' series), obviates the necessity of printing their texts here; the same is true of the British reviews reproduced in Frederick Anderson's *Mark Twain: The Critical Heritage*. Similarly, the California/Iowa definitive edition of the Works of Mark Twain will be a more appropriate place than this for a detailed and comprehensive collation of the texts, British and American, of individual titles.

A topic such as mine can only be treated adequately when there are very full records of the dealings between author and publisher. For the greater part of his career Mark Twain published with Chatto & Windus. The originals of many of their letters to him are available in American libraries (notably, of course, among the Mark Twain Papers in the University of California at Berkeley) and a few have appeared in print. My advantage, however, has lain in access to the copies of their entire correspondence with him in the firm's letter-books; for this privilege I am especially grateful to Ian M. Parsons, Mrs Norah Smallwood and their colleagues.

Had the firm retained all Mark Twain's letters to them as meticulously as they have preserved their own records, it would have been very useful. That they did not do so is paradoxically attributable to the high esteem in which they held Clemens: his personal friendship with Andrew Chatto (another aspect of my main narrative) led to many of his letters being regarded as belonging among Andrew Chatto's own papers rather than in the archives of the house. Consequently, after Chatto's death in 1913, they came into the possession of his daughter, Mrs Isabel Brocklesby, and were sold by her at Sotheby's on 29 June 1916 along with many other autograph letters, manuscripts, and a few books, from her father's collection. At least thirteen of the lots comprised or contained Mark Twain items: the catalogue makes it clear that there were more than 105 such pieces as well as two parcels of others. Many of these can be identified as autograph letters now in American collections, though the sale catalogue is naturally not specific enough for identification to be possible in every case. A significant number of Mark Twain's letters did, however, remain in the firm's possession and a few in the Chatto family's: by being allowed to draw on these I have been greatly helped in the piecing together that this study attempts. Nevertheless, even if all the letters had survived intact, the many transactions carried on orally between Chatto and Clemens on his visits to London, or between Chatto and Clemens's representatives, would still have been matters of speculation: the full story cannot be definitively reconstructed.

I say 'story' because my aim has been to present the material in a narrative as coherent and readable as possible. At the same time I am conscious of having drawn on material that other scholars will wish to consult, the whereabouts of which they will need to know. I have, at p.7 and in Appendix II, made acknowledgement of the help I have received from the many owners, public and private, of the material I have used. The problem remained of how to cite the authority for every statement in the text without overwhelming the less specialist reader with superfluous information or distracting him with a plethora of reference numbers. The solution I have adopted needs a brief explanation, amplifying a little what has been said in the Acknowledgements. I have, at Appendix II, provided a simple self-explanatory calendar of all the letters by Mark Twain, his wife, and his daughters, on which I have drawn. These are numbered serially, and an allusion to any letter in the text is immediately followed by its serial number in square brackets; an asterisk following the number indicates a copyright quotation of hitherto unpublished words by Mark Twain. The scholar seeking verification can, therefore, by consulting the calendar, immediately find the date of the letter, its recipient, its present owner, and where it has been previously published. The square brackets and their contents will, I believe, quickly become invisible to the reader concentrating on the narrative. The device is intended to minimise the bulk and the repetitiveness of the notes that would otherwise be necessary and to be very sparing with the sometimes irritating use of superior numerals in the text to refer to notes at the back that may or may not be of interest. Where such numerals occur, they are for one purpose only: to provide a finding reference for material other than Mark Twain letters that has been used. No reader, therefore, need be distracted into constant turning to the back of the book for fear of missing in a note some development of the argument.

In all extracts from letters, Mark Twain's and others, I have followed the original manuscript in spelling, punctuation, abbreviations and ampersands, even when these are at variance with modern usage. I hope that this statement of policy and practice will justify my reluctance to litter the text with more 'sic's than are absolutely indispensable.

I have not thought it necessary to identify precisely each of the hundreds of letters from John Camden Hotten, Andrew Chatto, and other members of their firms that I have consulted. Copies of all of these are in the possession of Chatto & Windus in the letter-books to which I have already alluded. This pre-Xerox method of duplication consisted of a quarto volume containing 1,000 serially numbered and specially treated flimsy leaves. The original manuscript (or, later, typescript) was placed face upwards under the dampened leaf, pressure was applied from above with a hot iron, and the impression thus left on the underside of the leaf was (and in most cases still is) quite legible through it. As most letters were on octavo paper two could be copied side by side on each leaf, and each book might thus contain up to two thousand communications. Addressees were listed alphabetically in an index in each volume, the serial number of each letter being then entered against the name.

Not the least interesting aspect of the research that has gone into this book has been the acquaintance one has made with the day-to-day business of a Victorian publisher, and I have tried to convey something of the flavour of this in the book. I have also tabulated, at Appendix I, publication particulars of every Mark Twain title issued by this house. There is, I believe, a great deal more of such work that could usefully be done in respect of other authors and other houses.

Manchester, 1977   DENNIS WELLAND

CHAPTER 1

MARK TWAIN, HOTTEN,
AND ROUTLEDGE

I

In the summer of 1873 a London publishing house changed hands on
the death of its proprietor. The business was bought for £25,000 by a
junior member of the firm, Andrew Chatto, who took into partnership
with him a minor poet named W.E. Windus. Chatto was the dominant
figure and it was he who ran the business, guided its policy and dealt
with its authors. As early as 25 November 1873, knowing that Samuel
Langhorne Clemens was in London, he wrote to him, introducing himself and naming 'Mr Bierce, Mr Tom Hood, and Mr. Stoddard' as having
promised to recommend him. He continued 'I am sincerely anxious to
establish more cordial relations as between Author & Publisher, than
have hitherto existed, between yourself and our firm'. Neither Chatto
nor Clemens could foresee how cordial those relations were to become,
and Clemens probably paid little attention to the letter. Not only had
he a perfectly satisfactory publishing arrangement with the London
house of Routledge, but he was unlikely to be attracted to a firm whose
lately-deceased head he had once called 'the missing link between man
and the hyena'.[1] Andrew Chatto's predecessor was, in fact, the
notorious John Camden Hotten whose unscrupulous piratical publishing
activities had earned for him many enemies besides Mark Twain, and
Clemens probably read Chatto's communication with amused
scepticism.

Yet two years and two months later he was to establish with Chatto
& Windus a business relationship which continued until his death, and
as time passed he was to develop for Andrew Chatto as a man a respect
that ripened into friendship. It would be too much to expect so volatile
a personality as Clemens not to have had occasional differences with his
publisher, but Chatto & Windus was the only publishing house, English
or American, with whom he published continuously for the greater part
of his creative life and with whom, for more than thirty-five years until
his death, he remained completely satisfied. They, in turn, remained
proud of him, and when in 1955 they celebrated the centenary of
Hotten's foundation of the firm by publishing an anthology of their
writers' work, *Huckleberry Finn* was one of the three novels that were
included in their entirety, when more than sixty other distinguished

missing completion

This mutual satisfaction is the more remarkable in the light of some of Mark Twain's celebrated and corrosive animadversions against publishers in general and many publishers in particular. In an after-dinner speech to the Authors' Club in London in June 1899 he told his audience: 'It is service to an author to have a lawyer. There is something so disagreeable in having a personal contact with a publisher. So it is better to work through a lawyer – and lose your case'.[2] His tongue must have been well in his cheek, for his visit to London on this occasion, as on so many others, had been entirely arranged by Chatto & Windus who secured a suite at the Prince of Wales Hotel, had 'an exquisite basket of roses and orchids' [292-6] in the room for Mrs Clemens on her arrival, traced his baggage which was delayed on the way from Vienna, and extended to Clemens a warm invitation to join them 'often at our frugal luncheon'. Far from his retaining a lawyer to save him contact with his publishers, it was his publishers who were currently retaining a lawyer to recover for Mark Twain a fee that was owed him by a recalcitrant editor.

He went on to tell the Authors' Club: 'I understand the publishers have been meeting together also like us. I don't know what for, but possibly they are devising new and mysterious ways for remunerating authors'. There was nothing mysterious about the ways in which Chatto & Windus had been remunerating him for nearly a quarter of a century by that date, although there had been an element of newness about it at one time: long before any international copyright law had existed between America and the rest of the world, Chatto and he had evolved a successful system for securing his rights in the United States, England, Canada and Europe. Clemens's long and vigorous campaign on both sides of the Atlantic for the protection of authors against pirates had not been dictated by mere self-interest, for his income from English publication had for many years been a very comfortable one – 'gaudy' was his own word for it [89] – and he had never had any serious grounds for complaint against his English publishers.

Mark Twain's relations with his English publishers are very well documented in letters and papers of which little use has hitherto been made, and it is in the study of these that this book takes its origin. It is not, however, intended as a conventional publishing history, although it may well throw incidental light on some aspects of the nineteenth-century book trade. What becomes plain from these sources is that Mark Twain's cultivation of a British audience was more deliberate and more extensive than is sometimes supposed and may be seen on occasions to have had a direct influence on his writing. It affected, and was affected by, his attitude towards Great Britain, which was always more complex than some writers have suggested. It brought him new friends, American as well as British, and introduces a side of his biography insufficiently explored so far. As a personality but even more as a great

American writer, Mark Twain has to be seen against an international background. It is with areas such as these that this book is concerned.

II

Mark Twain was introduced to the British reading public by Routledge & Sons, a London house that had begun by selling cheap and second-hand books in the Leicester Square area. Its founder, George Routledge, was a native of Cumberland. His enterprise and initiative took the firm to larger premises in Soho Square in 1845 when it extended its activities to reprints and remainders and then to the cheap editions which, because of their popularity with travellers, the Victorians knew as 'railway literature'. Forerunners of the modern paper-back libraries, these books sold at a shilling and were distributed through W.H. Smith's bookstalls on railway stations as well as through other agencies. Among the American authors printed by Routledge in this form were Washington Irving, Fenimore Cooper and Harriet Beecher Stowe, whose *Uncle Tom's Cabin* was reputed to have sold half a million copies. The house also had a good reputation for more expensive editions, especially illustrated volumes, and had brought out the first English editions of works by Prescott and Longfellow. This interest in American authors may have been one reason for Routledge's opening a New York branch as early as 1854. By the 1860's it was located at 416 Broome Street and the New York agent was Joseph L. Blamire. It was no doubt Blamire who brought to Routledge's notice the little book published in May 1867 by C.H. Webb entitled *The Celebrated Jumping Frog of Calaveras County, and Other Sketches* by Mark Twain, edited by 'John Paul', (a pseudonym for Webb).

There was already a taste for American humour in England, fostered largely by the popularity of Artemus Ward in the columns of *Punch* and on the lecture platform. His early death at Southampton in March of that year had left a void which Routledge may have hoped this new writer would fill; the copyright position was so fluid that no author's permission was either needed or, perhaps, sought at this stage. The book appeared in a form that was to become standard for Mark Twain's English editions for some years. Less lavish than the American, it had no bevelled cloth-cover, no goldstamped frog; instead, a somewhat garishly-coloured pictorial wrapper portrayed the eponymous hero, while the text was competently set in easily legible type on unpretentious paper. It was reviewed on 19 October 1867 in the 'Our Library Table' feature in *Fun*, a rival to *Punch* which Tom Hood was then editing, as 'one of the funniest books we have met with for a long time'. After explaining that 'Mark Twain' was a *'nom de plume*, like ARTEMUS WARD or ORPHEUS C. KERR' it praised the title story as 'too long to tell here and too good to spoil by curtailment'. It continued, with a printer's error particularly amusing in its context:

There are no misspellings, no contortions of words in Mark Swain; his fun is entirely dependent upon the inherent humour in his writings. And although many jokers have sent us *brochures* like the present from the other side of the Atlantic, we have had no book fuller of more genuine or more genial fun.

In 1868 Routledge published 'Cannibalism in the Cars' in his magazine *The Broadway*, and it may be this that Clemens had in mind in 1898 when, writing to Richard Gilder, he recalled his satisfaction at an occasion '31 years ago, when a now forgotten London magazine went down into its treasury and paid me $12.50 per mag page for a 4-page article' [272*]. If so, it was probably the beginning of his formal connexion with Routledges. He was certainly in touch with them by 1870 because on 3 March he instructed his Hartford publisher, Elisha Bliss, to send a complimentary copy of *The Innocents Abroad* to their New York office; he added that he had been in correspondence with them about obtaining British copyright [1]. If the complimentary was intended as bait Blamire does not appear to have risen to it, but Mark Twain clearly had aspirations towards an English market. 'Have you heard yet what the possibilities are in the matter of selling our book there?' he asked Bliss in a letter only a week later [2*]; but Bliss, who knew the American subscription trade well enough, was less familiar with techniques for promoting English sales.

III

Someone who was expert in this field, however, was quicker than Routledge to see the book's possibilities, and it was over the imprint of John Camden Hotten that it made its first British appearance in the summer of 1870. A Londoner of Cornish extraction, Hotten was an energetic and enterprising publisher who operated from premises in the more fashionable area, Piccadilly, on a site where the Ritz Hotel now stands. His diversity of interests and his frequently unscrupulous methods make him a very difficult figure to assess, but his importance in Victorian publishing as well as in the promotion of Mark Twain deserves fuller comment. To Clemens himself, to his secretary and biographer, Albert Bigelow Paine, and to his first bibliographer, Merle Johnson, Hotten was anathema (as indeed he was to many others), but their view of him was distinctly one-sided. Recognising this, a more recent scholar, Dewey Ganzel, has made a spirited attempt to restore the balance in an essay which, for all its vigour, goes unfortunately too far in the opposite direction.[3]

One cannot lightly dismiss a publisher who, dying at the age of forty-three, left behind him a flourishing business and a reputation as a scholar and antiquarian; the full list of his original works, because of his fondness for pseudonyms, can never be definitively established. Mr Ganzel rightly draws attention to Hotten's *Slang Dictionary*, his monumental *Handbook of Topography and Family History of England and Wales* with its annotated survey of 20,000 books, his histories of playing-cards and of sign-boards, and his many other historical and biographical writings and miscellaneous compilations. Hotten's lists reflect a publishing interest even wider than this, and he deserves full credit for taking over Swinburne's *Poems and Ballads* when the house of Moxon, fearing scandal, withdrew it from sale without consulting or compensating the author. However, what to posterity looks like the fearless championing and early recognition of a great poet probably looked to contemporaries rather differently. One side of Hotten's publishing and book-selling business was distinctly shady, as may be seen from Swinburne's now-published letters to him about books on flagellation, and it may have been the notoriety as much as the literary merit of *Poems and Ballads* that attracted him. There is no point in glossing over Hotten's ventures- in pornography, but neither should they be exaggerated or distorted: they reflect only one aspect of that sensibility to public demand that made him so successful.

Another aspect was his awareness of the market for humorous writing, especially American. He had spent eight years in the United States, going there with his brother at the age of sixteen, and he had obviously retained his contacts there as well as developing his flair for what would sell. He had spawned his own *Jumping Frog* by 1870, euphemising piracy by the bland statement 'from the Original Edition' on the title-page, and beginning the rivalry with Routledge that was to become acrimonious in a few years.

When *The Innocents Abroad* came into his hands he was not merely quicker than Routledge to recognise its value but was particularly well placed to exploit it. He was printing at that time a two-volume memoir of Artemus Ward by Edward P. Hingston, the English companion of the dead humorist, entitled *The Genial Showman*. Remembering from this a description of Ward's first meeting with Clemens in 1864 at the offices of the *Territorial Enterprise* in Virginia City, at which Hingston had been present, Hotten solicited from him an introduction to the English two-volume edition of *The Innocents Abroad*. The first of these was entitled *The Innocents Abroad : The Voyage Out*, and the second (which followed in October, 1870), *The New Pilgrim's Progress : The Journey Home*; the division occurred between Chapters 31 and 32.

Hingston presents Clemens as

> a flower of the wilderness tinged with the colour of the soil, the man of thought and the man of action rolled into one, humorist and hard-worker, Momus in a felt-hat and jack-boots . . . whose residence upon the fringe of civilization had allowed his humour to develop without restraint and his speech to be racily idiomatic.

One slip makes Orion Clemens Sam's father instead of his brother (*The*

Genial Showman states the relationship correctly), but Hingston's
rugged Western humorist was the Mark Twain who captured the British
imagination. Beyond praising the aptness of the Innocent as a personifi-
cation of Mark Twain the traveller and commending the spontaneity of
his response to Europe, Hingston is little concerned with literary
criticism, although in *The Genial Showman* he had described him as
'destined to distinguish himself in American literature'. 'John Paul'
introducing *The Jumping Frog* had paid tribute to Mark Twain's
avoidance of 'tricks of spelling' and 'rhetorical buffoonery' as well as to
his 'quaint similes, keen satire, and hard good sense'. Hingston recalls
that book as having been 'highly praised by Mr Tom Hood in the pages
of *Fun*' but he does not follow Hood in trying to define Mark Twain's
humour; he does not, for example, extend his reference to Clemens's
racily idiomatic speech into a comment on his prose style. Already
interest is being focused on Mark Twain as a funny man rather than as
an artist, and the demand for his short sketches flourished.

In 1871 Routledge brought out a sixpenny edition of *Mark Twain's
(Burlesque) Autobiography and First Romance*, possibly by arrangement with the author, who wrote to Bliss in June:

> Have you heard anything from Routledge? Considering the
> large English sale he made of one of my other books (Jumping
> Frog), I thought may be we might make something if I could give
> him a secure copyright. [3]

Hotten also issued an edition of this, including in it the apocryphal 'On
Children' and advertising it, with no apparent justification, as 'Author's
edition, containing twice as much as any other'. In the same year he
reissued the 'Autobiography' and the 'Romance', together with twenty-
five other sketches, as *Eye Openers: Good Things, Immensely Funny
Sayings & Stories that will bring a smile upon the gruffest countenance*.
A few weeks later came *Screamers: A Gathering of Scraps of Humour,
Delicious Bits & Short Stories*, another Mark Twain miscellany by the
industrious Hotten.

Screamers was reviewed belatedly and with some asperity in the
Spectator on 18 May 1872. The anonymous reviewer saw the humour
as less subtle than that of 'Bret Harte and Colonel John Hay and
Artemus Ward' and lacking their 'political and social irony'; nevertheless, recognising that Mark Twain might have an especial appeal 'in
countries where the politics, manners, customs, and tone of thought of
Americans are comparatively little known', he attempted a critical
assessment:

> The secret of his fun lies in the assumed childlike credulity with
> which he accepts the premises offered, and the real ability and
> assumed simplicity with which he follows them up to their logical
> but utterly absurd conclusions.

Yet, though containing 'a fair amount of excellent nonsense', the book seemed to him 'rather a hotch-potch, and of very unequal merit'; he found some 'amusing, though rather pointless satire', some pieces 'of a very vulgar type' and 'one or two . . . . such extravagant rubbish that they incline one to throw the book to the other end of the room'. He concluded sternly 'In a future edition, we trust Mark Twain will carefully weed out the vulgar papers, and the extravaganzas, and the nosense as distinguished from the nonsense'.

Routledge at once wrote to the *Spectator* to say that they were bringing out an authorised volume of Sketches that week and adding

> The Author's advertisement, which will be found in your advertizing columns, will explain the "unequal merit" of the papers in the volume called *Screamers*, many of which he had never seen till he found them fathered upon him in this collection.[4]

The letter was not published but its contents formed the basis of an editorial disclaimer in the issue of 1 June. Meanwhile the issue of 25 May had carried an advertisement by Routledge of a shilling edition of *A Curious Dream and Other Sketches* and an announcement of the Author's English Edition of his Sketches; it included the 'Author's Advertisement' referred to, which was subsequently prefixed to the volume:

> Messrs George Routledge and Sons are the only English publishers who pay me any copyright on my books. That is something; but a courtesy which I prize even more, is the opportunity which they have given me to edit and revise the matter for publication myself. This enables me to leave out a good deal of literature which has appeared in England over my name, but which I never wrote. And, as far as this particular volume is concerned, it also enables me to add a number of sketches which I *did* write, but which have not heretofore been published abroad. This book contains all of my sketches which I feel at all willing to father.
>
> Mark Twain
>
> Hartford 1872

Hotten was not slow to reply. On 5 June he wrote to the *Spectator* claiming that he had published as Mark Twain's nothing 'which has not already been published in the United States or elsewhere under *this* signature, or under that of "Carl Byng", another *nom de plume* of the same author'. Routledge's new collection of *Sketches* he attacked as 'simply my own revised editions transposed . . . and the stories in the "Jumping Frog" volume sorted in', instancing textual changes made by him and retained by Routledge. Publishing this letter on 8 June, the *Spectator* omitted a postscript in which the unregenerate Hotten

promised the publication of further fugitive pieces by Twain, but they
added this editorial note:

> All we can say is, that we have ourselves seen marked as
> "spurious" in what is alleged to be, and we believe to be, Mark
> Twain's own writing, one of the Essays in Mr Hotten's edition,
> and that we are told there are four or five more marked in the
> same way; and that we know on the same authority (Mark
> Twain's own handwriting) that Messrs Routledge's edition is
> revised by himself, and that he has received some payment for it
> by the publishers.

IV

There the matter might have rested, and indeed did rest for three
months until Clemens himself was in England. Merle Johnson flatters
the Piccadilly bookseller by describing this as 'a special trip' undertaken
because 'Hotten's activities became so pronounced'.[5] Clemens had no
legal redress against Hotten whose piracies could not be affected by the
author's presence in Britain. The author's presence could, however, be
conveniently publicised by reviving the press controversy over those
piracies, and this is exactly what Clemens did in a letter to the
Spectator dated 'London, September 20, 1872'.

Mr Ganzel rightly describes the letter as 'not so much a complaint as
a commercial' and justifiably draws attention to its many inaccuracies,
but I think he is mistaken in speaking of it as written 'in a style more
angry than humorous'. An angry man would have intervened in the
correspondence three months earlier, and in a different key from this.
It is also curious that Clemens confines his censures to two books that
had been on the market a year already. Had he really wished to
discredit Hotten or had he, as Hotten was to claim, been instigated by
Hotten's enemies, there was much better ammunition more
immediately available. Hotten had just issued another collection under
the unwieldy but deliberately ambiguous title *Practical Jokes with
Artemus Ward Including the Story of the Man Who Fought Cats by
Mark Twain and Other Humourists*. This volume certainly attributed to
Mark Twain pieces of doubtful authorship and it seems highly likely
that the 'Other Humourists' included Hotten himself writing 'fillers',
yet Clemens ignores it entirely and instead writes as follows:

> Sir,
>   I only venture to intrude upon you because I come, in some
> sense, in the interest of public morality, and this makes my
> mission respectable. Mr John Camden Hotten, of London, has, of
> his own individual notion, republished several of my books in
> England. I do not protest against this, for there is no law that
> could give effect to the protest; and, besides, publishers are not
> accountable to the laws of heaven and earth in any country, as I

understand it. But my little grievance is this: My books are bad
enough just as they are written; then what must they be after Mr
John Camden Hotten has composed half-a-dozen chapters and
added the same to them? I feel that all true hearts will bleed for
an author whose volumes have fallen under such a dispensation as
this. If a friend of yours, or even if you yourself, were to write a
book and set it adrift among the people, with the gravest appre-
hension that it was not up to what it ought to be intellectually,
how would you like to have John Camden Hotten sit down and
stimulate his powers, and drool two or three original chapters on
to the end of that book? Would not the world seem cold and
hollow to you? Would you not feel that you wanted to die and be
at rest? Little the world knows of true suffering. And suppose he
should entitle these chapters "Holiday Literature", "True Story
of Chicago", "On Children", "Train up a Child, and Away he
Goes", and "Vengeance", and then, on the strength of having
evolved these marvels from his own consciousness, go and "copyright" the entire book, and put in the title-page a picture of a
man with his hand in another man's pocket, and the legend "All
Rights Reserved". (I only *suppose* the picture: still it would be
rather a neat thing.) And, further, suppose that in the kindness of
his heart and the exuberance of his untaught fancy, this
thoroughly well-meaning innocent should expunge the modest
title which you had given your book, and replace it with so foul
an invention as this, "Screamers and Eye-Openers", and went and
got *that* copyrighted too. And suppose that on top of all this, he
continually and persistently forgot to offer you a single penny or
even send you a copy of your mutilated book to burn. Let one
suppose all this. Let him suppose it with strength enough, and
then he will know something about woe. Sometimes when I read
one of these additional chapters constructed by John Camden
Hotten, I feel as if I wanted to take a broom-straw and go and
knock that man's brains out. Not in anger, for I feel none. Oh!
not in anger; but only to see, that is all. Mere idle curiosity.

And Mr Hotten says that one *nom de plume* of mine is "Carl
Byng". I hold that there is no affliction in the world that makes a
man feel so down-trodden and abused as the giving him a name
that does not belong to him. How would this sinful aborigine feel
if I were to call him John Camden Hottentot, and come out in
the papers and say he was entitled to it by divine right? I do
honestly believe it would throw him into a brain-fever, if there
were not an insuperable obstacle in the way.

Yes — to come back to the original subject, which is the
sorrow that is slowly but surely undermining my health — Mr
Hotten prints unrevised, uncorrected, and in some respects,
spurious books, with my name to them as author, and thus
embitters his customers against one of the most innocent of men.
Messrs George Routledge and Sons are the only English publishers
who pay me any copyright, and therefore, if my books are to

disseminate either suffering or crime among readers of our language, I would ever so much rather they did it through that house, and then I could contemplate the spectacle calmly as the dividends came in. — I am, Sir,

Samuel L. Clemens ("Mark Twain")
London, September 20, 1872.

Conspicuous in this, surely, is the over-statement of the emotional effect the piracy is supposed to produce, the affectation of outraged morality, the denigration of the original as 'not up to what it ought to be intellectually', 'bad enough just as [it is] written' and disseminating 'either suffering or crime'; and the twice-used joke that the opponent has no brain. This is closer to the rhetoric of the frontier boast than to the rhetoric of a genuinely angry man: had Clemens really wished to join issue with Hotten he would have done it more pithily, without the extravagant emotional indulgence and without the elaborate obliqueness of hypothesis in the sustained 'just suppose' construction. Significantly he does not actually repudiate the 'Carl Byng' pseudonym but artfully creates the impression of doing so. The whole piece is an adroit, even cynical, 'puff' disguised as invective, as becomes transparent in the final paragraph, and an exercise in comic writing almost exhibitionist in nature.

Interestingly, the victim seems to have recognised this more quickly than some of the author's friends and champions. He replied in kind, in the *Spectator* of 28 September. Too long to quote in its entirety, Hotten's reply begins 'It was unkind of Mark Twain to write you that note last week concerning myself', refers to the correspondence of June and draws attention to the similarity between his text and Routledge's: 'the punctuation, English orthography, and even our printer's errors all appeared in the new "author's revised version" in a way that was simply marvellous'. Hotten goes on to deny 'in the interest of common sense' his own authorship of any of these sketches:

Mark Twain instances five papers as my composition. Whether American humourists as fathers are different to other men I cannot say, but in this instance Mark Twain has forgotten his own children. Three of these stories appeared in his own paper, the *Buffalo Express*, and the others were very generally circulated under his name without a single denial appearing. Anyone interested in the authorship can see the American originals at my office.

He disposes similarly of Clemens's equivocal denial of the 'Carl Byng' pseudonym and continues as follows:

But his taste for many *noms de plume* was curiously displayed only the other day. When Mark Twain called upon me with one of the greatest humourists of Fleet Street I gave the former a hearty welcome as "Mr Clemens, the famous Mark Twain", but observing that he looked glumpy his companion took me on one side, and in a hurried manner explained to me that Mr. Twain would be much better pleased if addressed as "Mr Bryce". I did so and he seemed greatly cheered up. We talked of the old and modern schools of humour, and after accepting a little book as a present "Mr Bryce" left me, and made his way back to Fleet Street.

The inference seems unmistakeable: Hotten is asking the reader to see the whole thing as an elaborate charade to which he is a consenting party as long as the basic rules are observed. It was only 'unkind' of Mark Twain to write the letter to the *Spectator* because the liberty it took with facts was bending the rules of the game; once the record is put straight the game can continue if that is how Mark Twain wants things, but one more fact has to be stated:

I have in three years written thrice to Mr Clemens, but never received one answer. As late as January I wrote offering equitable payment for any work he might do for me, and the editor of my English edition of the *Innocents Abroad* has also, I believe, been unable to get an answer. To any American authors who may either write or edit for me, I will make payment to the best of my ability; but if it is left for me to gather up newspaper trifles, trifles cast off and forgotten, and left to me to obtain a market for their sale in a collected form, with the cheerful probability of another edition appearing at one sixth of my price, – for such non-copyright raw material liable to such a contingency I am not prepared to pay anything, and I do not think any man in his senses would pay.
When Bret Harte's agent called upon me a few days since with a new copyright story we at once came to terms.
                                                                    John Camden Hotten

At its face value this seems to represent Hotten as the zealous business man, conscientious and misunderstood, but basically fair-minded. Taking his cue from Clemens, he even works in a puff for his edition of *The Innocents Abroad*, but keeps the discussion on a civilised level without rancour or abuse. His familiarity with the *Buffalo Express* and, implicitly, other American publications inspires a not-undeserved confidence. Unfortunately neither the case nor Hotten was as straightforward as the letter suggests.

Mr Ganzel is right in seeing some disingenuousness in Clemens's accusation that Hotten had pirated a *book* of his, but, although Hotten had certainly had the job of collecting these 'newspaper trifles' for his book, we now know (as will be seen in the next chapter) that Clemens had for nearly two years been trying to induce his American publisher to bring out a book of his collected sketches, so his deception is a little more venial. Routledge had already made it clear that at least one other 'man in his senses would pay' for the right to publish such a collection, and Hotten's alleged attempts to establish a business relationship earlier with Clemens are not wholly above suspicion. Nor were his dealings with Bret Harte and his agent quite as equitable as his final paragraph implies. Harte told Clemens the story in a letter three months later:

> You wrote me from London that you had heard that Osgood had taken £50 from Hotten and given him the copyright of my new book. I believe Osgood did it for the best, but as I had no idea of condoning that pirate Hotten's offenses for £50, I repudiated it at once. I told Osgood not to send him advanced sheets of my new story and to say that Mr Harte annulled the contract. He did so — and I see by the Spectator that Hotten has quietly reproduced all the book except that story, without ever paying the £50; and further has had the advantage of his previous announcement that he was "authorized by Mr Harte" &c. Further, the book contains somebody else's story foisted upon me.[6]

Yet Hotten's conduct could on occasion be more honourable than was publicly suggested. I have, for example, demonstrated this elsewhere in respect of his role in the abortive project, early in the 1870s, to publish in England a two-volume edition of Emerson's uncollected essays.[7] The sharpness of his epistolary style, however, in that affair and in others inevitably made enemies for him. To Henry Curwen, for instance, whose *History of Booksellers: the Old and the New* Chatto & Windus were to publish after Hotten's death, he sent a letter containing this passage:

> You wrote to me some time since, but in such an objectionable manner that I felt it did *not* deserve a reply. You and I could get on very well, but I can't stand cockiness — and I know very few people who can.

Curwen's reply is not available for quotation but can be readily imagined.

V

Beyond making it clear that Hotten was a tricky customer to deal with, all this does not put Clemens wholly in the right in his *Spectator* attack on the publisher. With the indefatigable resilience characteristic of him, Hotten still did not give up. On 1 November we find him writing to a Charles Watkins in an attempt to buy photographs of Mark Twain:

> Well, what *is* your price per doz and per 100 to a poor but honest bookseller?
> If you have an autograph of Mark Twain I wish you wd. send

it to me by bearer. I *will faithfully return* it in the morning. *I am a student of caligraphy.* [sic]

So eclectic were Hotten's interests that calligraphy may well have been among them, but one suspects that his interest in the autograph was more commercial than scholarly.

The next day he wrote to the Editor of *The Nation*, taking advantage of its being published in New York to be more maliciously outspoken than he had been in *The Spectator*:

> I have always believed the *Nation* to be a fair and manly paper, and when I saw, the other day, that the editor had given the substance of Mark Twain's attack upon me — an attack made at the instigation of a London publisher who had given him £10 — without waiting for my reply, I knew that the editor would also give my letter, or an abstract of it, when it appeared.

Enclosing a copy of his *Spectator* letter, he asked for it to be given the same prominence as the original complaint, a request that he may have regretted when he saw how fully *The Nation* acceded to it. On 10 October an editorial comment had described Hotten as American by birth: 'nobody but a Yankee would have practised sinful games such as Mr Hotten has been recently practising, and not for the first time either'. Mark Twain, it continued, had sent to the *Spectator* 'a letter which we assure that journal contains jokes', but they summarised its contents and spoke of 'a grievance for which Mr Clemens should have redress'.

On 21 November the *Nation* summarised Hotten's reply, ignoring the allusion to the £10, but claiming to find the logic of his argument difficult to understand. Gleefully alluding to the 'Mr Bryce' episode, they suggested that Hotten might have realised he was being made a fool of, and recounted an Artemus Ward story of a similar joke. Their conclusion was a fair one that puts Hotten's conduct in a fresh light:

> Perhaps Mr. Hotten ought to have reflected that some writers resent as an injury the gathering up of unconsidered trifles which they choose to disown and forget; and that being angered thereby they decline to answer his letters, and think it fair to attack him in ways not sanctioned by the usual laws of war. We do not know, but we suggest this as a solution to Mr. Clemens's indignation.

Moreover, they had a quarrel of their own with the unfortunate Hotten too: in the *Spectator* of 12 October he had advertised a new volume of humour with the claim that 'the New York *Nation* is struck with Dod Grile's wit'. This, they said, was the first acquaintance the *Nation* had ever made with the name of Dod Grile, let alone with his wit;[8] and, further to discredit Hotten's reputation as a connoisseur of

American humour, they were blunt in their disparagement of the work of 'the San Francisco *News Letter's* "Town Crier"' which he also proposed publishing. Then, for full measure, they corrected their previous statement about his nationality.

Meanwhile, on 8 November, Clemens had gone to Piccadilly to see Hotten, but had been unable to do so. Hotten immediately wrote him a long letter beginning 'I am vexed that I was out when you called this afternoon. Had I been at home I think the misunderstanding betwixt us might have been cleared away'. He enclosed a copy of a letter he claimed to have sent on 3 February 1872 to two different newspaper addresses, knowing Clemens to be away on a lecture tour. Earlier, he says, he had sent him a copy of his edition of *The Innocents Abroad* which he assumes Clemens to have received as he has named Hotten in print as its London publisher. The remainder of the letter merits reproduction for what it shows of Hotten's method of operation, the plausibility of his style, and his irrepressible self-confidence. He falls back again on the sorrowful tone of the misunderstood innocent and on the device of invoking the fairness of his dealings with other authors; he again offers payment; he again shows casually his first-hand knowledge of the U.S.; he underlines his reliability by drawing attention to the bank communication he is forwarding; and ends on a note of consummate flattery that almost over-reaches itself: is it unfair to call to mind the techniques of the confidence-trickster?

> From the message you left here this afternoon I am sorry to find you are under the impression that I am about to issue *with* your name, a work *not* written by you. You have said some very hard things about me — probably at the 'instigation of others who hoped to benefit by misleading you, but I do assure you in the frankest manner possible that *self-respect* — apart from my sincere respect for your inimitable talent — would not allow me to do anything of the kind. You have, unfortunately, fallen amongst people who dislike me, people who are jealous of me because I happen to be not quite so industrious, not quite so shrewd as they are. These people have misled you, the same as they tried to poison the mind of poor Artemus Ward against me. I say nothing more. *All I ask is for you to see and judge for yourself.*
>
> I may just mention that Mr Bierce was brought here for the express purpose of creating a disturbance. He saw that he was being made a tool of from jealous motives, and the result was that we became fast friends and I have had the pleasure of handing him money for material for a little book. It was my hope that *our* relations would have been of this character, and with the kindly message you have just left I do not despair of it.
>
> The advertisement you have seen — or rather, I suspect, to which your attention has been drawn — refers simply to an

elegantly printed volume of your scattered writings that we are preparing. The reason I was not more explicit in my announcement is that other members of the trade watch me as a cat would a mouse but after the frank message you have left here I at once tell you what I am doing, and I can only say that I gladly avail myself of your offer to revise it. I have just telegraphed for sheets, and these shall be with you tomorrow, when you can go over them and let me have back on Monday.

I did think of giving a short biography of yourself, taking your own outline sketch as my foundation. I suppose that story of the origin of your *nom de plume* is tolerably correct. I remember when I lived at Galena, Ill., and used to go down the river on the old Uncle Toby, the throwing − or casting − of the lead was accompanied by some such words.

As to payment for your editorial services − I am perfectly willing to give whatever you may think fair. I know you are a rich man, but that does not matter as my payment is concerned.

If you will kindly drop me a line I shall be obliged. Enclosed letter is from a *Bank*, and I sincerely trust that its stout proportions only represent so many bank notes.

Enclosed is a portrait of yourself which I prefer to any of the photographs yet published. I also send one of Bret Harte.

(The volume to which he refers was the *Choice Humorous Works*, about which more will be said in my next chapter.)

Hotten wrote again the next day saying that he had expected to receive a note in answer to his letter and apologising 'if my shopman misunderstood the messages you left; but anyway I am not sorry at the opportunity you have afforded me of correcting one or two misconceptions'. In fact, on 8 November, the day he had called at Hotten's, Clemens had written a letter to the *Telegraph* explaining that he had been called home by cable, would be unable to fulfil lecture engagements, but hoped to return the following year [17]. In the preparations for his departure, presumably, he ignored Hotten's olive-branch, and the question of how genuine that branch was must remain an open one.

Hotten's claim that he had 'thrice' written to Clemens before September 1872 should be verifiable, but there is no copy of such letters in his letter-books, though he seems generally to have been meticulous in this respect. The letter of 3 February, of which he sends a copy in November, does appear in the letter-book but only on the page following the November letter, not in its correct chronological position. It ends with a request:

I see you have a new book in hand "Roughing it" will you oblige *by mailing to me on receipt* of this some of the proofs − a few chapters. You may depend upon my dealing honourably with you and I will place to your credit whatever is fair and equitable.

This sounds like Hotten the fair dealer and the champion of copyright of Mr. Ganzel's picture.

Certainly there was that side to his character, and when he died on 14 June 1873 the *Bookseller* spoke of his 'keen knowledge of literature, shrewd manners, and great intelligence' as well as his indefatigable energy. A eulogy in the same issue over the initials R.H.S. developed this theme almost fulsomely, singling out his American interests especially:

> No new humourist or poet appeared among our Transatlantic brethren but he was imported and naturalized here for the delectation of English readers. Artemus Ward, Lowell, Holmes, Walt Whitman, Hans Breitmann, Bret Harte, Mark Twain, owe nearly all their reputation to him.

R.H.S. hints guardedly at 'the little jealousies and quarrels of the moment' which must not be allowed to sully Hotten's reputation any more than 'whatever may have been his faults and shortcomings'. In Hotten's industrious dedication to publishing the obituarist finds 'something heroic . . . if of a degenerate modern kind', but he commemorates in particular 'the kindness and encouragement he was always ready to extend to young beginners in literature'.

For others, however, Hotten's death prompted sentiments less generous. Swinburne with characteristic venom wrote 'When I heard he had died of a surfeit of pork chops, I observed that this was a serious argument against my friend Sir Richard Burton's view of cannibalism as a wholesome and natural method of diet'.[9] There is a story that George R. Sims and a friend, having at last collected a long-standing debt from Hotten, found their presentation of the cheque frustrated by his death, and that Sims thereupon coined the epigrammatic epitaph 'Hotten: rotten: forgotten'.[10]

Clemens, if he heard either of these stories, would have enjoyed their pungency, but that response would not have represented accurately his whole view of Hotten. Among the Mark Twain Papers at Berkeley are two manuscripts, one of six pages, one of nineteen, of vituperative attack on him. They date from 1872. The shorter, an ironical letter to the Superintendent of the Zoological Gardens, offers him 'one of the most remarkable creatures which nature has yet produced. For the sake of convenience I call it the John Camden Hottentot . . . I am *sure* that this singular little creature is the missing link between man and the hyena'. The longer diatribe documents Hotten's dishonesties of practice and cites Tom Hood as witness to one of them. Both are much more splenetic than Sims's aphorism; both exploit animal imagery with a fertile inventiveness beside which Swinburne's analogy seems mild and gentlemanly. Yet with both there is still a strong suggestion of a *jeu d'esprit*, in which a lay-figure 'John Camden Hottentot' is used as a substitute for the real Hotten whose business energy Clemens can respect while he dislikes his personality and deplores his methods. 'Hottentot' provides the excuse for a flight of vigorous literary creation and therapeutic hyperbole; the choice of soubriquet, though obvious, suggests an attitude towards the Negro less mature and sympathetic than that in *Huckleberry Finn* or *Following the Equator.*

In or about 1873 Clemens, at the request of Charles Dudley Warner, wrote a brief account of his own life and work. It contains this statement: 'In England the Routledges and Hotten have gathered together and published all my sketches; a great many that have not appeared in book form here. There are four volumes of these sketches'.[11] The total absence of rancour against Hotten in this passage which is the more reliable for not being written for effect, and the candid recognition of his important role in introducing Mark Twain to the English reader represents, I believe, Clemens's true and considered attitude to this remarkable and dynamic publisher, though it conveniently omits his distaste for the man.

CHAPTER 2

ESTABLISHING A REPUTATION

I

Routledge's *Sketches Selected and Revised* (1872) is bibliographically significant as the first collection of Mark Twain's Sketches to be published in book form with the author's approval. That it antedates the corresponding American volume by three years is surprising when simultaneous publication would seem to have offered such obvious economic advantages. The idea of publishing a collection of sketches in the United States occurred at about this time to the Boston publisher James R. Osgood: declining Osgood's proposal, Clemens wrote: 'I have just made up quite a portly volume of them for Routledge & Sons, London, but I have to leave my own countrymen to "suffer and be strong" without them' [5]. This decision was by no means a voluntary one on the part of Clemens who had long wanted such a volume. As early as December 1870 Bliss had been discussing its probable contents but by the end of January he had persuaded Mark Twain that to issue it too close to *Roughing It* would imperil its chances of success. Orion Clemens explained to his brother Bliss's view that 'few people want to buy two books from the same author at the same time' and so the *Sketches* were deferred until the fall of 1872 or 'another time'. By August 1872 Clemens was still urging Bliss: 'Hurry up your figuring on the volume of sketches' [9]; by February 1875 he had decided to let Osgood publish it until Bliss held him to a contract of 1870 and eventually brought out the volume himself later in 1875.[1]

The strange aspect of this is that the considerations which seem to have weighed with Bliss obviously did not affect the British market, for in 1872 Routledge issued *four* Mark Twain titles in quick succession: *Roughing It, A Curious Dream, Sketches Selected and Revised,* and *The Innocents Abroad.* He also reissued their *Jumping Frog* volume in the same year. Was Bliss being over-cautious? Was Mark Twain in fact already more popular abroad than at home? Were the book-buying habits of the British different from those of the Americans, or does Clemens's preference for the subscription method of publishing in the States explain the difference? There is no conclusive answer, only the fact that Routledge, who was too experienced a publisher to risk over-saturating the market, seems anxious to give his readers the opportunity of buying not two but five 'books from the same author at the same time', and the record of subsequent reprintings suggests that he was justified. Moreover, as has been mentioned, Hotten also published a collected *Sketches* in the following year, 1873, which Chatto reissued in a revised form early in 1874; the demand seems to have been insatiable.

It may be well for the moment to ignore chronology and the other Routledge publications of 1872 in order to complete the story of the *Sketches*. With the letter of 25 November 1873 in which he introduced himself as Hotten's successor, Chatto enclosed 'a set of the sheets of a volume of your writings, in order that you may (as I understand you expressed a desire to do) correct certain portions of the contents'. The sheets were of one of Hotten's last piracies which he had published earlier that year under the cumbersome title of *The Choice Humorous Works of Mark Twain, Now first Collected with Extra Passages to the "Innocents Abroad", now first reprinted, and a life of the author. Illustrations by Mark Twain & other Artists: also portrait of the author.* The biographical sketch was a compilation of Hotten's based largely on *Roughing It* and on Hingston's introduction to *The Innocents Abroad*; it is initialled 'J.C.H.' and dated 'March 12, 1873'. When Chatto reprinted the book in 1874 he gave it the more modest title *The Choice Humorous Works of Mark Twain, Revised and corrected by the Author with a Life and also a Portrait of the Author, and numerous Illustrations.* He omitted seventeen pieces from the earlier edition, and re-titled one other. The 'Life' is shortened by about four pages; the income Mark Twain was 'stated on very good authority' to have received from *The Innocents Abroad* is raised from 'seventeen thousand dollars' to 'twenty-four thousand dollars', this time on 'unimpeachable authority' and with the additional information that '112,000 copies of the book were sold'. There is no written proof that these changes were made at the author's direction, but Clemens not infrequently saved himself correspondence by a visit to a publisher and a conversation: being in London he may well have made these changes in this way. The eagerness with which he was to offer Chatto his next book, *The Adventures of Tom Sawyer*, and the fact that he never challenged Chatto's claim in the title of the 1874 selection would seem to point conclusively to his having personally authorised it.

Even so, the *Choice Humorous Works* gives rise to a number of questions of bibliographical significance. Were the seventeen omitted pieces dropped because Mark Twain had not written them, or because he no longer wished to own them? What is the status of the pieces — there are at least eleven — which are included here but not in the Routledge 'authorized' collection of 1872? Had they all been written in the interim? Given all the differences between the two volumes, should not Blanck differentiate them more fully than by merely listing the 1874 one as a reprint of the 1873 'with several omissions'? If Clemens's authorisation of this volume can be accepted, why did he allow

Routledge, as late as the spring of 1876, to issue *Information Wanted, and other sketches by Mark Twain* with the customary statement that he was Mark Twain's only authorised London publisher?

However these questions are to be resolved, the evidence of Mark Twain's popularity with the English reader is incontrovertible. It would also seem safe to assume that Routledge and Chatto were catering for a different type of reader from those who had been attracted by Hotten's catch-penny titles. As will be seen in the next chapter, the celebrities with whom Mark Twain became familiar on his first visit to England were not the sort of people whose staple literary diet was the ephemeral sketches of the many American humorists of the day. By then Mark Twain had shown himself capable of sustaining that humour over two full-length books, and the appearance of these in Routledge's lists of 1872 unquestionably widened the audience for it.

II

Roughing It was published in England early in 1872 (the British Library copy was accessioned on 15 February) and is described on the title page as 'Copyright Edition'. Jacob Blanck suggests that it may have appeared a few days before the American edition. A reference, in a letter to Blamire in New York, to 'the revised *Roughing It*' which Clemens is sending him seems to relate to a set of revised proofs and not to any authorial changes in the English text [4]. In England the book was published in two volumes, the first (chapters 1 to 45 inclusive) entitled *Roughing It*, the second *The Innocents at Home*. (On 9 March, however, the *Athenaeum* listed a one-volume edition containing both at 2/6.) Routledge omitted the three appendices to the American text, including instead 'Mark Twain's (Burlesque) Autobiography'. The English edition contains some printer's errors and some Anglicisations such as 'ploughed' for 'plowed', but no significant changes. Indeed, Chapter 44 retains the reference to 'the accompanying portrait' even though the edition was not illustrated.

The back cover advertised Routledge's American Library ('a series of the most popular American Books of Humour in fancy covers price 1/- each') comprising to date *The Jumping Frog, Roughing It* (*The Innocents At Home* was added as a separate title a few months later), Eggleston's *The Hoosier Schoolmaster*, a selection of Bret Harte's poems, and *The Luck of Roaring Camp*. That the last-named has 'an Introduction and Glossary by Tom Hood' indicates how exotic American humour seemed to the Victorian reader. The end papers list nineteen Fenimore Cooper titles at one shilling and twenty-eight at six-pence, as well as works by Washington Irving, Harriet Beecher Stowe, Artemus Ward, Oliver Wendell Holmes and James Russell Lowell. Mark Twain was in good company.

It was after publishing *Roughing It* that Routledge brought out *The*

Innocents Abroad. He followed Hotten in issuing it in two volumes, the second being titled *The New Pilgrim's Progress.* On 9 July 1872 Blamire told Clemens that he had sent *The Innocents Abroad* to London to be set; he enclosed a cheque for $250 in payment and acknowledged receipt of a preface which, he thought, would 'do capitally for one of the volumes and I think our People will be pleased with it, but they write me that they think it indispensable that *each of the vols.* should have a separate preface'.[2] Clemens, on holiday at Saybrook, Connecticut, replied at once that he was 'not feeling a bit industrious; but I like your suggestion so much that I mean to write the other preface at the very earliest possible moment' [7*]. The preface that he had already sent to Routledge ran as follows:[3]

Preface to the English Edition

Messrs. George Routledge and Sons pay me copyright on my books. The moral grandeur of this thing cannot be overestimated in an age like ours, when even the sublimest natures betray the taint of earth, and the noblest and the purest among us will steal.

This firm is truly an abnormal firm. If there is another in foreign parts with similar instincts I have not had personal dealings with it.

My appreciation of the moral singularity I am lauding is attested by the fact that at the request of this publishing House I have wrought diligently, here in oppressive mid-summer, until I have accomplished a thorough revision and correction of this book for republication in England, in defiance of the opinion of the great and wise historian Josephus, that "during the enervating season of summer, all persons so delicately constituted as authors and preachers ought to refrain from arduous employments of any kind and do nothing but worship nature, breathe the pure atmosphere of woods and mountains, and fool around".

Mark Twain

The emphasis on the writer as a professional, dependent on his pen for a living, was reiterated in a cancelled sentence complaining that other firms republish his books 'and refine and instruct and uplift whole tribes and peoples with them, yet never pay the benefactor a cent'. The note of burlesque introduced at the end of this preface in mockery of the Romantic, Transcendentalist view of the artist's sensibility chimes well with the tone of the book itself and its pawky irreverence, but its author had second thoughts. On 21 July he asked Blamire to destroy it as being 'not at all in good taste' and enclosed a piece that he thought was better suited 'to so reserved and dignified a people as the English' [8*].

His judgment was probably sound. The down-to-earth mercenary realism of his tone brings to mind the *Autobiography* of Anthony Trollope with its contemptuous rejection of inspiration, its insistence on the writer as a man with a job to do, and its satisfied preoccupation with the income his books had brought him. When the *Autobiography* was published posthumously in 1883 (it had been written at about the same time as *The Innocents Abroad*) its materialistic anti-Romanticism sharply alienated many of its readers. An American humorist might have been allowed a little more licence, certainly, than a Victorian social novelist, but a Preface suggests the author *in propria persona* rather than in the *persona* of the Innocent that excuses the irreverence of the text. Conscious that he was for the first time addressing himself directly to the English public, he seems to have wished to appear as Samuel Langhorne Clemens rather than as Mark Twain. With a characteristic excess of embarrassment at what he conceived to be a lapse of taste he wrote on the manuscript of the revised preface 'Please use this if it be *possible* — do try hard, anyway. Tear up the other. S.L.C.'[4] * (He was to suffer even worse agonies, on similar grounds and with more justice, of course, after 'that hideous mistake' of the speech he was to make at the Whittier birthday dinner in 1877.)[5]

Rationing himself to only one touch of humour, he becomes self-conscious almost to the point of obsequiousness in his revised preface. Here the emphasis is on his conscientiousness as a craftsman and on his desire to please the English audience.

Preface to the English Edition

At the request of Messrs. George Routledge & Sons, I have made a patient and conscientious revision of this book for republication in England, and have weeded out of it nearly, if not quite, all of the most palpable and inexcusable of its blemishes. At the same time I have wrought into almost every chapter additions which cannot fail to augment the attractions of the book, or diminish them. I have done my best to make this revised volume acceptable to the reader; and so, since I am as other men are, it would gratify me indeed to win his good opinion.

Respectfully,

Hartford, U.S., July 1872   The Author

Could this tone have been adopted in ironic flattery of an unsuspecting reader or in a cynical attempt to sell a two-year-old book by claiming for it revisions more extensive than had in fact been made? Numerous as the revisions are, they are not especially significant. A number of new footnotes appear: some explain allusions unfamiliar to the English reader as when the Smithsonian is identified as 'The national scientific institution at Washington'; others are purely facetious ('"Gob" is from the Greek'). A few may seem to be playing to the English gallery, as when, having praised the whole conception of the excursion, he adds 'NOTE TO ENGLISH EDITION — We were not then aware that the idea of this sort of expedition originated in England and was borrowed thence — M.T.'; similarly, the reference to the careful selection of the participants is glossed in a way that might confirm British prejudice: 'It presently transpired that any applicant was "select" enough who could pay his passage — M.T.' There are a number of omissions from and a number of additions to the American text, but all are brief and none is of major importance; they have already been fully discussed in a scholarly article by Arthur L. Scott.[6]

Probably the primary motive was to obtain an English copyright. The contract he had signed with the American Publishing Company on 29 December 1870 for a collection of sketches had stipulated that previously published pieces should 'be altered if possible to do so in such a manner that a new copyright will hold upon them',[7] and as Hotten had already pirated *The Innocents Abroad* it was necessary to give some authority to the claim on Routledge's title-page that this was the 'Author's English Edition'. This did not, however, give Routledge any monopoly in the title.

That Mark Twain was genuinely concerned, for reasons other than pecuniary, to appeal to a British audience is substantiated by the unusual modesty and self-deprecation of his preface to the second volume, *The New Pilgrim's Progress*, which again deserves reproduction in full:

To the English Reader

A long introductory speech would not become me, a stranger. So I will only say, in offering this revised edition of my book to the English reader, that it is nothing more than a simple record of a pleasure excursion among foreign peoples with whom he is doubtless much better acquainted than I am. I could not have made it learned or profound, if I had tried my best. I have only written of men and things as they seemed to *me*: and so it is very likely that the reader will discover that my vision was often inaccurate. I did not seriously expect anybody to buy the book when it was originally written — and that will account for a good deal of its chirping complacency and freedom from restraint: the idea that nobody is listening, is apt to seduce a body into airing his small thoughts and opinions with a rather juvenile frankness. But no matter, now. I have said enough to make the reader understand that I am not offering this work to him as either law or gospel, upon any point, principle, or subject; but only as a trifle to occupy himself with when he has nothing to do and does not wish to whistle.

The naive ecstasies of an innocent on his first voyage, become, in print, a matter of serious concern to a part of the great general world — to wit, the part which consists of that Innocent himself. Therefore, as nearly unnecessary as this book is, I feel a solicitude about it. Any American likes to see the work of his hands achieve a friendly reception in the mother country, and it is but natural — natural, too, that he should prize its kindly reception there above the same compliment extended by any people other than his own. Our kindred blood and our common language, our kindred religion and political liberty, make us feel nearer to England than to other nations, and render us more desirous of standing well there than with foreign nationalities that are foreign to us in all particulars. So, without any false modesty, or any consciousness of impropriety, I confess to a desire that Englishmen should read my book. That a great many Englishmen have already read it, is a compliment which I mention in this place with what seems to me to be legitimate and justifiable gratification.

Respectfully,
The Author

Hartford, U.S., July, 1872

Not all Englishmen, however, had read the book in ways to justify very much gratification. *The Bookseller* had reviewed Hotten's 1870 edition encouragingly, observing that 'Everybody knows the tale of "The Jumping Frog", which gave Twain widespread popularity' and predicting an increase in that popularity as a result of this account, 'brimful of fun', of a European visit 'made just as that of the "typical American" we meet on our travels'. The *Athenaeum*, though, had been much less sympathetic to the *persona* of the 'untravelled American': Mark Twain is 'ignorant of many of those things which would be familiar to an English tourist'. This would be pardonable, were it not that 'The greater his blunder, the more assurance there is in his language'. His pillorying of 'one of his fellow-countrymen for ignorance of French manners and assumption of native superiority' seems to the reviewer misplaced and almost hypocritical: 'Mark Twain is merely showing the prevalence of the faults which he satirizes', and the book 'reminds us of "The Book of Snobs", where the fancy picture of the author wholly eclipsed his characters'. To the *Saturday Review* he was 'a very offensive specimen of the vulgarest kind of Yankee'.[8]

The new introductions may have been influenced by these reviews, but certainly in them Mark Twain makes explicit for the first time a consideration that was to be of abiding importance to him throughout his career: it is illuminated by his reference to the English as 'so reserved and dignified a people' as well as by an undertone that runs through *The Innocents Abroad* as a counterpoint to the predominantly irreverent attitude that, in the candour of the English preface, he calls its 'chirping complacency'.

III

This undertone I once tried to identify, writing of 'Mark Twain the Great Victorian' and drawing a tentative comparison with Tennyson. I referred to T.S. Eliot's essays on the two (written at an interval of fourteen years from each other).[9] Tennyson's generation, Eliot complains, 'had, for the most part, no hold on permanent things, on permanent truths about man and God and life and death'. Except in *Huckleberry Finn* (as Eliot implies in his introduction to it) Mark Twain had no great hold on permanent things either. Of Tennyson Eliot also comments 'Temperamentally, he was opposed to the doctrine that he was moved to accept and to praise'. There is no doubt that this was as true of Mark Twain, but what is more significant is that the dichotomy Eliot finds in Tennyson is not that of the frustrated artist so much as of the frustrated moralist: 'I should reproach Tennyson not for mildness, or tepidity, but rather for lack of serenity'; and in *In Memoriam* 'His concern is for the loss of man rather than for the gain of God'. In a very real sense the same can be said of Mark Twain.

Diffuse and episodic as *The Innocents Abroad* undeniably is, there is one human quality for which Clemens's admiration is revealingly consistent, and it emerges most clearly in one of the best-told anecdotes in the book. This is the tale of Judge Oliver, who bore with patience every unbelievable hardship of pioneer life until for the third time his literary activities were interrupted by a cow falling through the roof. The judge's ejaculation when thus goaded beyond endurance — 'This thing is growing monotonous' — is, in its mildness, so inadequate to the situation that two interpretations are possible. Either the judge is being ridiculed as a man devoid of all proper emotional response, or he is being extolled as a man of remarkable self-control. The whole tone of the passage excludes the former; the insistence on Oliver's uniqueness shows that this is no burlesque of human nature in general. The quiet irony of this tale is directed rather at the reader's expectations than at the central figure. Fielding in *Joseph Andrews* and Johnson in *Rasselas* both tell this story, so to speak, in reverse. They describe the man who, having advocated to others a stoic acceptance of calamity, gives way to uncontrolled paroxysms of grief when touched personally by affliction. There is no doubt that Mark Twain's version springs from a greater belief in human nature. Oliver is *par excellence* 'a man that fortune's buffets and rewards/Hath ta'en with equal thanks' and Mark Twain's respect for him, like Hamlet's for Horatio, is the respect of the man whose own soul is divided for the man of completely unified personality.

In the next chapter comes the characteristically macabre description of the charnel house in the Capuchin monastery and once more, even as he recoils from the unnaturalness of it, Mark Twain cannot repress a grudging acknowledgement of the single-mindedness of the monastic self-mortification. Not even the touch of banter in the narration can detract from the fundamental seriousness of this wonder at man's power of self-discipline. 'Almost any exhibition of complete self-sufficiency draws a stunned tribute from me', admits Carraway in *The Great Gatsby*. Clemens might have said the same. The ambivalence of his attitude to John Camden Hotten, on which I have insisted earlier, may in part reflect a grudging recognition of that quality in him. Quite early in *The Innocents Abroad* the burlesque of European guides and European culture is temporarily suspended in favour of a comparison between the comfortable pace of European life and 'our restless, driving, vitality-consuming marts at home': here the tribute is so stunned as to be almost naive in its idealisation:

> They go to bed moderately early, and sleep well. They are always quiet, always orderly, always cheerful, comfortable, and appreciative of life and its manifold blessings. One never sees a drunken man among them. The change that has come over our little party is surprising. Day by day we lose some of our restlessness and absorb some of the spirit of quietude and ease that is in the tranquil atmosphere about us and in the demeanour of the people. We grow wise apace. We begin to comprehend what life is for.

Yet to Matthew Arnold the European scene meant 'this strange disease of modern life/With its sick hurry, its divided aims', the 'darkling plain' on which he could find 'neither joy, nor love, nor light,/Nor certitude, nor peace, nor help for pain'.

When Mark Twain meets the Czar of Russia there is again a naive over-simplification of response. As he realises that the Czar is not one of 'the tinsel kings of the theatre', he substitutes for his republican preconceptions another romantic idealisation which even rejects the possibility of mosquitoes in the royal fountain, but it is an idealisation completely consistent with the Mark Twain that I am describing. The Czar and his whole court impress him by virtue of their complete, unobtrusive control of the situation, their dignified self-possession which awakens a similar sense of responsibility in their guests; and the hushed awe in the description prompts in the reader a mischievous comparison with Disraeli or Tennyson contemplating Victoria and the Prince Consort. The Czar is Judge Oliver on a larger scale, the man who gains the respect of others by — the Tennysonian phrase is inevitable — 'self-reverence, self-knowledge, self-control'. These are the qualities Clemens has come instinctively to value; it is their conspicuous absence in the 'pilgrims' that evokes his most violent attacks on those whited sepulchres. The automatic defensive burlesquing of these 'royalist' emotions retrospectively in the next chapter shows that his acceptance of these moral values is not wholly conscious or complete; but the Mark Twain who left the Czar's presence could have said of himself with accuracy 'I warn't feeling so brash as I was before, but kind of ornery, and humble, and to blame, somehow — though *I* hadn't done anything'. If he did not use those words, it was because he had not yet attained to the self-knowledge and moral awareness that characterise the Huck who does use them, but he could recognise and envy those qualities when he saw them in others.

The Judge Oliver syndrome persists throughout Mark Twain's writing. In *Huckleberry Finn* Colonel Sherburn shoots down Boggs with callous inhumanity, and then, by sheer force of an oratory based on self-possession, utterly cows the crowd that has come to lynch him and draws from Huck and his author another stunned tribute. That the moral wrongness of Sherburn's position is thereby obscured reinforces my point. Scott Fitzgerald does not give Carraway's awed respect for self-sufficiency the status of a positive virtue, and indeed the development of the plot suggests a marked contrast between it and the self-knowledge to which he is brought by the end of the novel. This is a distinction which Clemens too rarely draws, and it is an index to his own insecurity that he attaches such importance to a show of self-sufficiency. When, in *Life on the Mississippi*, the quality is allied to professional expertise it is more acceptable in its incarnation in the river pilot, but even that paragon of men will strike many readers as being in large measure a creature of Mark Twain's imagination.

IV

To return to the prefaces to *The Innocents Abroad* and the letter to Blamire, we can see a parallel reflection of Clemens's insecurity in his awed respect for the 'reserved and dignified' English people – again, largely of his imagination. Envying them the self-possession with which he credited them, he was never satisfied merely to make them laugh. What he wanted – and the desire perhaps reflected an insecurity within himself – was their esteem, and when, at the end of his life, they signalised that esteem by conferring on him the Oxford D. Litt. the honour was one that he especially prized.

Much earlier they seem to have accorded him a serious hearing, if one random piece of evidence is to be trusted. I have a copy of *The New Pilgrim's Progress* (the second volume of *The Innocents Abroad*, that is) which, though undated, is almost certainly a Victorian piracy, though not one identified by Blanck. It was printed and published by Richard Edward King who operated in the East London district of Shoreditch; this copy was probably bought by the Manchester merchant, the rubber-stamped address of whose business premises survives on the inside cover and whose pencilled marginalia adorn the text. His interests seem to have been mainly in Biblical history and the Holy Land, and Mark Twain's references to either are the excuse for a profusion of assenting ticks or 'very good', an exclamatory 'No', and even an occasional reproach: 'Mark, you don't read your Bible'. Piety is his criterion, and even Mark Twain's 'd – n' is heavily scored through, his references to 'a god' corrected to 'God', and his amused allusion to the smallness of Palestine where 'the celebrated localities . . . occur that close together' prompts the footnote 'Yes, Mark Twain – but He made the United States and all your extraordinary large rivers'. The compari-

son between the Sea of Galilee and Lake Tahoe provokes the
sententious observation' 'Mark, the same Master created Lake Tahoe
but He honoured the Sea of Galilee with His presence'. Approval,
however, far outweighs these expressions of dissent, and it is interesting
to see the sense of easy intimacy that Mark Twain stimulates in this
reader right through to the pencilled comment at the foot of the final
page 'Well written, Mark!' This English reader at least would have
endorsed Mark Twain's claim, in the cancelled preface, that his works
'refine and instruct and uplift'.

The text of this edition seems to be that of the Routledge 'Author's
English Edition' but without the preface and without the 'Burlesque
Autobiography'. *The Innocents Abroad* was probably the most pirated
of all Mark Twain's books. Not only did Ward, Lock & Co., as well as
King and probably others, bring out unauthorised editions, but Chatto
& Windus reissued in 1875, in one volume at two shillings, Hotten's
Mark Twain's Pleasure Trip on the Continent of Europe (the title page
gives the title more accurately than the cover). They retained a version
of Hingston's introduction but updated it by removing his statement
that Mark Twain had never visited England. Their records (see Appendix I) show that it was frequently reprinted thereafter but it is not clear
whether any payment for it was made to the author.

Another anomaly in respect of *The Innocents Abroad* may be
mentioned at this point, though it relates to 1881 when Chatto &
Windus sought to follow up the success of *A Tramp Abroad* in 1880 by
issuing an illustrated *Innocents Abroad*. Their request to the American
Publishing Company for a set of electros of the illustrations brought
from Frank Bliss the reply: 'We are not particularly anxious to sell the
above as we have quite a considerable trade on the book in England and
the Continent which would be cut off if you issued an illustrated
edition'.[10] Routledge had by that date issued some forty thousand
copies and in the previous October had brought out a new one-shilling
edition of four thousand. It is presumably to this that Bliss refers, but
nevertheless in 1881 Chatto & Windus did issue a 7s. 6d. edition of *The
Innocents Abroad*, though whether it was illustrated is not clear from
their stock-book or their letter-book.

Routledge continued to print an average of four thousand copies a
year until 1902 when they printed twelve thousand, but there is no
evidence of any payment of royalties to Clemens on any of these sales.
The $250 they paid him in 1872 was presumably an outright purchase
of copyright, and although they subsequently allowed Chatto to
acquire their rights in some of Mark Twain's books, *The Innocents
Abroad* was never one of them.

V

Of the works so far discussed, only *Roughing It* was published almost simultaneously on both sides of the Atlantic. Mark Twain's next book, however, was likely to strengthen his reputation as a serious writer, and he attached considerable importance to its English publication. By now he had visited England and met the Routledges; indeed, it was from London on 16 July 1873 that he sent Bliss explicit instructions for sheets and illustrations for *The Gilded Age* to be sent to Routledge, signature by signature, 'by successive steamers always'. 'We shall issue a copyright edition of the novel here in fine style — three volumes' [22]. Routledge was to publish on the same day as Bliss or on the day before, so it was imperative that any change in publication date be telegraphed to him. For added safety, Clemens wrote to his Hartford neighbour and collaborator, Charles Dudley Warner, so that he might keep an eye on Bliss [23]. The contract with Routledge was not signed until 18 October; that with Bliss was dated 8 May, but whereas Bliss promised a five per cent royalty to each of the two authors Routledge offered double that sum. Again Clemens furnished a special preface for British readers, written while he was staying in London. His attitude towards them is more assured this time, and verging on the aggressive; he is eager to deny them the consolatory illusion that the British political scene is superior to the American system that the book castigates. A confidence in the American future replaces the deference to the English past shown in the prefaces to *The Innocents Abroad*; and the emergence of Mark Twain as social critic is reflected in the concentration on signs of reform and in the abrupt termination of the preface with none of the graces he had attempted in his earlier ones:

Author's Preface to the London Edition

In America nearly every man has his dream, his pet scheme, whereby he is to advance himself socially or pecuniarily. It is this all-pervading speculativeness which we have tried to illustrate in "The Gilded Age". It is a characteristic which is both bad and good, for both the individual and the nation. Good, because it allows neither to stand still, but drives both forever on, toward some point or other which is ahead, not behind nor at one side. Bad, because the chosen point is often badly chosen, and then the individual is wrecked; the aggregation of such cases affects the nation, and so is bad for the nation. Still, it is a trait which it is better for a people to have and sometimes suffer from than to be without.

We have also touched upon one sad feature, and it is one which we found little pleasure in handling. That is the shameful corruption which lately crept into our politics, and in a handful of years has spread until the pollution has affected some portion of every State and every Territory in the Union.

But I have a great strong faith in a noble future for my country. A vast majority of the people are straightforward and honest; and this late state of things is stirring them to action. If it would only keep on stirring them until it became the habit of their lives to attend to the politics of the country personally, and put only their very best men into positions of trust and authority! That day will come.

Our improvement has already begun. Mr Tweed (whom Great Britain furnished to us), after laughing at our laws and courts for a good while, has at last been sentenced to thirteen years' imprisonment with hard labour. It is simply bliss to think of it. It will be at least two years before any governor will dare to pardon him out, too. A great New York judge who continued a vile, a shameless career, season after season, defying the legislature and sneering at the newspapers, was brought low at last, stripped of his dignities, and by public sentence debarred from ever again holding any office of honour or profit in the State. Another such judge (furnished to us by Great Britain) had the grace to break his heart and die in the palace built with his robberies when he saw the same blow preparing for his own head and sure to fall upon it.

MARK TWAIN

The Langham Hotel,
London, Dec. 11th 1873

Discernible here are early glimmerings of what was to become, fifteen years later, *A Connecticut Yankee at King Arthur's Court*. Clemens has now sided, whatever the cost, with what, in *The Innocents Abroad*, he had censured as 'our restless, driving, vitality-consuming marts at home' and there is the implicit suggestion that, *per contra*, the English reader he addresses is the product of a greater social inertia. The faith in the legislature and the press as bulwarks against corruption in a truly democratic society informs *The Yankee* also, and Hank Morgan's choice of 'The Boss' as his title has led to the suggestion that Clemens still had 'Boss' Tweed in mind then. However, it is dangerous to oversimplify Clemens's attitudes at any given moment: while he was championing America in the preface to *The Gilded Age*, in his letters home he was still celebrating the virtues of the English in terms to which I shall refer in my next chapter.

On 12 December Routledge received the text of the preface and, from Bliss, a cable announcing the 23rd as the date of American publication. The price of the book was a matter of some discussion. Robert, one of the Routledge sons, notified Clemens of the decision to publish at 25s. instead of the conventional 31s. 6d. (half a guinea a volume): 'The late Lord Lytton adopted this price for his last novel, and we think it a good one, the object being to attract *purchasers* and not throw the book entirely into the circulating libraries'. The author was sceptical though acquiescent:

I am absolutely sure that you wont sell three thousand more copies at twentyfive shillings than you will at thirtyfive. I dont fancy that you can popularize the high pr..ced edition. I'm afraid it is only the low-priced editions that will have a large sale; but as I say, the price is the publisher's affair not the Author's and I'll endorse whatever action you take.[28*]

The next day he wrote to his wife that a 2s. edition would be immediately shipped by Routledge to Canada for sale there, and that he had himself urged the publisher 'to get out a cheap edition here just as soon as the libraries will consent' [29*]. The economics of Victorian book production, especially of fiction, was much influenced by the large lending libraries, and there is no doubt either that they increased the reputations of many authors by widening the audience they reached. The best-known library was of course Mudie's, founded in 1842, and Mudie's order alone for a single title could, if the author were well-known, run into four figures (1,000 for Charles Reade's *It Is Never Too Late to Mend*, 2,500 for George Eliot's *Adam Bede*). The three-decker novels that they preferred were expensive, and obviously it was not in the interest either of the publisher or of the libraries to jeopardise the circulation of these or indeed of any library title by the premature issue of a cheap edition. All publishers were naturally sensitive to library tastes, and Andrew Chatto, for example, was to keep in close personal touch with Mudie's as a matter of principle; he was also, in the 1890s, to play a prominent role in the re-shaping of policies affecting them.[11]

Although, on 29 December, the *Standard* reviewed *The Gilded Age* as 'a work which everyone should read', it was not destined in Mudie's or elsewhere for the big league: Routledge printed 500 of the 25s. edition in December 1873 and 8,000 of the 2s. edition in 1874. He did not need to reprint until 1877, and it was the first of the Mark Twain titles that he subsequently sold to Chatto & Windus.

VI

The more influential *Athenaeum*, however, was much less favourable. After reviewing rather patronisingly Trollope's *Phineas Redux* ('abundance of the light kind of intellectual gratification which may be drawn from seeing life-like portraits of common-place people'), the critic attempts a ponderous *jeu d'esprit* at the expense of Mark Twain's and Warner's suggestion in the American preface (which the English edition also included) that reviewers do not read the books they review; he then warms to the attack. There is some justice in his complaint that 'the authors have made the mistake of introducing far too many characters . . . There are, in fact, materials in this one book for several novels'. In 1965 Charles Neider extracted from it successfully *The Adventures of Colonel Sellers* and it is that piece of Mark Twain's comic invention that gives *The Gilded Age* most of what interest it has for modern readers. Without mentioning Sellers, this reviewer finds 'as might be expected ... plenty of funny things ... though, as might, perhaps, also be expected, the fun is now and again a little overdone. The negro's prayer at the sight of a steamboat verges on the profane, and the spitting joke is made rather too much of'. Had he remembered Mrs Trollope's reiterated censure of spitting habits in *Domestic Manners of the Americans* the reviewer would doubtless have moralised sententiously on how little American civilisation had progressed since the 1840s.

He dislikes 'the extraordinary fancy of heading the chapters with mottoes drawn from almost every language under the sun' and is not surprised by the textual inaccuracies in them since the authors are not even 'thorough masters of their own language'. The illustrations he considers poor and inaccurate, but his prejudices emerge most clearly in allusions to 'one or two odd little points of American etiquette' and his dislike of 'the spirit which brings to light all the *"linge sale"* of American speculation for the benefit of foreign readers'. He makes no attempt to compare it with *Phineas Redux* as political satire but merely allows himself the condescending conclusion: 'We think it just possible that the authors, one or both, may have it in them to produce a story which we may read without fatigue, and without constant jars to our taste, while it shall have no lack of humour; but we cannot say that in "The Gilded Age" they have reached this desirable consummation'.

The American reviewers were no more unanimous than the British in their reception. The extracts Charles Neider quotes in his introduction show how varied their response was, except for the zeal with which they identified the public figures on whom the characters were modelled. This aspect of the novel had less appeal for British readers, but not all of them agreed with the *Athenaeum's* strictures and at least one of them wrote to Clemens to tell him so. George Macdonald of Hammersmith had been in correspondence with him during 1873; that he was the recipient of a complimentary copy of *The Gilded Age* did not deter him from plain speaking, but his recognition of some of its qualities must have pleased its author:

> I am reading it now, and, although, to be honest, I do not think the action quick enough, I am delighted with the courage and honesty of the book, and provoked with the criticism in the Athenaeum ... Is it the part of a good American to cover the faults of his Country as if they were essential to America? ... Thank God, the congress is not America; it is but the very shabby hat which she happens to wear at present, which I hope she will soon see the propriety of changing for one of different material.[12]

Another friend whose good opinions of the book were especially welcome to Clemens was Dr John Brown of Edinburgh, author of *Rab and his Friends*. Acknowledging his 'commendations' on 28 February 1874, Mark Twain identified the thirty-two chapters he had written entirely and the three he had written in part. He also claimed that the forty thousand copies sold in America since publication gave the book 'really the largest two-months' sale which any American book has ever achieved (unless one excepts the cheaper editions of Uncle Tom's Cabin)'. Only 'the fearful financial panic' had, in his ever-optimistic view, prevented their doubling that figure, which had anyway given them £3,000 royalty. He did not expect the ultimate sale to exceed a hundred thousand copies [33].

A novel on such a subject would predictably have a stronger appeal to an American audience than to a British, yet when a few years later an anonymous novel called *Democracy* was published in London its reception was very different. The reasons for this may suggest some of the difficulties encountered by *The Gilded Age*. With obviously no knowledge of the author's identity the *Athenaeum* hailed *Democracy* as 'a short and bitter sketch of political life at Washington' which the reviewer was confident would be 'widely read on this side of the Atlantic'. His key comment is: 'There is no doubt of the writer's earnestness'. Without wishing to accept all the implications of Van Wyck Brooks's thesis that 'it was in consequence of pursuing his humorous writing that [Mark Twain] was arrested in his moral and aesthetic development' and that 'the making of the humorist was the undoing of the artist',[13] we can understand that in the 1870s Mark Twain's English reputation depended so much on his humour that earnestness was not a characteristic readily associated with him.

Humour and seriousness of purpose seemed hardly reconcilable to the Victorians, except perhaps in Dickens's work. They had, on the whole, little taste for satire. The dilemma was, as so often, epitomised graphically by Max Beerbohm in his delicious drawing of an enigmatically-smiling Matthew Arnold being asked by his little niece: 'Why, Uncle Matthew, Oh why, will not you be always wholly serious?' Henry Adams in *Democracy* was being wholly serious and they knew where they stood; Mark Twain they knew to be a humorist, and *The Gilded Age* was serious only in that, in certain places, it was slow-moving and boring. The *Athenaeum* did not question the taste of bringing to light in *Democracy* 'all the *linge sale*' of American politics 'for the benefit of foreign readers' because *Democracy* did so in a form that they could readily recognise: like *Blackwoods*, they immediately saw it as deriving from Alphonse Daudet's *Le Nabob*. The *Fortnightly* considered that '*Democracy* has nothing to fear from a comparison with any of Disraeli's political novels'.

All three journals measured it against Henry James; the *Edinburgh*, by reviewing it alongside three of James's novels and one by Howells,

serves to remind us that by the 1880s there was a sizeable body of
American social fiction which there was not in 1874. *The Gilded Age*
came before its time for the English reader and left him less sure of how
to place so confusing a novel. *Democracy* impressed by its knowledge-
able authenticity: for the *Westminster* 'its chief merit is that it shows an
intimate knowledge of the machinery of American politics' and
'portrays with a keen, unsparing touch that hideous system of corruption, which is the bane and disgrace of American democracy'. To the
British reviewers the novel was of no more interest as a *roman à clef*
than *The Gilded Age* had been, but they obviously responded more to
Adams's patrician attitude than to the more ambivalently democratic
note of the earlier novel. If they wished to be censorious or supercilious
about American politics and society, and all of them did in varying
degrees, they felt themselves on surer ground with *Democracy*. They
could say confidently, as the *Athenaeum* did, 'his chief characters and
the atmosphere in which they live are purely American' without having
to face the problem Colonel Sellers posed: how far was he 'purely
American', how far was he purely Mark Twain's comic imagination?
The *Edinburgh* in 1882 was to admit candidly that 'the slight knowledge we possess of the manners of American society is derived from
works of fiction'; in 1874 *The Gilded Age* was even more markedly *sui
generis* than it would have been eight years later, when readers and
critics might have known better how to cope with its crowded canvas,
its mixture of tones, and its undeniable variations of pace.[14]

Clemens's association with Routledge, except for *Information
Wanted, and Other Sketches*, ended with *The Gilded Age*, though, as
will be described later, they made three unsuccessful attempts to re-
capture him. Nevertheless this first chapter in Mark Twain's English
publishing history is important to his career and bibliographically significant. Of the books published by Hotten and by Routledge none is
identical with the American original. Some have new introductory or
prefatory matter added, others have typographical variations, one at
least contains minor revisions, while others represent the first publication in book form of fugitive pieces. They represent his determination to capture an English market and they illustrate the ambivalence of
his emergent attitude towards Britain at a time when he was making his
first visits to this country.

CHAPTER 3

THE LION IN LONDON

I

Mark Twain's prefatory suggestion that when he wrote *The Innocents Abroad* he 'did not seriously expect anybody to buy the book' is no doubt as greatly exaggerated as he was later to find the reports of his death. In other respects the modesty of the preface to *The New Pilgrim's Progress* is less artificial. 'I have only written of men and things as they seemed to *me*' could have been claimed by many writers, but for Mark Twain at this stage of his career it had a peculiarly literal application. His books rose directly out of his own experiences, so that for more books more experiences were needed, and more experiences necessitated more travel. It is a truism to say that he was never a great imaginative writer in the sense of being able to create great stories out of his imagination, given only a hint from life. Henry James's ability to develop a *donnée* into a full-length dramatic novel is a power Mark Twain never had, and such attempts as he makes at it (*Pudd'nhead Wilson*, for example) are uneven and more the product of the fancy than of the imagination. Nor was his imagination a 'shaping spirit' in the Coleridgean sense: for Mark Twain the natural form of a story was the picaresque concept of a journey fraught with incident. Like any generalisation this must be modified in the course of discussion, but even as late as 1895, confronted with bankruptcy, his immediate solution was a round-the-world lecture tour, gathering simultaneously fees from lectures and material for another book to make more money to pay his debts.

At the beginning of his career, having utilised the 'Quaker City' trip in *The Innocents Abroad* and his Western experiences in *Roughing It*, he was looking for fresh fields to explore. England would seem an obvious choice, given the popularity of his books there, and he had apparently had it in mind for some time, if Hingston may be trusted in his introduction to Hotten's *Innocents Abroad*:-

> I believe that Mark Twain has never visited England. Some time since he wrote to me asking my opinion relative to his giving an entertainment in London. He has appeared in New York and elsewhere as a lecturer, and from his originality would, I have no doubt, be able to repeat his lectures with success were he to visit this country. But I never met him in the character of a public entertainer, and can only speak from experience of his remarkable talent as a humorous writer, and of his cordial frankness and jovial good-fellowship as a friend and companion.

The letter which Hotten claimed to have sent Clemens on 3 February 1872 took this suggestion a stage further:

> From what my friend Hingston told me some time ago I thought we should have had the pleasure of seeing (and hearing) you in London before this. Your name is now very well known here and a large audience is waiting for you to amuse them. The Egyptian Hall where Albert Smith used to perform is now unoccupied and it was this Hall that we engaged for poor Artemus Ward.

Even if Clemens received this letter he would not have been tempted by it, for his mind was working along different lines.

In July 1872, sending Blamire the prefaces for *The Innocents Abroad*, he told him that he had declined an offer – presumably American – to lecture for a month for $10,000 (he could afford to be cavalier in those affluent days). Instead he intended to spend the winter 'either in the rural part of England or in Cuba and Florida – the latter most likely' [8*]. Blamire wisely suggested that winter was not the best time for a visit to England, but promised him a warm welcome from the Routledge family whenever he went and whatever the weather ' – if not, I am much mistaken in the estimate that I think they have formed of you from your writings'. He expected some indication from the Routledges by the end of August as to when a visit from Clemens would be most convenient to them, but, characteristically impetuous, Clemens must have been on his way eastwards across the Atlantic as Routledge's reply was travelling west. For the suddenness of the decision Blamire may have been in part responsible: he had written to Clemens on 6 August 'I cannot resist the temptation of saying that I think a Book on Great Britain would be ever so much more interesting than one on Cuba at present; besides, would you feel like trusting yourself there just now?' Clemens replied by return, asking for particulars of Cunard travel to England, and a week later Blamire had reserved for him a stateroom on the *Scotia*, bought his ticket, provided a letter of introduction to the Routledges, and made helpful suggestions about the journey. There is no record of Clemens's reply to Blamire's enquiry, on behalf of Cunard, as to whether he wished to appear in the passenger list as Mark Twain or Samuel Clemens, but however he was listed it was as a writer that he undertook this visit.[1]

Ten days before sailing he communicated urgently to Orion his latest fortune-making idea; 'Mark Twain's Self-Pasting Scrap-Book': 'Preserve, also, the envelope of this letter – postmark ought to be good evidence of the date of this great humanizing and civilizing invention' [10]. Having conferred this benefit on his fellows, he was now free to devote his attention once more to literature. As early as March 1870 he had written to Bliss from Buffalo: 'I have a sort of vague half-notion of spending the summer in England – I could write a telling book' [2*].

This idea Blamire had unwittingly re-awakened in 1872, and when, in 1907, Twain dictated his recollections of his first day in England he spoke of having taken 'a sudden notion to go to England and get materials for a book about that not-sufficiently known country. It was my purpose to spy out the land in a very private way, and complete my visit without making any acquaintances'.[2] Already, however, and no doubt to his own surprise, Mark Twain was too well known in England for privacy to be possible, and, far from making no acquaintants, he was, on that visit, to lay the foundations of many friendships.

II

He landed, as did most American visitors, at Liverpool, but, unlike many American writers, did not find that experience memorable enough to record. Washington Irving, Emerson, Melville, Hawthorne, and the conservationist Frederick Law Olmstead among others, did; T.S. Eliot, in a review of *The Education of Henry Adams*, drew a perceptive contrast between Adams and Henry James on the basis of their first impressions of Liverpool; it would have been instructive to have been able to add Mark Twain to the list.

The one thing he did recall, in 1907, was his eager expectation of 'an interesting time':

> The interesting time began at once, in the London train from Liverpool. It lasted an hour — an hour of delight, rapture, ecstasy — these are the best words I can find, but they are not adequate, they are not strong enough to convey the feeling which this first vision of rural England brought to me.

That this ecstasy lasted no longer than an hour might have been attributable to any of several causes. Henry Adams, on the same journey and after about the same length of time, was overwhelmed by the ugliness of the industrialised landscape in the Black Country into a drastic revision of his ideas of England. Hawthorne, leaving Liverpool by train in a slightly different direction, decided that 'English scenery is not particularly well worth looking at' and wearied of 'the never-failing green fields, hedges, and other monotonous features of an ordinary English landscape'. What disturbed Clemens's enjoyment, however, was something much more personal: delight in the discovery that the passenger opposite him was reading *The Innocents Abroad* was effectively dissipated when, by the end of the journey, the book had not raised even a smile on the face of the reader. 'It was a bad beginning, and affected me dismally. It gave me a longing for friendly companionship and sympathy'.

Whatever its basis in fact, this anecdote was obviously part of Mark Twain's stock in trade. Thirty years before dictating it, he had told it in a slightly different form (the journey this time is from London to Liverpool, the book *Roughing It*). For a humourist defensively to make a joke out of his fear that people will not find him funny is less noteworthy than is the context in which Mark Twain sets the joke. Fictitious though it may be, it is indicative of how, in 1872, he half-expected to be received by 'so reserved and dignified a people as the English'. When he landed in Liverpool he had no means of gauging the extent of his popularity in England. He had no contractual relation with any English publisher except Routledge, and the Routledge 'authorized' editions had been too recently issued for any reliable sales figures to be yet available. He knew that all his books had been pirated, but such reviews of them as had appeared in the British press gave no grounds for optimism; nor, at this stage of his life, did he have any correspondents in England, whether British or American, who could send him the detailed information about his reputation here that later he was to receive so regularly. Fear that the British might not be prepared to laugh at him would have made him more ready to laugh at them.

The dictation of his first impressions thirtyfive years after the event may have been prompted by his old friend Sir John MacAlister, to whom a typescript of it was sent as soon as it was done. An accompanying letter explained that 'It lacks smoothness in spots, but I seldom apply an after-polish, for dictated things are *talk*, and talk is all the better and all the more natural when it stumbles a little here and there' [330*]. If MacAlister's own reputation and ability as a talker were in Clemens's mind and perhaps putting him on his mettle as a raconteur, his next anecdote, for all its hyperbole, is not without significance. On the morning after his train journey the uneasiness induced by his humourless travelling-companion was still strong in him:

It was a dreary morning, dim, vague, shadowy, with not a cheery ray of sunshine visible anywhere. By halfpast-nine the desire to see somebody, know somebody, shake hands with somebody and see somebody smile had conquered my purpose to remain a stranger in London, and I drove to my publisher's place and introduced myself. The Routledges were about to sit down at a meal in a private room upstairs in the publishing house, for they had not had a bite to eat since breakfast. I helped them eat the meal; at eleven I helped them eat another one; at one o'clock I superintended, while they took luncheon; during the afternoon I assisted inactively at some more meals. These exercises had a strong and most pleasant interest for me, but they were not a novelty because only five years before I was present in the Sandwich Islands when fifteen men of the shipwrecked *Hornet's* crew arrived, a pathetic little group who hadn't had anything to eat for forty-five days.

In the evening Edmund Routledge took me to the Savage Club, and there we had something to eat again; also something to drink; also lively speeches, lively anecdotes, late hours, and a very

hospitable and friendly and contenting and delightful good time.
It is a vivid and pleasant memory with me yet.

That other nations eat more voraciously than one's own is a popular
superstition: among the domestic manners of the Americans that Mrs
Trollope disliked was their regular consumption of huge meals. The
Routledges, however jocularly Clemens describes them, evidently gave
him his first experience of two things that, perhaps because he had not expected to find them among 'so reserved and dignified a people as the English', he never ceased to relish: English hospitality and the English club.

His fears of rejection evaporated as his circle of acquaintance
widened rapidly and beyond his expectations, as his letters of the time
show. At a concert in the Albert Hall a Sheriff of London entered his
box to invite him to the Sheriff's Dinner, to the ceremony of electing
the Lord Mayor, and to the less convivial but instructive occasion of a
trial at the Old Bailey. Reporting this to his wife, Livy, Clemens had the
further satisfaction of being able to add 'He said that at the Lord
Mayor's banquet some time ago a number of big-wigs made my books
the subject of an hour's laudation. Very pleasant, isn't it?' [11*]. Not
surprisingly he recorded in his notebook[3] 'I find the English singularly
cordial in their welcome and hearty in their hospitality. They make one
feel very much at home'. He was prepared to like everything − to be
allowed to walk on the grass in Regents Park and at the Zoo, to be
given a privately conducted tour of the British Museum and to be left
to work undisturbed in the Reading Room, and to be taken on a
specially arranged nocturnal visit to Westminster Abbey. Here he
admired the tombs, especially 'the last one − Charles Dickens − there
on the floor, with the brass letters on the slab − and to this day the
people come and put flowers on it. Why, along at first they almost had
to *cart* the flowers out, there were so many' (Dickens had died on 9
June 1870). One of the great attractions of the day were the paintings
of Gustave Doré, exhibited in the Doré Gallery in New Bond Street
with the modest entrance fee of one shilling. Twain endorsed the popular taste; these paintings, he wrote 'fascinated me more than anything I
have seen in London yet', and he thought 'Christ Leaving the Pretorium'
'The greatest picture that ever was painted'. He enjoyed the Albert
Memorial: 'The finest monument in the world erected to glorify − the
Commonplace. It is the most genuinely humorous idea I have met with
in this grave land'. Edmund Routledge and Tom Hood took him down
to Brighton ('one of the favourite better-class watering places', he
noted, 'though in these days Scarborough is the boss watering-place').

The preoccupation with class that is hinted at here recurs frequently.
Thus in recording a meeting with the explorer Stanley he comments at
once 'He dined with the Queen last Saturday' and in October he writes
to Livy of having received invitations to lecture

from self-elected committees of *gentlemen*, who want to give me
their hospitality in return for the pleasure they say my pen has
given them. When *gentlemen* condescend in this way in England, it
means a very great deal. An English gentleman never does a thing
that may in the slightest degree detract from his dignity. [13*]

To recognise a possible hint of irony here cannot disguise the obvious
satisfaction he derives from the invitations, a satisfaction natural
enough to the barefoot boy from Hannibal but not so easy to reconcile
with the creator of Hank Morgan. It is nothing as crude as snobbery,
nor is it confined to his unpublished writings: I have already commented on manifestations of it in *The Innocents Abroad*.

It was the quality of control and assurance that Clemens was looking
for and seems to some extent to have found in England. In his London
notebook occurs the generous enthusiasm of 'I do like these English
people — they are perfectly splendid — & so says every American who
has staid here any length of time'. The old idea of 'a telling book on
England' receded in an Anglophile euphoria that admitted imperfections
only in minor matters. He professed to be mildly scandalised by the
number of wines served with English meals; there was gas-light everywhere except in hotel bedrooms, where 'they give you a candle five
inches long. But they *do* give you a power of coal on a cold day. In
American hotels they send it to you in a spoon'. Much English food he
found unappetising, but here too an honourable exception was
instantly made, this time for the sole:

> I never had a sole before. I believe it is a fish that is not known in
> American seas. But it is a delicious creature . . . He has his spine
> and radiating bones laid neatly in the middle of his person, like a
> fernspray in a hymn-book.

The inevitable pun on 'sole' and 'soul' prompts a delightful dialogue
between Twain and a waiter who thinks the fish ought to have been
differently cooked:

> "Perhaps it would have been better if I had never *had* a soul?"
> "Yes, indeed, sir. Kidneys is much better, sir. If you had 3 or 4
> kidneys. . . ."
> "Monstrous heresy! Can a multiplicity of kidneys supply the
> place of a soul?"
> "Some thinks they do, sir, Kidneys, with gravy on 'em."

Like a later Missourian writing *The Waste Land*, Twain has an ear for
the Cockney idiom, and if he could have sustained it the book on
England might have had Dickensian qualities. His burlesque piece on
Old St. Pauls would no doubt have gone into it, and he would have
worked up his notes on the Guildhall election of the Lord Mayor,
where again amusement is tempered by respect.

By the beginning of November he was feeling truly at home. 'I would like to stay here about fifteen or seventy-five years, a body does have such a good time', he wrote to James Redpath, the Boston organiser of the Lyceum lectures. He also told Redpath of having been invited to the annual dinner of the Whitefriars Club as the chairman's guest of honour; the 'gorgeous time' he expected to have was however denied him by his own carelessness:

> I got it into my head that Friday was Thursday so I staid in the country stag-hunting a day too long and when I reached the club last night nicely shaved and gotten up regardless of expense, I found that the dinner was *the night before*.

The lecture-platform too was beginning to lure him again, and he was reworking his *Roughing It* lecture to deliver in about a month's time twice in London 'just for fun'. Invitations and large offers from 'pretty much all the English and Scottish towns' he had turned down, 'not being fond of railroading'. He had not been, he said, fifty miles from London nor did he intend to 'till I budge homewards' [15*].

This was to happen earlier than he foresaw and before he had had a chance of lecturing. Five days after writing to Redpath he received a cable calling him home. Ever alert to the possibility of publicity he wrote at once to the papers:

> I desire to say to those Societies in London and other Cities of Great Britain, under whose auspices I have partly promised to lecture, that I am called home by a Cable Telegram.
> I shall spend with my family, the greater part of next year here, and may be able to lecture a month during the Autumn upon such scientific subjects as I know least about and may consequently feel least trameled in dilating upon. [17*]

To his mother he complained that, having come 'to take notes for a book', he had not 'done much but attend dinners and make speeches'. Nevertheless, he had 'had a jolly good time' and 'made hundreds of friends'; the English, he found, 'laugh so easily that it is a comfort to make after-dinner speeches here' [16]. The spectre of the dour passenger in the Liverpool-London train was becoming less of a threat already.

Even the voyage home was to furnish further unexpected food for Anglophilia. He sailed, on 12 November, on the Cunard liner *Batavia* (Emerson's son Edward happened to be a passenger on it also). On the voyage the *Batavia* rescued the crew of a dismasted vessel, and the gallantry of the ship's company was subsequently rewarded, at the instigation of the passengers, by the Royal Humane Society and the Cunard Company. Inspired by the news of this Clemens wrote at enthusiastic length to the *New York Daily Tribune*.[4] The letter is a characteristic

mélange of the serious and the comic. The plea for an American equivalent to the Royal Humane Society is bolstered by the assurance 'Why, it
is the next most noblest thing to sending moral tracts to Timbuctoo.
And would cost less money, too. Not that I object to sending moral
tracts to Timbuctoo; far from it; I write the most of them myself'.
Similarly his tribute to the Cunard Company breaks off with 'But
really, I can't advertise these parties for nothing. It isn't "business".'
Yet, just as *The Innocents Abroad* interjects into its humour serious
praise of virtue observed, so one of the highlights of this letter is this
passage:

> We are the offspring of England; and so it is pleasant to reflect
> that the very first thing that astonishes a stranger when he arrives
> in that country is not its physical features, not the vastness of
> London, not the peculiarities of speech and dress of its people,
> but the curious lavishness with which that people pour money
> into the lap of any high and worthy object needing help. It is not
> done ostentatiously, but modestly. It comes from nobody knows
> where, about half the time, but it comes.

Clearly it was not merely dining out and lack of time that inhibited the
writing of the 'telling book about England'.

III

Having made his mark as an after-dinner speaker to this congenial
English audience, Clemens returned the following year intent on
exploiting that talent on the lecture platform as well. His family accompanied him for the summer; they landed in April, and Mrs Clemens
found the Langham Hotel, where Regent Street and Portland Place
meet, every bit as comfortable as her husband had found it before. His
circle of English friends welcomed them cordially and many new ones
were added to the number.

Among these friends was an expatriate American with a somewhat
chequered past whose future was to cross and re-cross with his for more
than thirty years. Moncure Daniel Conway had been born in Virginia in
1832; he had become a Methodist minister but was later converted to
Unitarianism.[5] His Virginian origins had not prevented his becoming a
convert also to the anti-slavery movement before the war, but he could
not align himself wholly with the Union cause because he distrusted the
political motives of the North and abhorred the use of violence. In
1863, however, he was sent to England by the abolitionists, in the hope
that his oratory might swing public opinion towards support of them.
Idealism and good intentions outrunning both his discretion and his
mandate, Conway took it upon himself to open negotiations with John
Mason, the Confederate envoy in London. His proposal had the merit
of simplicity, and the drawback of political naiveté: if Mason would

induce the Confederacy to agree to the emancipation of the slaves Conway would persuade the abolitionists to cease supporting the war and to bring pressure on the Government to end it. Mason's response had been to publish in the *Times* the letters which Conway had been unwise enough to write, with the result that abolitionist support was promptly withdrawn, not from the war, but from the now discredited Conway. Realising that there was no longer a place for him in America, Conway settled in London, accepting a ministry in South Place, Finsbury; he also diverted into less controversial channels his efforts to promote Anglo-American understanding. His admiration for Emerson led him to collaborate with Hotten on the project for publishing Emerson's uncollected essays. He began to publish articles on contemporary American writers in the *Fortnightly* and other English periodicals, as well as drawing on them in his sermons and addresses and later publishing monographs on both Emerson and Hawthorne. When *Leaves of Grass* first appeared in 1855 he had sought out Whitman in Brooklyn and 'came off delighted with him'. He met the poet again in 1857, and ten years later helped William Michael Rossetti with his edition of Whitman, undertaking the negotiations with Whitman over the omissions in that edition. As a result of this Whitman asked him in 1868 to become his English agent, a role that he was later to fill for Mark Twain as well.

Conway's two-volume *Autobiography* illustrates anecdotally his intimacy with many men of letters on both sides of the Atlantic, but its main preoccupation is with his progress from Methodism through Unitarianism to free thought; its account of his relationship with Clemens is brief and demonstrably inaccurate. A letter from Clemens addressing him as 'my dear Sir' is dated from the Langham Hotel on 6 October but, like so many letters between them, inconveniently omits the year. It declines rather formally 'the opportunity of going to Stratford and enjoying the hospitality of Mr Flower so kindly offered' [12*]. On 2 November 1872, in a letter to his American friend Mrs Fairbanks, Clemens spoke of being unable to accept this invitation 'as I was too busy to visit him now'; he hoped, however, to take it up the following summer with Olivia and Mrs Fairbanks herself [14].

The visit duly took place, though without Mrs Fairbanks, on 8 July 1873. Clemens warned Conway that a pressing piece of journalistic business might prevent his being back from Paris 'in time for Hepworth on the 8th' [20], but in a letter dated 7 July Conway greets him 'On the eve of the glorious and never-to-be-disremembered-or-underestimated day when we are to visit Hepworth, the birthplace of a great man'.[6] The obliqueness of this is explained by Conway in his *Autobiography* (though his memory plays him false as to the year and the place name); an innocent deception was being practised on Mrs Clemens to heighten the surprise of her first visit to Stratford by pretending that their destination was Epworth. Conway's letter tells Clemens that they are to meet at Paddington at 2 p.m. (exhorting him not, 'in the role of the "early bird"' to 'step in at 2 a.m. at Paddington'), to travel via Oxford and to be met at the station by 'Mr Charles [Flower]'. In the *Autobiography* Conway describes Livy, finding herself at Shakespeare's tomb, ejaculating 'Heavens, where am I?' It is indicative of Clemens's tenderness for his wife's memory that, in his copy of the book, he has scored out 'Heavens'.[7] The success of the visit is attested by Clemens's letter of thanks to Flower: 'No episode in our two months' sojourn in England has been so void of alloy and so altogether rounded and complete'. The visit had included more than sight-seeing, for the writer speaks of 'having learned all about how ale is made', and of his 'new and ferocious interest in consuming it'. (Flowers are still the Stratford brewers.) The Clemenses had also made new friends, and desired 'to be remembered to all the Floral host and to thank each bud and blossom' [21*]. Charles Flower, a prominent Stratford citizen and its mayor, founded the Shakespeare Memorial there in 1874, and a letter of Clemens's (which again omits the year) seems designed to raise funds for that [34]. Although, as will be seen later, he did not contribute himself, he retained his affection for the Flowers [35], and in 1876 Conway relayed greetings to them from the Clemenses.[8]

Perhaps even before their Stratford outing (again the letter is undated) Mark Twain gave Conway the manuscript of 'a heavy job, & roughly done' which seems to have been the text of his address to the Savage Club on 28 September 1872; he asterisked the various London landmarks so that Conway 'could explain the allusions – an American reader would not understand them'. Presumably Conway was to arrange its American publication, but the letter passes quickly to a casual mention of Clemens's having lost £40 on his way home the previous evening [18]. Whatever became of the manuscript, the letter's tone bespeaks the easy informality that characterises their correspondence throughout the long friendship to which this narrative will frequently recur. Conway's sense of humour, little in evidence in his other writings, blossomed in all his contacts with Mark Twain, not merely as a reflection of the latter's radiance but because Clemens's gift for friendship brought out in this rather solemn, even self-important, minister and critic, qualities that others could not.

A British friend to whom Conway probably introduced Clemens was William Kingdon Clifford, a brilliant Cambridge Wrangler and Fellow of Trinity, who had been appointed to the Chair of Applied Mathematics at University College London in 1871 at the age of 27. When, eight years later, he died of consumption, he was described by Huxley as 'the finest scientific mind born in England for fifty years' and his lectures and essays were collected and published by Leslie Stephen and Frederick Pollock. The prefatory memoir credits Clifford with 'an inexhaustible

sense of merriment' and 'a keen perception of the ludicrous', adding a
description that could well apply to Clemens: 'There was an irresistible
affectation of innocence in his manner of telling an absurd story, as if
the drollery of it were an accident with which he had nothing to do. It
was hardly possible to be depressed in his company'. Pollock also tells
of Clifford in 1875 cancelling a class in order to attend his own
wedding and giving his students merely the Twain-like explanation that
'he was obliged to be absent on important business which would
probably not occur again'. His fondness for children and his nonsense-
story which Pollock prints suggest a delightful personality and a parallel
with that other unusual mathematician, Lewis Carroll, whose acquaintance Clemens was to make a few years later.[9]

An enduring friendship that certainly began in the summer of 1873
was occasioned by Livy's indisposition on a visit to Edinburgh in
August. Clemens recorded of John Brown:

> I stepped around to 23 Rutland Street to see if the author of *Rab
> and His Friends* was still a practicing physician. He was. He came,
> and for six weeks thereafter we were together every day, either in
> his house or in our hotel.

The letters to him in Paine's selection indicate the respect in which they
continued to hold him; Clemens spoke of him as having 'the face of a
saint at peace with all the world'.[10] Among the many other British
authors that he met were Browning, Trollope, Tom Hughes, Charles
Kingsley, Charles Reade and Harrison Ainsworth; his circle of acquaintance also included Henry Irving and the medium, Home, the model for
Browning's Mr. Sludge.

In Edinburgh Clemens acquired 'the famous "Abbotsford Edition"
of Scott's works — 12 huge volumes elaborately illustrated. Pretty
scarce book'.[11] Whatever strictures he was later to pass, in *Life on the
Mississippi*, on Scott's harmful influence in the old South, he at least
had access to his work in a collector's edition. Similarly, however much
his Connecticut Yankee might later condemn the pomp of feudalism,
Clemens was delighted to acquire a twelve-foot high carved oak mantel-
piece from a Scottish castle to grace the library of his new house in
Hartford. After visits to Ireland and Paris he took his family home to
America in October at the end of the first of their many visits to
England. A week later he sailed back to London for two months' lecturing and to secure the copyright of *The Gilded Age*. He had already
made a successful debut on the English lecture-platform in October. His
wife was reconciled to his going back only for the effect his lecturing
was expected to have on his literary reputation.

IV

The way had been prepared for him as early as 18 October by Mr. Punch in his 'Welcome to a Lecturer':

" 'Tis time we Twain did show ourselves". 'Twas said
By Caesar, when one MARK had lost his head:
By MARK, whose head's quite bright, 'tis said again;
Therefore, "go with me, friends, to bless this TWAIN".

Fred W. Lorch has described very fully Mark Twain's publicity devices, the content of his lectures, and his platform manner. Hal Holbrook, on stage, television screen, and recordings, has re-created that manner for us. By this time Clemens had engaged as a secretary-companion Charles Warren Stoddard, a California friend who happened to be in London, and he too has recorded his memories of these lectures, so that it would seem otiose to rehearse it all again.[12] A little may be added to Lorch's account by focusing on one particular point in the lecture programme, the substitution of the 'silver frontier' lecture for the popular 'Sandwich Islands' one.

Clemens had decided on the change by 3 December, when he wrote to Livy that he was 'revamping and memorizing my "Roughing It" lecture, because I want to use it next week' [26*]. On Monday 8 December the *Daily News* carried this item:

Advertisement for Mark Twain at Hanover Square Rooms tonight. Stalls 5/- Unreserved 3/- Admission 1/- New Humorous Lecture entitled "Roughing It on the Silver Frontier".
The Lecture will commence at 8 o'clock, & be repeated every evening (except Saturday) at 8 on Wednesday & Saturday afternoons at 3.

Lorch is wrong, then, in saying the lecture was first given on Tuesday 9 December, but this is unimportant: what matters more is the impact the lecture made, and on this we have several witnesses. Conway was in the audience and on 10 December he wrote to the lecturer:

My dear Clemens,
    I would have liked much to have wrung your hand on Monday evening for that admirable speech of yours, but having a bonnet-less lady along could not manage it. It (the lecture) is even better than the Sandwich one, and that is saying a great deal. Your audience was limited by Sir Sam Baker, who was to be welcomed that night by the Prince, but I have no doubt your lecture will be a favourite with the public — especially as the Baker and Tichborne affairs prevented the papers publishing all your best plums.

That this was not mere flattery was independently attested by another American, G.W. Smalley, who wrote to congratulate Clemens on the same lecture and added in a postcript 'Conway sat beside us & laughed

till the bench shook. I thought his conduct most improper'.[13] Clemens
was aware of the success of this lecture even before these letters
reached him for he wrote to Livy immediately after it on the 9th:

> I never enjoyed delivering a lecture, in all my life, more than I did
> tonight. It was so perfectly jolly. And it was such a stylish
> looking, bright audience. There were people there who gave way
> entirely & just went on laughing, & I had to stop & wait for them
> to get through . . . . Those people almost made me laugh myself,
> tonight. [27*]

Whatever else is hazy in Conway's autobiographical reminiscences, his
memory of Mark Twain's platform manner is undimmed after thirty
years and his racy account of it is still delightful reading. Into his own
copy of Conway's *Autobiography* Clemens inserted an unidentified
newspaper report on the 'Sandwich Islands' lecture which extolled its
informative value and its descriptive powers, as well as its humour, and
praised its 'language which a Ruskin might envy'. Whether it was from
Conway's own pen must remain conjectural – he contributed
frequently to British newspapers and periodicals – but it suggests that
the lecture's 'intellectual treatment' of its subject was as well received
as its 'outcroppings of quaintness'.

A rather different impression, however, lingered with another
member of one of these audiences, the Reverend H.R. Haweis who, in
an otherwise favourable essay on Mark Twain nine years later, spoke of
his having lectured 'without I believe striking success':

> I heard him once at the old Hanover Square Rooms. The
> audience was not large nor very enthusiastic. I believe he would
> have been an increasing success had he stayed longer.
> We had not time to get accustomed to his peculiar way, and
> there was nothing to take us by storm, as in ARTEMUS WARD
> . . .
> His appearance was not impressive . . . He spoke more slowly
> than any other man I ever heard, and did not look at his audience
> quite enough.
> I do not think that he felt altogether at home with us, nor we
> with him.

None the less, Haweis records his surprise at finding that an hour and
twenty minutes had elapsed, and not merely the ten minutes he had
supposed.

> It means that Mark Twain is a consummate speaker.
> If ever he chose to say anything, he would say it marvellously
> well; but in the art of saying nothing in an hour, he surpasses our
> most accomplished parliamentary speakers.[14]

Haweis's verdict unintentionally supports Smalley's praise in the
letter the postscript of which has been already quoted:

Dear Mark Twain

　　We have to thank you for your kindness in sending us tickets, and still more for the delight of hearing you. Mrs Smalley and I agreed in thinking the lecture capital, both in itself and in the manner of its delivery, which was simply inimitable. I admired your way of leading up to your points, and your great good sense in giving a slow-witted English audience time to take them in. That they enjoyed so many of them was a proper tribute to you and some credit to them also, for the average Englishman does not take kindly to the peculiar humour in which you excel. I was sorry to see you so wretchedly noticed in the *Daily News* — what a donkey the man must be to be able to spoil things so.

Yours ever,
G.W. Smalley

The *Daily News* that morning had noticed the lecture in non-committal terms, its main cause for dissatisfaction being the failure to make clear 'what was, or where was, the "Silver Frontier".' It had itemised some of the contents of the lecture and allowed itself as comment only the somewhat equivocal remark 'Intermixed with his word-play and jests, Mr Twain gave some very eloquent descriptions of the country. He began and concluded his lecture last evening amidst loud applause'.

If Mr Smalley opened the *Daily Telegraph* that morning he was no doubt more pleased at their report, but the emphasis was still on the eloquence of the description of Lake Tahoe and the vivid depicting of 'the natural grandeur of the scenery of the Sierra Nevada'. The *Telegraph* at least had the geography clearer than its contemporary and also had its emphasis more accurate: 'throughout the hour and a half occupied by the lecture much substantial information was imparted in the pleasantest form, while the tendency of the speaker was always towards the droll instead of the didactic'. The *Telegraph* particularly enjoyed the way in which Clemens ended his 'entertaining discourse' with the hope 'that he had said nothing which might lead to the dispopulation of England by a flood of emigration setting in towards the country he had described, and the apologetical tone of the remark was in thorough harmony with the quaint, sarcastic humour which pervaded the whole recital of his personal experiences'.

Punch too remained loyal, and on 14 December its editor, Shirley Brooks, wrote to Clemens 'I feel desirous to do something more useful to your lecture than perhaps the article would be, and I have therefore written . . . a strong incitation to the public to make haste and go and see you'.[15] The article is possibly one referred to in a note from Clemens 'To the Editor of Punch' dated 23 September (no year specified) requesting permission to submit 'a brief article for acceptance or rejection' [25]. Brooks's puff ran thus:

"TWAIN CAN DO'T"
Antony and Cleopatra

Again we have, as J A C Q U E S   P I E R R E observes in the *Midsummer Night's Dream,*

"Twain, at large discourse;"

but, as the same eminent Frenchman says in the *Winter's Tale,* 'twill be only a case of

"Mark, a little while"

In fact, the distinguished humorist's stay is to be so brief that if we were not now upon such extraordinary sweet terms with America, we should write unpleasantly about such auto-schediastic treatment of us. But for a few times MR MARK TWAIN is to be visible to the naked eye, (fog permitting) in Hanover Square, and because his visit is so short, *Mr. Punch*, who extracts something good out of anything objectionable, performs the philanthropic act of hereby encouraging and inciting his friends to go and hear MR TWAIN'S new lecture.

The fog was no figment of Mr Punch's imagination. It rolls as densely through Stoddard's pages as through *Bleak House* and he recalls the lecturer reassuring his audience 'Perhaps you can't see me, but I am here'. Thirty years later when he read Conway's account of these London lectures, Clemens immediately and instinctively pencilled on the margin 'The fog'.

He was very conscious of the honour of *Punch's* recognition and sent home to his wife, urging her to preserve it safely, Shirley Brooks's invitation to him to spend New Year's Eve with them. Many years later he was invited to follow the tradition of carving his initials on *Punch's* editorial table and declined by indicating Thackeray's initials, WMT, and saying that two-thirds of Thackeray would do for him.[16] The *Athenaeum* had been reminded of *The Book of Snobs* and *The Innocents Abroad* but in a spirit different from this: here the diffidence of the American rings more true than it had done for the reviewer.

One of Clemens's publicity stunts had taken the form of a letter to the *Post* explaining his failure to arrange for the attendance of great public figures at his lectures:

> I was afraid of it for the reason that those great personages have so many calls upon their time that they cannot well spare the time to sit out an entertainment, and I knew that if one of them were to leave his box and retire while I was lecturing it would seriously embarrass me.[17]

He had, however, sent out complimentary tickets to some great personages despite the disdain for them affected in this letter as a whole, and one of them had honoured him with a reply:-

16 December 1873

Dear Sir,

I saw some of your countrymen last Sunday, who spoke so highly of your Lectures, that I longed to come and hear you; but whether I come or not, I am equally beholden to you for your kindness.

Yours with all thanks
A. Tennyson

This letter too was sent to Livy with the comment 'An autograph from *him* is a powerful hard thing to get'.[18]

Charles Kingsley had written to him on 26 November asking to introduce himself and extending an invitation:

. . . if you care to make a closer acquaintance than the multitude can make with our English Pantheon the old Abbey here — it would give me — and mine for my ladies are even more fond of your work than I — extreme pleasure to act as cicerones to some strange & remote spots in our great Stone Mausoleum.[19]

The visit was duly made and enjoyed, and when some three months later Kingsley was visiting the States Clemens wrote cordially to him inviting him to Hartford. His wife, he explained, was 'a trifle scared', thinking that 'meeting such a personage as a Canon of Westminster is something like encountering a King or a Colossal Grand Duke', but she had been 'this long, long time a most appreciative and admiring reader' of Kingsley and was anxious to entertain him. Clemens's final assurance that he will 'be on hand at *any* train you come by' emphasises the respect they felt for the distinction of this acquaintance [32]. Four days later Clemens had to introduce Kingsley to a Boston audience, and it may have been awe of the Canon as well as of the audience that explains the mediocrity of his speech. The editor of *The Twainian*, reprinting it, described it rightly as 'not a sample of Mark's best style'.[20] Though in better taste than the notorious later one in that city, and though it may in delivery have been better than in print, it is merely a laboured anecdote leading up to the obvious canon/cannon pun; he had utilised this much more easily in the letter by suggesting that Olivia thought a Canon 'a new and peculiarly destructive, sort of artillery'. Clemens seems to have been constitutionally incapable of expressing in speeches the respect he genuinely felt for others.

By Christmas 1873 he had become so well known in England and so well publicised that he was a celebrity, and he wrote proudly to his wife:

The photographs are so good, and they are around everywhere, so it seems as if 3 out of every 5 I meet on the street recognize me. This in London! It seems incredible.[30*]

At about this time too he was elected to membership of the Savage Club, a privilege that he valued highly. His connection with it is described in the Club's history and twenty-five years later they were to make him an honorary member.[21]

His third visit to England was now drawing to a close. Christmas 1873 he spent at Salisbury in scenes which he told Livy, 'naturally recall Coventry Patmore's books' — an interesting sidelight on his reading tastes [31]. On 17 January 1874 the *Athenaeum* told its readers 'MARK TWAIN sailed on Wednesday last from Liverpool for New York. He is expected shortly to revisit England'. In fact five years were to elapse before his return, but, despite the sadness of his mood at Liverpool as Stoddard describes it, his memories of and affection for England remained very strong.

In the summer of 1873 he had, not surprisingly, been invited to deliver an after-dinner speech to a Fourth of July gathering of Americans in London.[22] He prepared it enthusiastically but in the event was not able to deliver it, because 'our minister, Gen. Schenck' who presided, spoke at inordinate length and then cancelled all other speeches: '44 perfected speeches died in the womb . . . Gen. Schenck lost 44 of the best friends he had in England'. Mark Twain's would have been a light-hearted contribution with jokes about the American legal system, its railways, 'and a United States army which conquered sixty Indians in 8 months by tiring them out — which is much better than uncivilized slaughter, God knows'. His main theme was the great improvement in 'kindly and mutually appreciative relations' between England and America, as evidence of which he instanced the settling of 'the last two misunderstandings . . . by arbitration instead of cannon' and the fact that 'England adopts our sewing machines without claiming the invention'. He anticipated the preface to *The Gilded Age* (English edition) by finding 'hope for the future in the fact that as unhappy as is the condition of our political morality today, England has risen up out of a far fouler since the days when Charles II ennobled courtezans and all political place was a matter of bargain and sale. There is hope for us yet'. His feelings towards England at this time are perhaps best epitomised by this rhetorical question, stifled by General Schenck's verbosity: 'With a common origin, a common language, a common literature, a common religion and common drinks, what is longer needful to the cementing of the two nations together in a permanent bond of brotherhood?' It was a bond which, by the end of 1873, his own writings, his platform appearances, and his clubbable sociability had also done much to strengthen.

CHAPTER 4

TOM SAWYER IN ENGLAND

I

In 1875 Moncure Daniel Conway was at last able to fulfil a long-deferred hope and return to the States on a lecture tour which also enabled him to visit old friends, and by now the Clemenses were in this category. For them there was the double pleasure of repaying his kindness to them in England and exhibiting the new house in Hartford into which they had moved in 1874. 'One of the oddest looking buildings in the State ever designated for a dwelling, if not in the whole country' was the verdict of the *Hartford Daily Times* on 23 March 1874. What may have seemed to this journalist and to passers-by a piece of wilful extravagance on the part of a *nouveau-riche* writer, or even Mark Twain's latest and most enduring joke, had a rationale which the newspaper evidently did not know. That there were 'no less than five balconies about this building, beside that of the west tower' was due to Clemens's instructions to the architect to get some suggestion of a Mississippi steam-boat into his designs. One visitor likened the top-floor billiard room with its balcony to the pilot-house and deck; another saw the open porch at the back as 'fashioned after a "Hurricane Deck"'. Some interior features such as the stairway and the folding doors also kept alive his memories of the riverboats; others were of more recent inspiration.

At its west end the library opened into a semi-circular conservatory of a pattern which his friend and neighbour, Harriet Beecher Stowe, had popularised in the district; it contained a fountain, and its vines and plants were set direct into the ground. The folding doors separating library from dining-room could be opened to allow amateur theatricals in the library to be watched by an audience of more than eighty. Stencilled wall decorations, glass tiles and stained glass windows were by Tiffany. The unusual siting of the service wing at the front to face on to Farmington Avenue left the seclusion and the vistas at the rear for the family's enjoyment, though Clemens claimed to have done it 'so the servants can see the circus go by without running out into the front yard'.[1]

Other features of the house reflected his travels. The fireplace in the library had been brought over from Ayton Castle near Edinburgh, and the dining room fireplace incorporated a feature that may have been British-inspired. Instead of the conventional chimney-breast, there was a window immediately above the fire so that Clemens could enjoy the appearance of snowflakes falling into rising flames. Charles Barry had embodied a fireplace like this in the Reform Club when he designed it in 1837, and Clemens would have seen it if he had been entertained there by one of his many London friends. (Frank Finlay, editor of the Belfast *Northern Whig*, seems the most likely, for he spent a good deal of time with Clemens in London in 1873.) In the Hartford study an L-shaped divan was modelled, said Clemens, on one he had seen in 'a Syrian monastery'. A few years later a massive carved bed was imported from Venice: Clemens used it for the rest of his life, preferring to sleep with his head at its foot so as to be better able to enjoy the carved angels at its head.

The wonders of the house were to be described for the English reader in 1877, when *The World* carried an unsigned article on 'Mark Twain at Hartford' in its series on 'Celebrities at Home'. It referred with approval to 'his richly-furnished library, to whose beauty and artistic completeness half the lands of Europe have contributed', but perhaps over-stated its case by speaking of 'the mansion with its quaint old English architecture'. The use of red brick may be more characteristic of English than of American domestic building, and its chimneys have a hint of the Elizabethan, but its Gilded Age eclecticism is its most marked characteristic. The *Hartford Daily Times* was more accurate in alluding to 'the novelty displayed in the architecture' which, with 'the oddity of its internal arrangements, and the fame of its owner, will all conspire to make it a house of note for a long time to come'.

A hundred years after it was built it is fulfilling that prediction as the Mark Twain Memorial. More than most tourist-attracting homes of artists, the Nook Farm house contributes positively to an understanding of its owner as a writer and not merely as a man of property. 'The whole style of the house was Mark Twain' said one contemporary. *The World* defined it as 'a gradual and organic outgrowth of the owner's mind which gives you a delightful peep into the inner recesses of his character'. Mark Twain made the same point in his own way in the same year as the publication of the essay in *The World*: in a parody of 'This is the House that Jack built' he celebrates the eccentricity of the house and the idiosyncrasy of its owner ('An extravagant wag that none can tame'), identifying him with the *personae* and principal characters of all his works to date. More than a gratuitous piece of self-advertisement, the doggerel encourages a view of the house and the writings as the product of their times and a challenge to them. A monument to the ostentation and conspicuous consumption of the day, the house is also something of a *jeu d'esprit* in its calculated mixture of tastes. Neither a slavish imitation (or importation) of a baronial castle, nor a pseudo-Colonial mansion, it belongs as much (and as little) to the Old World and the New as did its ebullient owner; like his books, it assimilates a variety of disparate elements and stamps the result with its own individuality.

The indulgence of such architectural whimsy cost time and money: Clemens was at once eager and grudging in his outlay of both. Fulminating at being 'bullyragged all day' by builders, decorators and furnishers, he begins to exhibit the impatiently autocratic superiority that was to become more overt and more significant later. A letter to Mr. Flower explained that when they were with him at Stratford anxiety about the mounting costs was preying on their minds: 'So we didn't even venture to subscribe £5 to the American window in Shakespeare [sic] church! We did feel *so* poor!' [35*].

Whatever their financial standing, the Clemenses were always rich in friends and lavish in hospitality. Inscribed on their Scottish mantel was the appropriate aphorism 'The ornament of a house is the friends that frequent it', and the catalogue of their guests would be as impressive as the tributes many of those guests paid to house and hosts. But friends can be of use as well as ornament, and in December 1875 Moncure Daniel Conway was doubly welcome. Receipts from the English sales of Mark Twain's books had, up to then, contributed only modestly to the meeting of his prodigious Hartford expenses. With *The Adventures of Tom Sawyer* he must have hoped to increase that revenue substantially, and Conway's long expatriation had made him very familiar with the English market.

II

On 12 December 1875 Conway wrote to Clemens from New York proposing to visit Hartford on the 28th or 29th.[2] The letter concluded with a graceful reference to Howells whom Conway had known since 1860, and especially during Howells's consulship in Venice:

> I have had a charming little visit at the Howellses in Cambridge. Said I to them, says I, "Do you know and adore the Clemenses?" Says they "We do!!" Then, says I, Let us embrace! We did.
>
> Ever yours,
> Moncure D. Conway

The warmth of this tribute must have pleased its recipient who pasted it into his scrapbook and replied by return of post with an equally cordial invitation:

> Good! Give us both days – can't you do that? Just do your level best once more, & see if you can't manage to come the 28th & stay several days. My wife & I will be delighted. Take the train that leaves at 10 a.m. – it is the best one – and telegraph or write & I will be at the station to receive you. Come! – is it a "go"? [39*]

Evidently it was, and if Conway's later recollections of 'their beautiful home' echo sentiments he expressed at the time his hosts must have been much gratified by his enthusiasm:

> The grounds, with their gardens, trees, flowers, were such as one might look for in Surrey, England, as the result of centuries of culture, but the house they surrounded represented the consummate American taste and art. In showing me to my dainty room Mark pointed out the various tubes for calling up servants, coachman, fireman, etc. "There's one somewhere for the police, I believe", he said, peering around.

Conway also recalled Clemens showing him a letter from an autograph-hunter with whom he was 'playing a game. Mrs Clemens has been writing my replies'.[3] Again, sensitive about his wife's memory, Clemens noted in the margin of his copy of Conway's *Autobiography* 'No. She never dealt in deceptions'.

On this, or on one of his other visits, Conway was taken across the lawn to the house of Harriet Beecher Stowe with whom he was able to talk about English friends they both knew. The conversation was interrupted for charades in costume, introduced by Clemens who 'began with a knight in full armour, saying as if aside, "Bring on that tin-shop" ' and continuing with 'a romance of this knight's gallant achievements'.[4] It does not occur to Conway that he may have been witnessing the birth of the idea that was to come to fruition more than a decade later as *A Connecticut Yankee at King Arthur's Court*: the notebook entries Clemens was to make in that connection are in a very similar key.

The only contemporary reference to this, Conway's first visit to the Hartford house, is a plaintive postcard from him after the event, asking that his overshoes be expressed to him in Boston. Reporting on 5 January that he had 'started them', Clemens invited Conway to visit Hartford again before sailing:

> I want you to take my new book to England, & have it published there by some one (according to your plan) before it is issued here, if you will be so good. [40*]

The book was, of course, *The Adventures of Tom Sawyer* and the overshoes had evidently been forgotten in the excitement of discussing that. By a happy coincidence the same post brought Conway an invitation to deliver three lectures in Hartford between 18 and 23 January, news which he at once communicated enthusiastically to Clemens. His closing paragraphs indicate at least three bonds that joined the two men: respect for Olivia, enjoyment of billiards, and a relish for puns that were neither subtle nor delicate. (Clemens told Howells that he had been 'under the doctor's hands for four weeks on a stretch' [41] and Conway's word-play makes clear that the malady was dysentery):

Now your dear wife, just because she is Amiability slightly disguised in flesh & blood, shall not be imposed upon by another long visit. It is probable that between 18th and 22nd I shall be lecturing somewhere else (I hope in New Haven). But I think you & she must prepare yourselves for *some* further invasion of your household. I hope you are diligently mastering that Dissenter's trouble of yours (which reminds me of the man who entered a bookshop & asked for Pepys' Diarhee [sic]).

We will talk over the book when we meet in the intervals of b-ll-r-ds. By the way, we think b-ds a good Sunday pastime in London — especially holy (perhaps because our tables have holes) — but I suppose that at Farmington we should make the old Puritan gods turn over in their graves by the click of anything that did not give pain.

This anti-Puritan attitude comes strangely in one who in 1858 had curtailed his chess-playing because he felt it an indulgence and who was to note the 'curious survival' in him up to his 'twenty-seventh year of the Methodist dread of card-playing'.[5]

Clemens was obviously bringing out the human and the humorous elements in his ministerial friend, for a postcard from Conway in New York on 17 January reports 'Unless there should be a bluff [sic] trip slip 'twixt the cup and the lip I shall be with you tomorrow by the train leaving here at 10 a.m.'. Evidently Clemens had introduced him to the insidious rhythms of

Conductor, when you receive a fare,
Punch in the presence of the passenjare,
A blue-trip slip for an eight-cent fare,
A buff-trip slip for a six-cent fare,
A pink-trip slip for a three-cent fare;
Punch in the presence of the passenjare.

CHORUS

Punch, brothers! Punch with care!
Punch in the presence of the passenjare.

'A Literary Nightmare' which enshrined this horse-car jingle had been completed the previous November and was to appear in the February *Atlantic*. (Clemens alludes to it in his 'House that Jack built' parody.) Its popularity spread to London, again probably with the help of Conway; he told Clemens in a letter in May: 'Wish you could have heard Professor Clifford sing 'Punch in the presence' at a dinner party Wednesday, (at the piano — tune composed by himself). It was real fun'.

The manuscript of *Tom Sawyer* that Mark Twain proposed entrusting to Conway had been read by Howells in November 'sitting up till one a.m., to get to the end, simply because it was impossible to leave off'.[6] The author, however, did not bring himself 'to the dreary & hateful task of making final revision' until 16 January, and then, profiting from Howells's pencilled comments, he completed it 'at a single sitting' [42]. His delightful letter of thanks to Howells was written on the day of Conway's visit, perhaps at the same time as Conway was writing to his wife in England a letter headed 'Hartford, Conn. Jan 18' which deserves reproduction: [7]

Mark Twain has written a remarkable book called "Tom Sawyer", about which I wish you to try your hand in preparing the way for negotiations with Chatto Windus [sic]. He (Mark T.) would like to follow our plan − pay for the manufacture of his own book and pay the publisher for each copy sold. You had better arrange by letter to have Andrew Chatto come to see you, as he will be glad to do that if you say in a note addressed to him (with Esq. after it!) that it relates to a new book by Mark Twain. If *Chatto wishes to know it* you can inform him that Mr. Clemens (Mark T.) is under no obligation legal or moral to Routledge who for some time has been publishing his works; and that Routledge has no ground whatever upon which he could object to any other publisher being contracted with by the Author. You can also inform Chatto that the story is very important & illustrated with 150 engravings, & that plates can be sent over at once for the early May publication. You can tell Chatto that I suggested him to Clemens provided his firm is willing to publish on the plan mentioned. And if they incline to that let them state to you to be transmitted to me what they think will be a fair royalty for them − Clemens paying everything in the way of manufacture & advertising. Of course you can go to see Chatto if that strikes you as preferable, by appointment. You must avoid giving to the interview any force beyond a consultation; there should be nothing for the present in the way of a contract or a promise to let Chatto have the book. If Chatto inclines to anything else than the suggested arrangement, you will listen, take down what he says, and let me know at once. When I come over in March I shall bring the Manuscript (of which two copies exist) with me. It is probable that two editions will have to be issued, one cheap. Address as usual at the Literary Bureau.

Your loving husband,
M.D. Conway

Mrs Conway had been, until their marriage in 1858, Miss Ellen Dana; she was born in Cincinnati, Ohio, of parents of Massachusetts origin. A loyal wife during seventeen uneasy years, she had found their English exile less easy to bear than had Conway whose opportunities and intellectual resources were probably greater. She was unhappy at his absence in America where, her letters suggest, he was attracting neither the fees nor the audiences they had expected. Her one hope was that he might be offered a post in Boston, for she felt his Finsbury congregation was less appreciative of his letters to them than they should have been, and unsympathetic to her personally. It may have been to give her some active interest that Conway employed her on this errand to Chatto: the meticulousness of his instructions implies that she had not regularly undertaken such missions, and his parenthetic reminder of the formal mode of address argues her unfamiliarity with English life outside the domestic circle. Conway might more expeditiously have written direct to Chatto, but the employment of an intermediary — especially one so obviously unofficial — avoided any commitment to Chatto before Clemens was ready.

Conway's plan of publishing by a method other than the conventional royalty system probably appealed to Clemens's speculatory temperament with especial force at this time. In the previous July he had told Howells he could not afford to sell *Tom Sawyer* to the *Atlantic* for serial publication: 'You see I take a vile, mercenary view of things — but then my household expenses are something almost ghastly'. He quoted enviously the terms *Scribners Monthly* was giving Bret Harte for the serialisation of *Gabriel Conroy*, and the fact that in England Harte was getting ten per cent for serial rights and also for book rights, as well as an advance of £500. Terms such as these, coupled with the reflection 'it is likely I could do better in England than Bret, who is not widely known there', prompted Clemens to think more carefully about exploiting the British market [36]. By November 1875 this was crystallising into a conviction that a change of publisher might be beneficial and he had evidently asked Bliss to explore this possibility. On 5 November Clemens enquired of him:

> What have you heard from England in the way of a proposition for Tom Sawyer? I have an offer from the Routledges (which I haven't answered), & if you have heard nothing from over there, I propose to write the "Temple Bar" people. [37]

Temple Bar was a periodical published and edited by Richard Bentley, to whom Mark Twain had promised some sketches in 1873 which he had not sent.

Conway's fortunate arrival in December, his personal knowledge of Chatto, and his zeal on Mark Twain's behalf must undoubtedly have influenced the latter's decision to allow Conway to explore the possibilities more fully for him. That Conway should have recommended Chatto so strongly says much for the publisher's personal integrity. Conway's experiences with Hotten over the publication of his own books had been less than happy, and his collaboration with him in the abortive scheme to publish Emerson's essays had ended stormily. After Hotten's death in 1873, the outcome being still unsettled, Chatto had driven a fairly hard bargain with Conway, requiring him to guarantee Emerson's delivery of a manuscript and to buy back the copies of his own introductory essay which could no longer be used. Since then, however, he had been used by Chatto as an intermediary in at least one transatlantic negotiation in March 1874 in connection with Mrs Lynn Linton's *Patricia Kemball* which was running in *Temple Bar*:

> We will take 100£ for early sheets of the complete work for simultaneous publication in America on the 20th of November next, provided we hear from you that it will be accepted, before Messrs. Lippincott & Co. shall have made us a better offer.

Conway presumably was to give his American publisher Henry Holt the opportunity of outbidding the Philadelphia firm: now he was about to play Chatto off against Routledge for better terms for Mark Twain.

Having sent Mrs Conway her instructions he left Hartford once more, this time apparently remembering his overshoes but neglecting to arrange for his mail to be re-directed, which necessitated another light-hearted postcard to his host. Mail was important because the YMCA at Elmira had paid him only $100 of a stipulated $125 lecture fee and he was still hoping for the balance. On 9 February, from Louisville, Kentucky, he wrote to ask Clemens whether he had 'an influential acquaintance in Elmira' who could bring pressure on them: they were now 'coming the dodge of not answering letters'. Ever-buoyant and still remembering the horse-car jingle, he told Clemens:

> I have been for some days haunted by paragraphs in the papers saying that Mark Twain is about to take a blue trip ship — alas, what am I writing; that you mean to go to England to "lecture in London in May and June", etc. Is there any real substance in this rumour?

There was not, but there was substance enough in his own lecture tour which took him from Louisville to St. Paul, Minnesota, then back to Chicago, and by 21 February to Cincinnati where a letter from his wife reached him: 'I went down at once to Chatto & send enclosed the results of our talk. I told him I had no right to make any contract only to consult'. The enclosure was a letter from Chatto & Windus dated 31 January:

> We shall be happy to undertake the publication of Mark Twain's new work upon the terms suggested by you this morning — viz. that he should bear the entire cost of production, and pay us a royalty of 10 per cent upon the entire amount of sales.

If they had lost no time, neither did Conway: the letter was despatched to Clemens with a note written at 1 a.m. on 22 February. Conway was to lecture again in Hartford on 8 March and would call on the morning of the 9th for final instructions before sailing for England on the 11th. No record of the meeting survives but Conway left with the manuscript, recalling later 'I read it on the ship and then recognised that Mark Twain had entered on a larger literary field'.[5]

III

It was a literary field even larger than Conway could possibly have recognised at the time. *The Adventures of Tom Sawyer* is Mark Twain's first single-handed attempt at sustained fiction, but it is more than that — more, too, than his first excursion into that dream-world of remembered Missouri boyhood that was to fascinate his imagination for the rest of his life. It was the product of a new literary personality: the 'wild humorist of the Pacific slope', famous in print and on the lecture platform as the droll raconteur of racy and irreverent anecdotes, had become not merely a novelist but a family novelist. The persona he had so successfully adopted in *The Innocents Abroad* and *Roughing It* had been that of the irresponsible bachelor with no ties of home or class and, for all his mockery of Europe, only the loosest of ties to country and to institutional religion: he was, in his own phrase, 'one of the boys'. However, when Howells described *Tom Sawyer* as 'altogether the best boy's story I ever read'[9] it was not that sort of 'boy' that he had in mind. Mark Twain was beginning to take life and himself seriously beneath the surface gaiety of this new book. *The Gilded Age* had seen him tackling a serious subject and adopting to some extent the standards and situations of the sentimental novel of his day; in the preface he had lamented the acquisitiveness of the age and the corruption of American politics, but his creative imagination had failed to respond to these large national issues in the way they merited; the prefatory assertion of 'a great strong faith in a noble future for my country' is a tacit admission of this, for there is little in the novel to support it. That his imagination did respond to his material in *Tom Sawyer* is a truism, and like many truisms its truth may have become a little blurred.

Perhaps the blurring started before the book ever got into print. Howells's prediction of 'an immense success' for the book had been accompanied by a warning: 'I think you ought to treat it explicitly *as* a boy's story. Grown-ups will enjoy it just as much if you do'. Always willing to accept Howells's advice, Clemens, in thanking him for it, narrowed the remark in a way that its author does not seem to have intended: 'Mrs. Clemens decides with you that the book should issue as a book for boys, pure & simple — & so do I. It is surely the correct idea' [38]. The editors of the Mark Twain-Howells correspondence suggest that Howells meant only that publication in the *Atlantic* would seem to be directing the book at an adult audience. His comment 'I shouldn't think of publishing the story serially' may have been in part a graceful acceptance of Clemens's earlier refusal to give it to the *Atlantic*, but it is much more a logical development of his praise for the compulsive quality of the book that he had experienced in reading it.

The Clemenses took him literally, and it was in this spirit that Clemens accepted all Howells's suggested emendations, coming to speak of it as 'now professedly & confessedly a boy's & girl's book' [42], and losing sight of the appeal to an adult audience with which Howells had also credited it. Howells certainly toned down some of the racier aspects of the diction, and Mark Twain's ready acceptance of this may be interpreted in several ways: always unsure of his own taste he deferred meekly to Howells's, prudish at times and genteel as that was; or it may be seen as an instance of Samuel Langhorne Clemens sacrificing Mark Twain on the Hartford altar of middle-class respectability; or it is Mark Twain capitulating too easily to the inertia which made the final revision of the book a 'dreary & hateful task' for him. All these have some validity, but the crucial factor was more probably Mark Twain's own view of his role in this book, unconscious as that may have been.

Perceptively Howells remarked that his 'corrections and suggestions in faltering pencil' were 'almost all in the first third. When you fairly swing off, you had better be let alone'. It is the humorous, episodic scenes of that first third, more than the book as a whole, which have earned for *The Adventures of Tom Sawyer* its popular reputation as a celebration of happy, unfettered boyhood, the antithesis of the 'improving' type of juvenile literature embodied in the contemporaneous Horatio Alger novels. These are the chapters in which Tom is the engagingly mischievous scapegrace whose ingenuity gets him out of the difficulties that his boyishness gets him into. Somewhere after Chapter VI, realising that a novel has to be more than a string of anecdotes however amusing, Mark Twain begins to get a story under way. As he does this the devices he employs become increasingly fraught with serious implications. Tom's calf-love for Becky is amusing because the perspective on it is adult, parental: his agonies are never made as real to us as they are to him. Yet, as the Tom/Becky plot develops, Tom's 'nobility' in taking her punishment, his comforting of her in the cave, and his eventual rescue of her are as assertive of the desirable virtues as any Horatio Alger novel. The other plot that begins comically with Tom, Huck and a dead cat in the churchyard modulates quickly into a more serious key in its consequences. The experiences to which the boys are exposed are comic only because they are satisfactorily delivered from them unharmed: the serious and horrifying elements in them are played down but not eliminated. If at times we are reminded of the traumatic scene in *The Innocents Abroad* where Mark Twain remembers his boyish self finding the corpse on the floor of his father's office at night, it is obviously not coincidental.

Conway, on his return to England, wrote to tell Clemens that it was the best book he had done: 'The cave scenes are written with the highest dramatic force. I don't think it would be doing justice to call it a boy's book and think it had better be left people to form their own conclusions whether it is for young or old'.[10] In reply Clemens gave him *carte blanche* to omit the preface, to alter it, or even to substitute a new one over his own name: 'Fix it any way you want to, if as you say, it will be best not to put it forth as a book for youth' [43]. This readiness to accept the judgments of others argues a lack of confidence in his own judgment rather than in the book itself. That he should defer to Howells is not surprising; that he should give Conway such freedom and responsibility indicates his respect for Conway and for Conway's knowledge of the English market.

Perhaps remembering his unhappy experience over the abortive Emerson volume, perhaps out of natural reluctance to appear as Mark Twain's sponsor, Conway wisely decided that any change by him 'would have been impertinent' and as the author's 'little preface reads excellently' wisely let it stand. In it Mark Twain speaks of the book as 'intended mainly for the entertainment of boys and girls': it is rather like Graham Greene's use of the term 'an entertainment' for something that was later to be elevated into 'a novel'. Although with some justice Howells thought that 'to put it forth as a study of boy character from the grown-up point of view' would be to 'give the wrong key to it', his suggested revisions may have appealed more to Mark Twain as paterfamilias than to Mark Twain as social climber, uncertain artist, or indolent proof-reader.

The book is 'for the entertainment of boys and girls' only in that it recounts amusing and exciting adventures that have a happy outcome because Tom accepts his responsibilities when they confront him and is allowed to revert to boyishness at the end. 'Part of my plan', Mark Twain continued in his Preface 'has been to try to pleasantly remind adults of what they once were themselves', but he does this in a way to remind them even more sharply of what they now are — no longer children, but adults who can watch the growing-pains of childhood with affectionate indulgence. They can enjoy the book as the 'study of boy character' it so delightfully is, but they will have a sense of distance from its happenings that will not trouble its younger readers. This double-vision is the book's strongest feature. Reminded 'of what they once were themselves', the adult readers are tacitly reminded of a parental responsibility to provide for childhood a framework of security in which it can flourish. Mark Twain never allows this to become didactically overt: Aunt Polly's solicitude for Tom is often misplaced and comic, but it is none the less genuine and admirable. It is this, too, that dictates his benevolent shaping of the story and his acceptance of Howells's corrections.

Much of his correspondence with Howells at this time is an exchange of anecdotes about the progress and the sayings of their children. While the book was in the press in America Clemens, writing on a totally unrelated subject, told Howells revealingly 'When a humorist ventures upon the grave concerns of life he must do his job better than another

man or he works harm to his cause' [48] . The world of *Tom Sawyer* is
a world made safe for children, despite all its threats to their innocence.
Tom never becomes the unattractively dissimulating manipulator that
he is in the closing chapters of *Huckleberry Finn*, but neither is he the
narrator of this story as Huck is of his. This St. Petersburg is unlike the
altogether tougher south of the later novel, but it has anticipatory
glimpses of that world in the Injun Joe plot. The corpse that has met a
violent end and is stumbled upon unawares is an increasingly recurrent
symbol in Mark Twain's writing. In this novel its implications are
played down and do not disrupt the story or fracture its unity as they
do later, but they are none the less there. This view of the novel was
charmingly, if not wholly consciously, adumbrated by one of its first
readers and staunchest champions: Moncure Daniel Conway, newly
landed in England, began his first progress report to Clemens with a
graceful recollection of 'a certain house on the brow of a wooded hill —
a beautiful room with three fairies flitting about in it, and guarded by a
dragon whom I vainly tried to subdue with a billiard-cue'.[11] *The
Adventures of Tom Sawyer* is the first work of Mark Twain the family
man, and the family was as dear in Victorian England as to America.
Clemens's fondness for the writings of Coventry Patmore must have
taught him as much.

IV

This letter of Conway's is a long one, largely devoted to explaining
the differences between the alternative forms of publishing in terms so
confusing that Clemens might have quoted Byron: 'I wish that he'd
explain his explanation'. The weariness of which he complains at the
end of the letter is evident throughout. His exposition is obscured by a
wordiness unusual for him and by a re-emphasising of many points, but
even more by his arithmetic: he begins by basing his illustrative calculations on a hypothetical retail price of five shillings but by the end he
has silently and probably unwittingly changed this to the more usual
price of seven shillings and sixpence. The distinction between the two
methods of publishing is not difficult to draw: on the royalty system
the publisher bore the cost of production, advertising and distribution,
paying a percentage of the proceeds to the author, whereas on the
commission system these costs were borne by the author who then
took all the proceeds and paid the publisher a percentage commission
for his trouble. Conway's own preference was decidedly for the second:
'No publisher likes it. I do'.

Having persuaded Clemens to let him explore its possibilities for
Tom Sawyer, he had had 'two long sessions with the Routledges, father
and son; found them much opposed to publishing on 10 per cent commission, but finally willing to undertake it in a spirit that did not
impress me as enthusiastic enough'. His own enthusiasm had been

stimulated by his shipboard reading of the manuscript and he was convinced that 'with an earnest man to take hold of it . . . there is money in it, if not millions'. Nor, apparently, was he alone in his belief. 'I have had several hours interview with Chatto . . . and they are so anxious to get the book, so plainly determined to make it their leading card, that I have resolved that they are the men for our work'.

His reasons for this, apart from his personal prejudice in Chatto's favour, are compelling: Chatto was willing to print on a commission basis and 'presumably because of lower production costs' quoted a profit for the author rather higher than Routledge's estimate. He had also promised Conway 'freedom to examine all of his books & printers accounts', but, most important of all, had offered an alternative of royalty payment and was prepared to begin printing as soon as Clemens authorised it and while he was deciding which method of financing it he preferred. On Conway's calculation the ten per cent commission system would net Clemens, on a sale of ten thousand copies of a 7s. 6d. edition, approximately £1,000, whereas a royalty on that sale would amount only to £750. However, the commission scheme entailed Clemens's meeting all costs of production and advertising, which required an immediate payment of £500 and another £500 later: to a man who a year earlier had described his household expenses as 'something almost ghastly' such an outlay must have seemed prohibitive, even though his profits would rise encouragingly on reprints and cheap editions. The choice was made easier for him by Conway's news that Chatto's royalty proposition was 'more liberal than usual': 1s. 6d. on every copy of the 7s. 6d. edition and 3d. on every copy of the 2s. 6d. cheap edition. 'These', Conway told him, 'are as fair propositions as have ever been gained by an American author since I have lived in England'. Foreseeably, Clemens accepted them at once, though characteristically telling Conway that the decision was Olivia's [43] .

If he wanted proof that he could secure better British terms than Bret Harte's ten per cent, here it was. Chatto & Windus were offering Mark Twain double that figure on the more expensive edition, even though they stayed at ten per cent on the cheaper one. His letter to Conway bespeaks his satisfaction; it also shows the generosity of spirit and impatience with detail that were to bedevil so many of his later, more ambitious business ventures. Conway had suggested 'with a wince' a five per cent commission for himself: Clemens agreed at once, and Conway proceeded to give him good value for it. The contract he signed with Chatto & Windus on 24 May defined Clemens's royalties thus: 1s. 9d. on 7s. 6d.; 1s. 2d. on 5s.; 10d. on 3s. 6d.; 7d. on 2s. 6d.; and 5d. on 2s. The absence of correspondence implies oral negotiations, and Conway drove a hard bargain: the royalty on the 7s. 6d. edition had now risen to nearer twenty-five per cent, while that on the 2s. 6d. edition had been more than doubled and brought into line with the others. By what means he had achieved this is a less interesting question than why Chatto was prepared to make such concessions when Routledge was making no effort at all to retain Mark Twain. Chatto, in the letter forwarded by Mrs Conway, had agreed to 'publication by commission' without any clear idea of the nature of the book, so he must have been confident of the author's ability to sustain his English reputation. Ironically, the feud with Hotten may have given Mark Twain a higher prestige value for Chatto than for Routledge: after all the publicity attracted by that quarrel his decision to have his new book published by Hotten's successor would look like an assertion of confidence in the new management and a tribute to the business acumen of that successor in healing such a breach. Neither party could foresee with what mutual profit this new connection would develop, but the agreement to publish *Tom Sawyer* in England was effected much more smoothly than was the publication itself, and there must have been occasions when Chatto wondered whether it was worth all the trouble.

Conway's original letter on the subject had authorised his wife to tell Chatto that he would bring the manuscript with him in March, that there ought to be two editions, one a cheap one, that the book would be 'illustrated with 150 engravings, & that plates can be sent over at once for the early May publication': this in mid-January. In March, in his 'several hours interview with Chatto', more detailed plans were agreed. A 7s. 6d. edition with pictures would be followed, when the market was right, by a 2s. 6d. one, but there were in any case problems of format to be overcome:

> It will be positively necessary [Conway told Clemens] for the book to appear here in a difft shape from the American — (which here is fatally unorthodox). I send you by bookpost a copy of Tom Hood's Nowhere & North Pole as an indication of the kind of book we shall have to make here.

Conway assured Mark Twain that if the change in format necessitated reducing any of the original illustrations 'it will be done with artistic care so as not to impair the figures'; he promised to watch 'all these details like a hawk' and to revise the proof personally after Chatto's proof reader. If any picture could not be safely adapted they would 'either leave it out or reduce it by photography & recarve it'. With his characteristically optimistic confidence, Conway immediately cabled Clemens to send him electros of the illustrations, amplifying this in the letter:

> They ought to arrive here in about 15 days. The type will be set up & waiting for them, it being very important here that the book should appear about the middle or third week in April to catch the great Spring sales . . . in which case May 1 would be a good time for your American appearance.[12]

Conway's proposed production schedule was less unrealistic than might be thought, though April publication can hardly have been feasible. On 29 March Chatto acknowledged receipt of the manuscript which 'is now in the printer's hands to be set up'. Some of the surviving galleys are dated: apparently Spottiswoode, the printer, had the first set of proofs back to Conway by 11 April, the seventh set two days later, and the seventy-ninth set (down to Chapter XXIV) by 1 May. On 3 May Conway returned 'the last revise of the last proof' and on 10 June the book was advertised in the *Athenaeum* as 'New copyright work by Mark Twain. Now ready'. An impressive rate of book production by any standards, it compares especially favourably with Bliss's dilatoriness.

In mid-April Clemens had cabled Conway that the American edition would not appear until the autumn, and Conway had replied

> All right. We shall come out here just so soon as we can get hold
> of the electros of pictures which we are anxiously expecting.
> They wd. naturally have been sent after my first long letter to
> you.

Unfortunately the electros were still in Hartford. A letter was on its way to Conway, dated 16 April, in which, with no sense of urgency, Clemens was suggesting that 'Chatto may see *his* best market in waiting till fall' also. Ignoring the arguments for a difference of format in the two countries, he quoted to Conway alternative prices for a full set of plates ('pictures, letter press and all') or a set of 'picture-electros alone': 'Write or telegraph me which you want and I will send them' [44].

On 6 May Conway told him categorically that Chatto & Windus were 'convinced that they can make no use of the American letter-press in this country' where books of the American shape were known 'only in connection with "toybooks" or 2d. [second] class things like Cassell's'. There does seem to have been a genuine preference in England for a format smaller than the American. In this instance, the dimensions of the English *Tom Sawyer* cited by Blanck are $7\frac{9}{16}''$ x $5\frac{1}{2}''$ as against $8\frac{7}{16}''$ x $6\frac{9}{16}''$ for the American. This consideration, as well, probably, as copyright law, explains the preference for setting a book anew (on either side of the Atlantic) from a second manuscript or proofs rather than publishing from borrowed plates or imported sheets.

V

It must have been at this stage that Chatto decided to wait no longer but to bring out an unillustrated edition immediately and follow it with an illustrated one to catch the Christmas trade. Conway had told Clemens in April 'Everybody here frantic with curiosity, and threatening a mob if there be any delay'. That Conway was himself zealously fanning that curiosity is clear from the conclusion to his letter to Clemens of 27 April:

I have just given to a big audience (for London) about 1500 of
the best people here a lecture on "America Revisited", in which,
speaking of the younger generation of American authors, I selected you as a type, and took up the burthen of prognostication in
Tom Sawyer, and said that I must purloin one scene from the
work whose MS. had been rashly entrusted to me (Loud
applause). I then read, having previously practised it over, the
scene of Tom whitewashing the fence and farming out the privilege. The audience roared like a bull. They laughed till eyes
streamed – floors were pounded – and such a gust of cheers was
raised at the end to fill the sails (& I hope *sales*) of that book as
never before delighted the heart of your friend, M.D. Conway.
P.S. – Chatto was charmed and says no book could have a better
send-off & he is getting it out as quick as may be. I have just
revised and sent back proof down to the point when Muff is in
gaol.

No sooner had Conway finished reading the proofs of the whole book
than he wrote again to its author (6 May 1876): 'I am preparing some
notices of [sic] the press, at whose criticisms I expect to be much surprised, and for whose authors I shall enquire diligently among my
literary friends'.

The first English review of *Tom Sawyer* appeared in the *Examiner*
on 17 June, the second in the *Athenaeum* on 24 June. Both were unsigned, but the *Examiner's* was considerably longer than that in the
Athenaeum (approximately 2000 words, as against 450). It gave the
reader a foretaste of the book by two sizeable extracts (approximately
260 and 860 words respectively), and was altogether more knowledge-
able, constructive and comprehensive in its discussion of all Mark
Twain's work to date. This review was in print and on sale only seven
days after the date on which *Tom Sawyer* was advertised as 'ready', but
the writer had evidently familiarised himself with the text remarkably
well to have been able to write so fully about it, for the lengthy quotations are clearly not there merely as padding. There is strong presump-
tive evidence that the writer in this instance was Conway himself,
'puffing' the book from a position of convenient anonymity.[13]

Among his other activities Conway was London correspondent to
the *Cincinnati Commercial* and because of this Ohio readers were able,
on 26 June, to make the acquaintance of Tom Sawyer in a 'London
Letter' dated 10 June, initialled 'M.D.C.', and occupying forty-six
column inches on page 5. The *Examiner* review must have been written
on or about 10 June to be in print by the 17th, and comparison of the
two pieces suggests very strongly that they are by the same hand.

That both quote exactly the same extract describing the discovery of
Injun Joe's body might be a coincidence; the second passage which the
Examiner reproduces is the church scene with the dog and the 'pinch-
bug' which Conway singles out for praise, though not for quotation, in

the *Commercial*. The parallels between the following passages are more striking: turns of phrase, the same topical allusion exploited in almost the same way, and similarities of tone that half-suggest the tone of the original:

> 'Tom Sawyer' carries us to an altogether novel region, and along with these characteristics displays a somewhat puzzling variety of abilities. There is something almost stately in the simplicity with which he invites us to turn our attention to the affairs of some boys and girls growing up on the far frontiers of American civilisation. With the Eastern Question upon us, and crowned heads arrayed on the political stage, it may be with some surprise that we find our interest demanded in sundry Western questions that are solving themselves through a *dramatis personae* of humble folk whose complications occur in a St Petersburg situated on the Missouri river. Our manager, we feel quite sure, would not for a moment allow us to consider that any other St Petersburg is of equal importance to that for which he claims our attention.
>
> *(The Examiner)*

> It is, as I think, the most notable work which Mark Twain has yet written, and will signally add to his reputation for variety of powers. His *dramatis personae* are mainly some boys and girls residing in the magnificently small village of St. Petersburg, somewhere on the Missouri, the Czar of which village is Tom Sawyer, who settles his Western question more satisfactorily, I suspect, than the chief of the larger St. Petersburg is likely to settle his Eastern one. Under pretext of this boy-and-girl's romance, Mark Twain has written a book which will not only charm elder readers . . . but will be of value to philosophers.
>
> *(Cincinnati Commercial)*

In the *Commercial* Conway suggests 'the survivals of ancient Oriental and Greek myths and beliefs in the elaborate folk-lore of Tom Sawyer and his comrades'; in the *Examiner* the 'Injun Joe' extract is followed by the comment: 'In such writing as this we seem to be reading some classic fable, such as the Persian sadi might point with his moral, "Set not your hearts on things that are transitory" '. Both make the mistake of locating St Petersburg on the Missouri instead of the Mississippi. Both question whether the term 'humorist' is any longer adequate to describe a writer capable of the range Mark Twain has now mastered; both lay emphasis on his 'philosophy'; and both apply to his writing the phrase 'innate refinement'. Where the *Commercial* commends 'the stately and dignified way in which he deals with the seemingly small subject which has excited his sympathy', the *Examiner* observes:

> Nor is this feeling of the dignity of his subject absent when the author is describing the most amusing incidents. Indeed, a great deal of Mark Twain's humour consists in the serious — or even at

times severe — style in which he narrates his stories and pourtrays [sic] his scenes, as one who feels that the universal laws are playing through the very slightest of them.

That Conway was the author of both seems indisputable. A closer analysis of the two essays would show that he made some attempts to slant each towards its particular audience, and he deserves credit too for singling out for special commendation in the *Commercial* 'a unique and vigorously-drawn character called Huckleberry Finn, the juvenile Pariah of the village'. In publishing the piece in the *Examiner* Conway may have been motivated by friendship and a desire to make his own five per cent commission as large as possible, but he marks a new departure in Mark Twain criticism. For the first time in England Mark Twain is treated as a serious writer with claims to literary merit.

The Athenaeum was still patronising, but its reference to *Tom Sawyer* as 'consecutive, and much longer than the former books' implies a familiarity on the reviewer's part with only the *Sketches* (the only title he mentions is *Screamers*) and not *The Innocents Abroad* or *Roughing It*. Both it and *The Times* were generally favourable to the book but in a heavy-handed way. Both found it genuinely amusing, but belonging to a world totally different from their own. Neither could accept its picture of childhood as wholly convincing, but neither knew quite how to handle it. *The Times* finds Tom 'a portentous phenomenon' of 'unprecedented precocity'; ' "Cuteness" is scarcely the word for Tom's ingrained artfulness'. Then, exemplifying this by extensive reference to the fence-painting incident and other episodes, it seems to succumb to the book's charm and to find 'the ludicrous individuality of Tom himself' the key to its success. Neither recognises, as Conway did in his *Cincinnati Commercial* piece, that there is an essential innocence in the idyllic aspects of the book that would arouse envy in the English child and nostalgia in the adult.

The other feature of *Tom Sawyer* to which neither does justice is its idiom. *The Times* praises the originality of Tom's 'quaint felicity of picturesque expression' but is later troubled by 'the queer Americanizing of the language'. To the *Athenaeum* reviewer, what is now commended as 'the vernacular tradition' was evidently as great a mystery as were the rules governing the use of the double negative in English:

> With regard to the style, of course there are plenty of slang words and racy expression, which are quite in place in the conversations, but it is just a question whether it would not have been as well if the remainder of the book had not been written more uniformly in English.

In one respect Conway achieved a greater anonymity than he intended. Other American papers quickly plundered the *Commercial* article for extracts without bothering to acknowledge its authorship. Long before the American edition appeared, Mark Twain was mystified to discover passages from the book in the American press. In July, evidently forgetting Conway's May letter, he told him with surprise:

> I've found out where the wildly-floating extracts that puzzled me so much, come from. From your Cincinnati letter, you shrewd man! I happened to run across the entire letter in a Hartford paper, extracts & all. Much obliged to you, but you know that.*

He added that Charles Dudley Warner, newly returned from England and enthusiastic over the book, had reported that Conway even read it to his congregation on Sundays [45]. Warner may not have been exaggerating, for Conway yielded to no one in his admiration for the book. Howells's review in the May *Atlantic* he thought 'good' but objected to its comparisons with Thomas Bailey Aldrich: ' "A Bad Boy" is not to be mentioned on the same day with Tom S.' He was also embarrassed lest the American sales be damaged by the premature publication of his extracts.[14]

Absence abroad prevented Conway's earning the £50 Mark Twain offered if he could find him an English collaborator in the dramatising of *Tom Sawyer* [45] [15]. Conway was, however, in all probability the author of 'Mark Twain at Hartford' in *The World*.[16] Its first-hand acquaintance with the appointments of the house is less significant than its emphasis on the owner's cultured taste, warmth of personality, and seriousness of purpose. Its declaration that 'The much-abused term, "professional humorist", can hardly apply to Mark Twain', and its justification of this, are entirely consistent with Conway's *Examiner* review; the presentation of Mark Twain as 'the father of two beautiful little girls of whom he is very proud ... like the amiable prince of tradition' chimes with Conway's letter of 24 March 1876; and the reference to his fondness for billiards echoes that letter and a number of others. The anecdotal approach, the almost ecstatic respect for Clemens, and a number of features of style and tone all support the probability that this was from Conway's hand. Frank Finlay's reference to it as 'A well-meant but imperfect sketch of one Mark Twain'[17] may have been directed less at its adulatory tone than at its attempt to define Clemens's political stance: 'he at first impresses you as an indifferentist, with perhaps a leaning towards pessimism ... Probably his political creed is not very different from that of the Independents'. Finlay may well have credited his friend with views closer to his own Liberalism.

VI

Even when the English edition was on the market Chatto's troubles were by no means over, for he wanted to get ahead with the Christmas illustrated edition. Whether or not Bliss had sent the electros is not entirely clear, though Clemens had reminded him of it on 24 June, but

Chatto seems to have considered Bliss's price too high and to have asked Conway to raise the matter with Clemens. This gave rise, on 1 August, to a letter from Clemens that is an archetype of a whole series over the next twenty years and that fully justifies that author's earlier description of himself as 'a man who loathes details with all his heart'. Time and again Clemens would take insufficient notice of a request made to him, give Bliss either confused instructions or none at all, and then, when Chatto remonstrated, Clemens would explode into righteous indignation as a means of blurring the whole issue.

The letter to Conway of 1 August 1876 is a perfect example. It takes the offensive at once and warms to the attack in a string of illogicalities and inconsistencies almost too obvious to need enumeration. There are conflicting statements as to whether the quotation was sent in time for the first edition or not, and no indication of when (if at all) the electros were despatched. The inconvenience to himself is ludicrously overstated ('I would have to go to work and correspond with Bliss every three days for a couple of weeks, before a comfortable and satisfactory result could be reached. Life is too short. Manuscript is too valuable'). The use of Bliss as a scapegoat is disingenuous: 'If I ask Bliss to favor Chatto by reducing the contract price of the electros, what argument (not sentimental, but commercial), am I to offer him to that end?' Bliss's dilatoriness over the American edition would surely have been a cogent argument, had Clemens bothered to use it, for maximising the chances of success with the English edition. And to the comment 'You have already issued your high-priced edition – there is no money in another one' Conway could legitimately have retorted that that was Chatto's business.

Then, abruptly, the irascibility disappears. The letter ends with a glowing account of the peace of Elmira, an invitation to the Conways to spend a week there sometime, and the news that, though *Tom Sawyer* proofs come in slowly, he is 'booming along with' his new book and has completed a third of it already [46]. The next letter, addressed to Eustace Conway, as his father was in Paris, is completely conciliatory in its acknowledgment of the safe arrival of copies of the English edition ('very handsome and attractive, they are') and in the statement

> Please tell your father I am not going to allow him to do the thousand splendid things he is doing in behalf of this book & then worry over those electrotype pictures besides. He must do the thing that is the *least trouble* to him, & charge the damage to me. Use them – destroy them – whichever is the least trouble.*

No attempt this time to deny that the electros were ordered: only a final phlegmatic 'Well, mistakes are bound to occur – folks can't help them', which adroitly avoids awkward identifications of folks who might have done [47*]. The one curious fact is Chatto's request to

Conway on 25 August 1876 to obtain either proof sheets of the American edition or a set of impressions of the illustrations so that they could plan the English illustrated edition 'which we may now consider as certain that we will bring out'. It sounds as though Mark Twain, not uncharacteristically, had erupted into anger without checking his facts and that, despite his instructions, Bliss had never sent the electros.

However, the whole incident ended happily enough with a very gracious letter of apology to Mrs Conway who apparently had also written to him, probably while Conway was abroad, in August. Clemens's letter of 28 October (Hamlin Hill is wrong in attributing it to 1877) exonerates everybody by assuming that his 'estimate of cost of plates was not received', reiterates his gratitude to the Conways for all they have done for him, and assures his correspondent:

> I feel like a scoundrel of the blackest dye, Mrs Conway; I am coming to England (in April, Mrs Clemens puts it,) with the entire family – mainly to apologize to you & Mr Conway. One can't do these things to one's satisfaction in a letter.*

Generosity of spirit is matched by material generosity too:

> As to Chatto, his case is simple & easy. I will pay Bliss for the plates, & if they are worth re-shipping home, we'll do it. If not, we won't. And moreover, I shan't have any hard feelings toward Chatto. I couldn't afford it at that price.[49*]

Blanck records that Chatto's illustrated edition was advertised on 9 December 1876; it was still some weeks before Bliss eventually issued the first American edition. This lack of synchronisation, which Mark Twain tried very hard never to repeat, aggravated another problem that had arisen (it will be more fully discussed in Chapter 11). The Canadian publisher Belford had brought out a cheap pirated edition and was, Clemens told Conway in November, 'flooding America' with it: he estimated that Bliss could not 'issue for 6 weeks yet, & by that time Belford will have sold 100,000 over the frontier & killed my book dead. This piracy will cost me $10,000' [50].

Thus when Bliss eventually brought out *The Adventures of Tom Sawyer* in America it was the fourth publication of that book: Chatto had already published an illustrated and an unillustrated edition, and there was Belford's piracy. Bibliographically, however, the situation is even more complex than that suggests. Both authorised editions had been printed from a manuscript, but the first to appear, the English edition, was set from an amanuensis copy with corrections by Howells. The proofs had been read by Conway. Bliss, however, had worked from an autograph manuscript and Clemens had presumably read the proofs. Which, then, constitutes the *editio princeps*? For, as Jacob Blanck notes, there are textual differences. The example he cites is from Chapter 1. In one text Tom promises himself ' "but I bet you I'll lam Sid for that. If I don't, blame my cats".' In the other he remarks more circumspectly "'But I bet you I'll lam Sid for that. I'll learn him!" '. The school of criticism that sees William Dean Howells as perpetually emasculating in the interests of gentility Mark Twain's vernacular raciness would probably detect Howells's influence behind the second of these and attribute that version to the Howells-corrected English manuscript. Unfortunately for theory, the reverse is the case. Howells took no exception to 'blame my cats' and the English text contains the phrase, though it is one unfamiliar to the English ear. 'I'll learn him!', which the English reader would more readily have understood, appears in the American text. Presumably Mark Twain had second thoughts about it before the later edition was printed. Yet in another instance the English edition appears to follow the author's second thoughts more closely than the American. In Chapter XX Becky comes upon the teacher's anatomy book with its frontispiece of 'a human figure, stark naked': that, at least, is how the manuscript originally read. 'I should be afraid of this picture incident' wrote Howells in the margin, and Mark Twain cancelled 'stark naked'. The English edition observed this cancellation; the American edition, although proof-read by the author, retained the phrase.

Howells's corrections to the manuscript have been discussed by other scholars, though problems of legibility make it hard to establish a definitive reading in all cases. Only a few points need to be quickly restated here. First, the changes were not all adopted by Mark Twain. Second, they were not always designed to make the diction more genteel: in the phrase 'wealth of short curls' Howells took exception to 'wealth' as 'a lady author's word', and queried 'eclat' and 'gloomed the air with a lurid lie'. On two occasions he criticised what he regarded as Anglicisms: 'jolly' in Chapter VII and 'Sawbones' in Chapter IX. Both these he marked as 'English'; both of them Mark Twain allowed to stand. It is tempting to suggest that as early as 1876 Clemens's interest in and knowledge of England had made him more cosmopolitan than Howells in his attitude to language. Certainly his English audience seems to have found less difficulty with the language of *Tom Sawyer* than did their reviewers, and the book quickly established itself as a favourite.

CHAPTER 5

A WORKING RELATIONSHIP

I

If *Tom Sawyer* won Mark Twain countless friends among the reading public, it also cemented his friendship with Conway and won him, in Andrew Chatto, an able and enthusiastic business associate who soon became a friend as well. This much can be plainly inferred from their correspondence. It would be misleading to judge by modern standards the formality of their mode of address ('Dear Mr Clemens . . .', 'Dear Mr Chatto . . .'). Mark Twain's habit of beginning letters to his American publisher 'Friend Bliss' may sound more intimate but in reality betokened little genuine affection, whereas Mr Clemens and Mr Chatto obviously had for each other a liking and a respect that easily survived all the occasional misunderstandings and contretemps of their professional dealings. Through the correctness of Chatto's business letters glimpses may be caught of a personality attractive enough to have been the subject of a full-scale study, but there is none, and unfortunately the personal letters and testimonies needed to round out such a study are probably now irrecoverable.[1]

Six years younger than Clemens, he was born in 1841, the youngest child of William Andrew Chatto. On his mother's side he was descended from Samuel Birch who had been Lord Mayor of London in the year of Waterloo. His father was the author of *The History of the Art of Wood Engraving,* and *The Origin and History of Playing Cards;* and, under the pseudonym 'Stephen Oliver the Younger', of books on angling and country life. If this range of interest, antiquarianism, and literary activity parallels Hotten's in some respects, it extends like his into the field of humour too: in 1844 the elder Chatto founded the short-lived comic daily, *Puck.* It was probably at his father's instigation that the fifteen-year old Andrew Chatto was apprenticed to Hotten in 1856, the year after the opening of the bookseller's premises at 151b Piccadilly.

The boy began as a 'runner' at book auctions, but, as Hotten diversified his interests into publishing, Chatto was able to learn the profession at the same time as his employer. Shrewd and able as both men were, publishing was to them, as to any good publisher, much more than a livelihood. Chatto acquired the interest in transatlantic writing that Hotten, lately returned from an eight-year stay in the States, had brought back with him: in 1913, when Chatto died, it was said of him that he 'knew more of American authors than any other publisher'. He knew a great many other things as well, and, although it was for the promotion of fiction that he became best known, his interests were almost as catholic as those of his father and Hotten. That, unlike them, he did not himself write is probably due less to lack of aptitude than to the pressures of a successfully expanding business, and to a nature essentially unassuming.

Seventeen years after joining the firm Chatto acquired it on Hotten's death in 1873. It was, presumably, in order to raise the necessary £25,000 that he went into partnership: his father (who had died in 1864) is remembered in the family as 'working on commissions, and having many children and no money'. In the subsequent history of Chatto & Windus W.E. Windus certainly played no role more active than might be inferred from his residing, for some of the time, on the Isle of Man. A contemporary, at Oxford, of Ruskin, Windus was a water-colour painter, though less well known than W.L. Windus, the minor Pre-Raphaelite, to whom he was perhaps related. He wrote for magazines and for the press, but it was probably as a poet that he first made Chatto's acquaintance when, in 1871, Hotten published his first volume, *Under Dead Leaves*. Most of these poems might be described as sub-Tennysonian narratives and lyrics with echoes of Rossetti and Poe. His second collection *Broadstone Hall and Other Poems* (1875), carried the Chatto & Windus imprint. Its range is wider than its predecessor's, extending to satire and parody (particularly of Poe), but it is hardly more distinguished, though Alfred Concanen's Pre-Raphaelitish engravings give it a period charm. Advertising it, Chatto quoted the *Morning Post's* praise of its 'robust, manly tone of thought' which 'gives muscle to the verse and elasticity of mind to the reader', as well as its 'thoroughly practical knowledge of and love for sea-life'. Windus was, indeed, a keen yachtsman, and Chatto's enthusiasm for sailing must have constituted another bond between them. Their partnership survived until Windus retired at the age of 81 in 1909, the year before his death; but though he published two dramas with an Isle of Man setting and a third collection of poems none of these was issued by his own house.[2]

In the same year that Chatto acquired *Tom Sawyer* he also acquired a new partner who, though his name was not added to the house's title, probably contributed more practically to its reputation and development than did W.E. Windus. Percy Spalding may not have had Chatto's flair ('a rattling good story' appears to have been his chief literary criterion), but he was a capable businessman and a congenial colleague for the firm's head. 'You do not need to be long in the society of the pair (Mr Spalding manages the commercial department) to perceive that their union partakes more of that of the Brothers Cheeryble than it does of that of Spenlow & Jorkins', was the comment of one Dickens-minded contemporary. Spalding was plainly a 'character', beginning his sentences with a sound like 'Nce', jingling his keys and loose change in his pockets and cheerfully whistling popular songs. People who are remembered for such mannerisms are usually remembered with affection and respect, and Clemens among others warmed to Spalding's geniality.

It was in 1876 too, shortly after Spalding's arrival, that the firm bought up, for £20,000, the stock and copyright of Henry G. Bohn. Although George Bell & Sons had forestalled them in the acquisition of Bohn's well-known and lucrative 'Libraries' series, the transaction was an important one, increasing their list impressively and extending it into science, in which Chatto himself had an interest that was more than merely amateur.

It was, nevertheless, in fiction-publishing that they were to establish their primary reputation, not only for their discovery and encouragement of new novelists but also for pioneering the production of copyright novels at cheap rates. Hitherto cheap fiction had been restricted to the works of obscure authors and to books out of copyright either for legitimate reasons or because of inadequate international arrangements. It was Chatto's achievement to market for two shillings a copy works by the most popular novelists of the day. Known as 'yellow-backs', these appeared in distinctive yellow boards, as a compromise between the expensive cloth-bound book and the paperback.

It was a policy that commended itself to authors as much as to the public, and Chatto never underrated the importance of his authors. When the firm had been in existence just over twenty years, he estimated that he had paid out more than a quarter of a million pounds in royalties on copyright works. The authors, he said, 'have had the lion's share of the profits, and they had a right to it'. Had more publishers shared Chatto's views there would have been less need for writers to be banding together to protect their rights; as it was, Sir Walter Besant, who founded the Society of Authors in 1883/4, later made an honourable exception of him by the remark 'I should like to see my friend Chatto driving in a gilded coach'. Chatto bought Besant's novels outright for eight hundred pounds each; many writers less popular in their day than Besant as well as others, like Robert Louis Stevenson, whose reputations have outlasted his, paid their own tributes to Chatto's methods, and when the publisher died his good relations with authors attracted especial comment in almost every obituary.

It was essentially on Chatto's judgment that the house's reputation was built, for, especially with fiction, he always acted as his own reader. He looked first for something that held the attention, then for imagination and novelty of invention with an appeal to human sympathy, and also for literary aptitude and power of expression. Mark Twain would have scored well on all counts: Hotten's training and his own subsequent visits to the United States must have persuaded Chatto earlier than many of his contemporaries that power of expression was not the sole prerogative of the Queen's English. His habit of conducting the firm's business as far as possible himself would have appealed to Clemens, even if the efficiency with which he did it might have aroused the envy of that more mercurial businessman. One of Chatto's employees was later to say of him that he 'simply oozed confidence': it was a quality to which Clemens would always respond warmly. Frank Swinnerton the novelist, a very junior member of the firm at the end of Chatto's life, also testifies to his kindness to writers: ' " In the present parlous state of the publishing trade" was his excuse for rejection; "I have the cheque in my pocket" was the usually irresistible bait to demurring authors'. That cheque might be for as little as thirty pounds, but his offers seem generally to have been regarded as very fair.

Of course he made mistakes. Swinnerton mentions his 'failure in younger days to snatch the chance of publishing Kipling', and the later loss of Arnold Bennett (whose talent Chatto had been the first to recognise) after *Sacred and Profane Love* (1905), 'which he had published under protest'. When Swinnerton knew him Chatto was nearing retirement: 'My only memory of direct contact with him is that when Bennett sold the balance of a yellowback edition of Bierce's *In the Midst of Life* by praising it in *The New Age* he gave me a copy of that old book with a slightly quizzical endorsement of Bennett's enthusiastic praise'. Although he feels that the old publisher was inevitably losing his touch, Swinnerton has, in his autobiographical writings, given several very sympathetic accounts of him, including one of his physical appearance:

> A very kindly man of middle height, with a not very big grey beard, who I think always wore a frockcoat, he would walk slowly and with a rather rolling gait along the warehouse-corridor, smoking a cigar and smiling and nodding to any member of his staff whom he met. He was of the old school, and his memories went back to halcyon days when publishers offered booksellers superb banquets at the beginning of a season, and took orders *after* their guests had sufficiently dined.

That such a personality would appeal to Samuel Clemens is as certain as that Chatto must often have used of Mark Twain his favourite formula of approval, 'He has the power of the pen'.

Two novelists not mentioned by Swinnerton who might have been added to Chatto's list were Henry James and George Gissing. James offered him *Confidence* in September 1879, when it was running as a six-part serial in *Scribner's,* for a cash payment and a royalty; the letter does not specify the sums he had in mind, nor why he was not dealing with Macmillan who had published *Daisy Miller* and *The Madonna of the Future* that year, but explains that he was making the approach 'rather tentatively'.[3] Chatto immediately offered £100 for the English rights for three years from the date of publication provided that it would run to two volumes and would appear in England before its American publication: there was, he explained, always a risk of piracy with 'a story running through an American magazine'. The offer was accepted at once and proofs of the first five instalments were in Chatto's hands by mid-October. If the sixth part were perceptibly longer than any of the others, the publisher thought, the whole might stretch to 'two volumes in rather displayed type'; he proposed issuing on 3 December, before Scribner's had completed the serialisation. *Confidence* duly appeared in this form, with the volume division occurring between chapters nineteen and twenty; though the title-page date is 1880, the British Library copy was accessioned on 13 December 1879. There does not, however, seem to have been any proposal to prolong the connection between James and Chatto & Windus.

It was in January 1884 that Gissing offered them *The Unclassed*; he sent a reader's report on it and reviews of an earlier story, but these did not tempt Chatto to ask for the manuscript. He had, he wrote, too many works of fiction on hand already. Characteristically this rejection was less blunt than that of George Bentley who told the author that he thought it 'not wholesome' to write about such things.[4] Hindsight may regard as errors of judgment the loss of James and the turning down of Gissing, but they are consistent with Chatto's middle of the road taste. The growing subtleties and sophistication of the later James would have been little to his liking; and though, as will be seen later, his social conscience could often guide his publishing decisions, he tended to prefer a sharper distinction between fiction and non-fiction than Gissing usually observed and would have been uneasy at Gissing's bleak and aggressive manner.

Not that Chatto was unfamiliar with aggressive authors; he had, after all, inherited from Hotten the irascible Swinburne. The shadier side of Hotten's activities which may first have attracted Swinburne (his pornographic and flagellatory publications) had been discontinued by Chatto, but even before purchasing the business he had assured Swinburne of his desire to continue as his publisher and had sent him an advance of fifty pounds as a token of good faith. When, despite this, a quarrel developed between them at the end of 1873, Chatto's dignified handling of it and his offer to open his books to the inspection of Swinburne and Theodore Watts cemented a relationship that was to last for the rest of Swinburne's career. Indeed, at the age of sixty-eight Chatto travelled to the Isle of Wight in order to attend Swinburne's funeral. At the earlier point in time, however, which this narrative has reached, the 1870s, the poet must have been a serious burden on the publisher's patience. A series of querulous letters, in which Swinburne's high-pitched voice is almost audible, orders books (for the book-selling side of the business still continued), complains at the non-arrival of others, asks to borrow a copy of the current *London Quarterly* ('as I suppose you have one'), and even, as 'our books here are not unpacked', seeks verification of a remembered quotation from *The Merchant of Venice*.[5] Andrew Chatto, like Mark Twain's Judge Oliver, 'never complained'; indeed, he does not even seem to have allowed himself the luxury of observing 'This thing is getting monotonous'.

When, in August 1879, Swinburne was reading the proofs of *Edward III*, he launched at Chatto the following tirade:

> I am much dissatisfied & might properly use a stronger word at finding after incredible pains on my part (to which I need not & should not have been subjected) to ensure correctness in the page already published, the disgracefully careless & scandalously incompetent printers whom you employ have not even yet observed in all cases my corrections of their execrably bad punctuation.[6]

If it did nothing else, it might have prepared the publisher (if preparation were needed) for the equally intemperate letters (often on this same subject) that he was from time to time to receive from Mark Twain.

II

The two men met in New York in the summer of 1877. *Ah Sin*, that product of stormy collaboration between Mark Twain and Bret Harte, had its New York opening on 31 July before a distinguished audience that included Andrew Chatto. Clemens wrote ebulliently and over-optimistically to Conway of the play's success (the critics 'all abuse the play, & that fills the house'). Vilification of his collaborator ('Bret Harte & I are cordial enemies . . . He is an incorrigible literary thief – & always was') alternates with praise of Chatto as 'a fine man & gentleman. I like him. We had a chat at the Lotos Club next day'. Evidently he did not yet know Chatto well enough to ask him the sort of favour that he would not have hesitated to ask in later years: the letter opens with a request to Conway to 'do a fellow a kindness' and acquire for him 'a gold watch that will tell the minutes, the hours, & the *days of the month*' for not more than £100. Livy is to make him a present of such an object, if it is obtainable, and Conway is asked to look out for it, when he is 'down in the city or over in Switzerland or Paris'. One wonders how the principled Conway reacted to Clemens's final characteristic proposal 'If you succeed I'll send the money & you wear the watch till you find a friend willing to wear it over-sea & gouge the duty' [54*].

The chat at the Lotos Club would certainly have touched on Mark Twain's future publications which Chatto was bent on securing. By the time *Tom Sawyer* had made his belated appearance in America, the first English edition of 2,000 was almost exhausted. Sixty copies had been given away, 1,858 had been sold by 14 December, and Conway had received £162.10*s*.8*d*. on Clemens's behalf. 'You can by no possibility do so well elsewhere', Conway assured him. When the remaining eightytwo copies had been sold, the first edition, Conway estimated, would have brought in 'nearly $900 in greenbacks'; this, he admitted, was a rather better return than would have been realised by the alternative method proposed of publishing at the author's expense.

By now Mark Twain was news. On 25 November 1876 the *Athenaeum*, between announcements of forthcoming works by Harriet Beecher Stowe and William Cullen Bryant, sandwiched a report that Mark Twain was working on a new book to be called 'The North Pole and How We Didn't Get There'. The item was picked up by the *Newcastle Weekly Chronicle* on 2 December, and probably by other provincial papers too, but Chatto, always keen to promote a successful author, was even more prompt. Three days after the *Athenaeum* appeared, Conway told Clemens that 'Chatto writes in some anxiety about your new book on the North Pole. I told him you would naturally let him have it'. The similarity of title between this book and Tom Hood's *Nowhere and North Pole* which Conway had sent him earlier that year suggests the possibility that a passing reference by Clemens to Hood's book had been misunderstood and misreported by a journalist eager for literary gossip. A disgruntled reply came back:

> It is a mistake, I am not writing any new book . . . and if I can make a living out of plays, I shall never write another book. For the present I have placed the three books in mind, in the waste basket, but if I should write one of them, Chatto shall have a say in it.[51]

This 'lugubrious letter', as Conway termed it, was prompted by the financial loss that the Canadian piracy of *Tom Sawyer* had caused Clemens and by his frustration at the apparent ineffectuality of copyright laws.

It was not only books, however, in which Chatto was interested. 'I really wish you would try & write an article for Chatto's excellent magazine — "Belgravia" ' Conway has scribbled in the margin of his letter of 16 November, intimating that he spoke for the publisher. In December he returned to the point; 'Chatto has not failed to notice that you have in the last Atlantic an article for which he would have given *money*'. The explanation was predictable but less than adequate:

> I promise to simultane Atlantic articles in Temple Bar, but I have always forgotten to do it, except in a single instance. I had abundant time to do it in the case of this last Atlantic article, but

as usual never thought of it, until it was too late. So I threw
away ... [52*]

The loss of the remainder of this letter prevents our knowing whether
it was money or publicity that he regretted losing; but in any case
Temple Bar was published by Richard Bentley, not by Chatto, who,
still under the misapprehension about the new work, again jogged
Conway's memory in January 1877: 'If Temple Bar simultanes with
the Atlantic I wonder why Mark Twain's "How we did not reach the
North Pole" was not reprinted? I wish we had had the early sheets
of it. I hope Mark Twain will not forget us. We now have two Magazines; the "Gentleman's" as well as "Belgravia" '.

Chatto may well have raised the matter with Clemens in New
York. A postscript to the letter telling Conway of their meeting reads:

Have offered to "simultane" 4 Atlantic articles with Temple
Bar, beginning with October number. You look out for them.
The two last are *good*. I wish there were enough for Chatto or
Bentley to make a 6d primer out of. [54*]

Subsequently, however, he asked Bentley to transfer them to Chatto
for publication in *Belgravia* [56]. They appeared in four consecutive
issues from October 1877 to January 1878 and together formed 'An
Idle Excursion', to be followed in the March issue by 'The Loves of
Alonzo Fitz Clarence and Rosannah Ethelton'.

Paying him for the last two 'Excursion' articles Chatto regretted
'that you have brought them to a close so soon, but hope that you
may let us have something else every month, even if you do not simultane it in America'. If this is a measure of the commercial significance
Chatto attached to Mark Twain, the exchange of letters is also indicative
of the informality that their relationship had already acquired. Sending
cheques for the first two articles, Chatto apologised for an error that
the book-selling side of the firm had evidently made with an order from
Clemens:

I am indeed sorry that we should have mistaken your burst of
economy for a burst of bibliographical luxury and so sent you the
"crack" edition of the "Arabian Nights" instead of the working
one; especially I am vexed that our people should have been the
means of the U.S. customs robbing you of 9$. If you will accept
the work from me burthened with this outlay it will give me
great pleasure to be so relieved from the consciousness of having
blundered which now oppresses me.

His correspondent was not to be outdone in magnanimity:

It is a right-down generous offer you make & if the books didn't
cost much I accept with pleasure. But if they were expensive it

would not be fair to let you pay the whole cost of a blunder which was not yours but a subordinate's — in which case let us divide the expense & shake hands across the bloody chasm.*

The payment for the first two 'Excursion' pieces prompted this encomium:

> Have received your checks for 5 guineas and £7.10.0 Thanks, they are satisfactory, especially the latter. The larger a check is the more I like it; & the more I honor & glorify the sender, & the more it stirs me up to high literary achievement in that man's behoof. [57*]

Chatto reciprocated by paying for the third and fourth pieces at the rate of £7.10s.0d. each, but would accept no payment for the *Arabian Nights*. Thanking him for this, Mark Twain promised another article soon [59].

In the same exchange of letters Chatto reported the sale of another eight hundred copies of *Tom Sawyer* from December to (presumably) June, and the imminent publication of 'a new cheap edition for which we anticipate a large sale'. Clemens explained that he had requested the figures only in order to know 'if Conway had paid himself his royalty [his five per cent commission] or if you had paid it to him . . . I did not care anything about the details, I only wanted to know that he got it' [57*]. This relaxed note of mutual confidence continued throughout their lives, broken only on rare occasions by Clemens and then more over details of book production than over substantive or financial matters.

In reviewing the arrangements made for Conway's remuneration, Clemens looked through his letters of a year earlier, thought he had discovered an omitted payment of expenses and at once authorised Conway to deduct £3.11s.0d. from the next payment from Chattos [58]. He seems also to have instructed him to negotiate the British publication of *An Idle Excursion*, for on New Year's Day 1878 Conway wrote to say that he had received Clemens's note that day, had 'consulted & bargained' with Chatto, and come to an agreement. Publication would be deferred a little so as not to interfere with the two-shilling *Tom Sawyer* ('the cheap edition on which it is hoped the money is to be made', as he had earlier described it). *An Idle Excursion* would be issued at two shillings and Chatto offered a royalty of fourpence per copy; Conway assured Clemens that this was 'the biggest available royalty . . . which can be got in a cheap book'. Having sent the letter with his usual enthusiastic promptness, he then had second thoughts. Although, as he had told Clemens, 'Chatto means to sell lots of the cheap books' he would need to sell three thousand before the author got fifty pounds. He therefore persuaded Chatto into the alternative offer of a single

payment of eighty pounds for the English rights of the book, leaving
the choice to Clemens. Communicating this to the author, Conway's
son Eustace also explained why his father had earlier urged the turning
down of the offer Routledge had apparently made for the book: 'As
Mr Chatto had already printed the Bermuda sketches we thought he
had a better right to publish them, in book form, than Routledge'.[8]

Routledge had made a bid for another Mark Twain book in April
1876. Belford, the Canadian publisher, had pirated, in book form from
the *Atlantic, Old Times on the Mississippi*, and had then offered for sale
in this country the stereo plates. Disdaining this method of acquiring
the book, Edmund Routledge wrote to Clemens to ask whether he would
authorise re-publication in England.[9] How – and indeed whether or
not – Clemens replied, is not known but in the event Ward Lock &
Tyler pirated the book as *The Mississippi Pilot*, announcing it in the
Publishers' Circular of 16 March 1877. Presumably, as the volume does
not contain the other pieces included in the Canadian edition, they had
not bought Belford's plates either. They had already pirated at the same
price of one shilling per volume *The Innocents Abroad, The New
Pilgrim's Progress, The Jumping Frog, Eye-Openers, Practical Jokes* and
Screamers – all, significantly, from Hotten's lists and none from
Routledge's or Chatto's. A preface 'puffed' this book as 'a very humorous account of the life of a Mississippi pilot' by an author who 'appears
to have studied piloting' and whose nom-de-plume it then explains.
The reassurance that it thinks necessary to offer the audience may argue
an unfamiliarity with Mark Twain greater on the part of the preface-
writer than of the readers:

> . . . under the thick veil of quaintness and American drollery,
> there lies much practical knowledge . . . And although "MARK
> TWAIN" does not shrink from some forcible word-painting in
> his book, there is nothing to offend even the fastidious reader
> in the pages now offered for his perusal.

Surprisingly, Chatto seems to have missed all this, for only in January
1878 did he voice to Conway his fear of an unauthorised edition appearing, a fear which Eustace Conway immediately relayed to Clemens in
his letter. Clemens accordingly decided to send to Chatto the Mississippi articles and three others published in the *Atlantic* together with
one accepted for March publication there 'which Chatto can also put
into one of his magazines & also into the new book (or books)'. He had
also, he told Conway, made clear to Routledge that Conway had 'sole
power over there to make book contracts' on his behalf and that 'Whatever arrangement C. makes will be satisfactory to me' [60*]. This
letter (unusual, in that it is signed 'Mark') expresses no opinion on the
alternative forms of payment, but the contract which Conway signed
with Chatto on 19 February 1878 was for the fourpence royalty.

An Idle Excursion and Other Papers appeared in the spring of 1878. In addition to 'Random Notes' and 'Old Times' it contained 'A Literary Nightmare', 'The Recent Carnival of Crime in Connecticut', and 'Tale of a Canvasser' (all named in Clemens's letter to Conway), together with 'The Loves of Alonzo FitzClarence and Rosannah Ethelton' and 'Speech on the Weather'. It also carried a two-page advertisement for Mark Twain's Patent Self-Pasting Scrapbook. Eustace Conway had expressed to its inventor his family's gratitude for the gift of one of these: 'It has been of very great use & we are going to get some more'. Meanwhile Clemens's good intentions about simultaning continued at least a little longer, enabling the May *Belgravia* to carry, as 'Fables and their Sequels', the piece that the May *Atlantic* published as 'About Magnanimous-Incident Literature' [61].

III

In 1878 Clemens began the visit to Europe that was to give rise to *A Tramp Abroad*. Elisha Bliss's son Frank was trying to establish a rival subscription-publishing house of his own, and while his father tried to secure the book for the American Publishing Company Frank had come to a clandestine agreement with the author for the rights. By March 1879 he was urging Mark Twain 'take your time & fix the Ms. to suit yourself' and simultaneously 'get the thing in shape so I can get the book out in the early fall & have the benefit of a long season's sale'. Memories of the havoc Belford had wrought with *Tom Sawyer's* sales prompted the thought 'I wish we could manage to get a twist on those Canadian fellows by securing an English copyright, don't suppose we can, but *if* we could it would make a vast difference to the sales'.[10]

Reticence about his activities may have inhibited Frank from the direct approach to Chatto that might have produced results, and Clemens was too engrossed in the book and its problems. When he wrote to Chatto it was to order urgently such books at Edward Whymper's *Scrambles Among the Alps* or to request the despatch of a copy of *Roughing It* to Ivan Turgeniev in Paris [65,66], evidently forgetting that the title was on Routledge's list, not Chatto's.

Then in July 1879 the Clemenses came to London, remaining in England until September. In some respects, to which I shall return in my next chapter, it was a less happy visit than the one they had paid six years earlier, but this was not the fault of either Chatto or Conway. Such evidence as we have of his activities on this visit come from his notebooks, for there are no letters even to Howells on the subject.[11] As in 1873 he met men of distinction. At Windermere, a laconic note-book entry recalls, he 'Talked with the great Darwin'. The same source mentions, in no more detail, visits to Mr Reginald Cholmondeley at Condover Hall near Shrewsbury where Millais the painter and his family were fellow-guests; and to Oxford where Mr Edward Wyndham showed them round the colleges. Another entry reminds him to ask Chatto 'if Conway's in town'. Evidently he was ('Go to Conway's' says another note), and he would have been able to report receipt, on Clemens's behalf, of a cheque for six months' royalties in the sum of £227.11s.6d.

'Ask Chatto what terms he gives for new book', Mark Twain's notebook reminded him in July; this he no doubt did in person and to his satisfaction. In August he wrote amiably to Chatto from Windermere, describing a Whistler etching the family had seen in a shop adjacent to the Haymarket Theatre and which they wanted to give to their travelling companion, Clara Spaulding. Chatto was requested to acquire it and get it to Liverpool in two days, as their ship was due to leave then. The picture was priced at seven guineas ('Possibly *you* may be able to get it for *less* than seven guineas – and that I would prefer, of course'). Not surprisingly the letter ends 'With many thanks for your many kindnesses' [67*].

Before leaving Paris Clemens had begun, with Frank Bliss, the discussion of rather grandiose schemes for preparing the illustrations to his new book – schemes which lay well outside the younger man's financial resources; he was also trying to sell his American Publishing Company stock, but the market was by no means favourable. By September, when he was home again, the book was well enough advanced for its author to apply to the Librarian of Congress for its title to be copyrighted [68]. In November Chatto told him that he had taken a similar step at Stationers' Hall; the only way of copyrighting the book to protect it from Canadian piracy, however, was by depositing an actual copy and this of course was impossible. Expressing pleasure at news of the book's progress, Chatto reported the arrival of electros of four illustrations from Paris and he must have assumed from this that production schedules on both sides of the Atlantic were to be better synchronised than they had been with *Tom Sawyer*. By now Frank Bliss had abandoned his breakaway scheme and rejoined his father's firm who were to publish the book, but in January 1880 no publication date had been fixed. Clemens's natural impatience at this comes out in a letter to Conway on the 19th, but is offset by the knowledge that subscriptions already taken out are worth between twelve and fifteen thousand dollars [70].

Another draft from London, this time for £219.1s.6d., elicits the tribute 'Prosperity to Chatto! – since he helps the prosperity of others – mainly the humble & deserving, like you & me'. He writes from Elmira, N.Y., whither he had taken Olivia to recuperate, away from the children, after a period of ill-health; yet even this news is related less portentously than usual: 'poor old lady, she can't well write her acknowledgement herself, as the doctor confines her pretty strictly to resting'. The whole letter, in fact, has a relaxed, expansive tone that testifies to his affection for his correspondent. Conway's removal to a new house (it

was in the newly-developed Bedford Park) and his wife's good taste are
commented on favourably, and a reunion with the Clemenses in America
is urged on them; but what must have pleased Conway especially is
the appreciation expressed for his *Necklace of Stories*. It was the gift
of a copy of this that Mrs Clemens was unable to acknowledge; the
children 'had laid hands on it as a sort of right, & walked it off to the
nursery'. Clemens thinks it a 'beautiful book' and 'if I enjoy it as much
as I have enjoyed your devil-lore [*Demonology and Devil-Lore*, 2 vols.
1879] I shall know it is a happy success'. He can even write of his
worries over *A Tramp Abroad* in a relatively light-hearted way: 'Dod-
rot the new book – as John the Baptist would say – it hangs along
drearily' [70].

That his correspondent was a minister, and a minister he enjoyed
teasing, may explain the inconsequential 'John the Baptist' reference.
It is a reminder too that one impetus behind *A Tramp Abroad* had been
his enjoyment of the company of another minister, Joe Twichell. The
religiosity that Clemens always abhorred was obviously no part of their
personalities, and the liberal humanitarianism of Conway's position in
particular was completely compatible with Clemens's hostility to
institutionalised religion. Nevertheless, the evident pleasure he derived
at this period from his contacts with them may, as will be suggested
later, have a further significance for an understanding of his state of
mind.

However drearily it was hanging along, *A Tramp Abroad* was at
least in the press. 'Bliss has been instructed to furnish advance sheets
to Chatto as fast as possible', Clemens assured Conway, '& I don't
doubt he does it' [70]. Rough proofs were indeed reaching Piccadilly
(up to page 570 by 11 March) but what Chatto could not get was an
idea of the length of the whole book or of the intended date of publication. Even more disturbing was the non-arrival of any electros for
illustrations since the first batch from Paris. On the same day that
Chatto was writing to call Clemens's attention to the implications of
all this for the English copyright, Bliss, in Hartford, was writing to
Chatto with remarkable nonchalance:

> We have mailed you all the sheets of Mark Twain's new book
> *A Tramp Abroad*. Mr Clemens wishes us to notify you that you
> can publish as early as you please. We shall not wait for its
> publication there. We trust you will have a successful issue of
> the work.[12]

This letter is dated 11 March and presumably the final batch of sheets
left Bliss on the same day. It is indicative of Chatto's efficiency that he
brought out the English edition on 9 April (without illustrations, of
course), but as Bliss had published on 13 March the English edition had
technically no title to copyright. Bliss may have realised his error in

advance, for an unusual feature of his edition is the inclusion on the title page of the British publisher's name as well as his own: he may have hoped that this would afford some protection to the English edition.

Clemens's initial response to Chatto's predicament over the failure to simultane was as casual and as imperceptive as Bliss's:

> Dr Sir: Yours just received. O dear! Bliss promised to be sure & attend to everything right along — proofs, electros & all — and he also promised to *cable* you date of publication, at my expense, two or three weeks before issuing. We issued, here, a week ago. Too late to telephone him, tonight, but I will hurry your note to him.
>
> Yrs truly
S L Clemens [71*]

Written on 27 March, this is not even accurate in its reference to the American publication date: it should have read 'two weeks ago' but he may have been reluctant to admit how great the discrepancy between the two editions would have to be. He is, however, already firmly persuaded that it was Bliss who was at fault and not himself.

Bliss, more predictably than convincingly, tried to transfer the blame to Chatto in a letter which manages to ignore the crucial difference between the date of despatch of material from America and the date of its receipt in Britain, and to imply that there had been no previous reference to illustrations:

> Upon sending a few sheets completing Mr Clemens work we wrote you we should publish at once. Your later letter to him makes mention of electros for cuts. We have been informed by Mr C. last fall that if you wanted such you would communicate with us about them. We had supposed you had given the idea up. A set of electros could be given you for $450. We presume however you will not bring out an illustrated edition first, at least. The book is now issued here.[13]

Chatto knew the facts, but the person who was persuaded by this version was Clemens, who was never averse to finding himself more guiltless than he thought. Throughout April letters to and from Chatto were crossing the Atlantic (and crossing with each other) so frequently that it is pointless to attempt a chronological reconstruction. Unfortunately the only one so far published is Clemens's lively invective of 20 April, the readability of which far exceeds its factual accuracy. Such explosions as 'Jesus Christ, how mad I am! This man is *forever* ignoring Bliss & writing *me* about electros & matters strictly within Bliss's province' and 'This is simply a hell of a way to do business' are entertaining but utterly misleading. Yet even here honesty compels the admission 'I like Chatto exceedingly, & shall continue to like him' [72].

Chatto's letter which triggered off this diatribe, though cooler and more formal than usual, had been essentially constructive. It expressed 'dismay' at the 'precipitancy' of the American publishers which had prevented simultaning and also necessitated a rushed English edition without illustrations; this jeopardised the English copyright as much as the English sales, but 'we will do our very best with it'; finally, he asked for a set of electros so that 'a new illustrated edition' could be prepared at once. 'This entails considerable needless expense upon us and the sharp edge of expectation concerning the work has already been taken off by the necessity of our issuing the unillustrated edition'. Neither its tone nor its content merited Clemens's aspersions of unbusinesslike inefficiency, and if it asked for his intervention with Bliss it did so very much in his own interests.

It is apparent, however, that Clemens had already taken an attitude on the matter in an earlier letter to Conway before Chatto's was written, and felt obliged to sustain it. Chatto's letter just quoted is dated 7 April: on the 16th he sent another which calmly summarised the whole comedy of errors in terms that again reflect favourably on his equanimity of temperament and natural dignity: 'I have just seen your letter of 31st March to Mr Conway, and although as he says there is no use in crying over spilled milk it is not through any indifference or lack of interest in the work that we had not put ourselves into communication with your American publishers'. The crucial passage is this:

> I was never quite sure who were to be the publishers of your new book. The proofs came without any accompanying letter or other indication and I always fancied that they were posted by yourself and that you were keeping all the lines for the production of the work in your own hands. I only recently heard the name of Mr Bliss in connexion with the American Publishing Co. and never dreamed of it being requisite to communicate with him concerning the electros after having spoken to you about them and receiving a first batch implying that the matter was arranged on an agreed basis. We never received the prospectus book or any information to guide us as to the plan of the work.
>
> I post a copy of our edition which was rushed through the press in three days in order to keep the ground if possible against pirates. I hope there may not be too many heart-breaking misprints in it – some of them no doubt will be owing to the uncorrected proofs we had to print from.

It is as well that an unusual prudence had dissuaded Mark Twain from completing and despatching the draft letter to Chatto that he had begun earlier [72a].

Evidently Frank Bliss's machinations and the secrecy they entailed lay at the root of the trouble, and Clemens began to recognise that the inefficiency was not Chatto's. He wrote to Chatto again on 25 April:

> It is too bad. I can't see how the mistake could have occurred. If you or Mr. Conway ever wrote Bliss about electros & date of issue, he did not get your letters. I naturally supposed that at least the date of issue had been agreed on, on both sides of the water. I received your unillustrated edition yesterday; it is very handsome, and the proofs were well read. I told Bliss, the other day, to go right to work making pictures for you, & inform you by cable. [74*]

IV

Chatto, however, was uneasy at Bliss's price of $450 for the electros and asked Clemens to use his influence 'to obtain them for us at a rate more in accordance with the cost of their manufacture, as we understood was to be the case at the commencement'. Bliss, he suggested, 'has contrived very seriously to emperil [sic] your English copyright' and put Chatto to a lot of unnecessary trouble and expense, so that 'it is only right' that he should supply the electros immediately 'and at the cost of production, without any additional profit'. Bliss did not see it in this light, especially as Clemens, forwarding this letter to him, scribbled at the top:

> How could *I* have an "understanding" about what the Co. would charge for electros, when I could by no possibility know?
> I *must* blame you for not telling me, in time, that you had not informed Chatto what date you meant to issue on. Of course I would have cabled him. [78*]

Bliss despatched the electros on 10 May but adhered to his price which he claimed, was already lower than usual

> on account of Mr Clemens's interest in the book. Of course we don't know what arrangements he has made with you about it, but we certainly should never have furnished you or anyone else electrotypes of our engravings for the mere cost of electrotyping them.
>
> [31 May 1880] [14]

With no help from Clemens Chatto argued no more, but only allowed himself the satisfaction of keeping Bliss waiting for payment until October and then sending him a draft at four months 'as we cannot spare you a cheque at the present moment'.

In May 1880 Chatto & Windus had some cause to fear that a pirated edition at one shilling might be marketed 'but by keeping a bold front we hope to scare off intruders'. There was also the problem of the circulating libraries like Mudie's who expected to be allowed a discount

on the copies they took: to cope with this, Chatto told both Conway
and Clemens, he was pricing the book at 10s.6d. Clemens's royalty was
to be 'upon the same terms as on "Tom Sawyer" '. There seems to have
been no formal contract for *A Tramp Abroad* between Chatto and
Conway, and the exact date of publication of the English illustrated
edition is not clear, but it was probably on sale by the end of August
(Blanck errs in describing this as a one-volume reprint of the two-
volume April edition, because that was unillustrated).

By November the two English editions had earned their author
£1,245.17s.6d. Thanking them 'for the pleasant surprise which so handsome a sale of the book furnished me', he announced 'I mean to have
the "Atlantic" people delay my articles hereafter, so that I can "simultane" with you' [80]. Chatto, pleased by this letter, sent it on to
Conway and he, returning it, equally pleased, suggested that they should
revert to their former custom of dealing with Clemens through him
rather than direct: 'In that way there will never again be any chance of
further worry such as we got into about the pictures &c.'[15] To Clemens
he commented with his usual ebullience 'Chatto's four notes to you
[the drafts by which the royalty had been transmitted] are harmonious
notes, but I hope they will prove a small quartett [sic] compared with
the choral glory to come. Their new edition (7/6) is going off finely, I
believe'; and to the *Athenaeum* he contributed a note reporting that
'though by no means cheap' the book had been 'a remarkable success
in a pecuniary sense'.[16]

So the contretemps was over, and good relations were restored all
round. In a brief allusion to it Hamlin Hill remarks — with some justice,
on the evidence available to him — that 'friendly arbitration was not
in evidence' during the argument.[17] In fact Clemens's conscience was
beginning to trouble him as early as 23 April when he sent Howells
'A Telephonic Conversation' for publication in the *Atlantic* and added
'If you will send me 2 proofs, I'll send one to Chatto myself & write
him a soft-spoken letter & mollify him a little, — though it is through
his own carelessness that he is out behind us with the new book &
therefore has doubtless lost his English copyright' [73]. (It is odd that
Clemens ignores that fact that it is *his* English copyright and income
that are threatened, whoever may originally have been at fault.) Six days
later he changed his mind, returning the proofs to Howells 'for transmission *at the proper time*'. He voices two contradictory fears: that
the piece 'might get back here in the English mag. before it had appeared in the *Atlantic*' and that someone else might bring out a similar
piece 'while we fool around waiting on an English mag.'. After Chatto's
promptness with the Bermuda pieces this latter comment is less than
fair, and there seems to be no reason other than pique over the *Tramp
Abroad* confusion for the remark in the same letter 'I'm not particular
about simultaning now-a-days, though I used to was' [75]. Chatto was

still pressing him in November 1880 'not [to] forget our Magazine "Belgravia" for any short stories that you may wish to *simultane'*.

Between writing these two letters to Howells he had, of course, sent to Chatto the more conciliatory note of 25 April reproduced above and on 1 May he followed it with this (neither of these letters was available to Hill):

> Dear Sirs:
>
> I never attend to any business of my own myself — either with my publisher or other parties — because I *know* I shall get it all wrong. My lawyer attends to everything that is business, for me. Therefore you must do me the charity to consider that when I promised to attend to the electros & advance-sheets I was not in my right mind. I *never* do so thoughtless and dangerous a thing when I am "at" myself.
>
> Of course, I *meant* to perform all I promised. I frequently warned Bliss to forward clean, thoroughly revised and corrected proofs to you, therefore it is likely that I ordered the electros *in the beginning*, & then dismissed the matter from (what I call) my mind. I don't know. If memories were merchandize, I think mine might bring ten cents — & swindle the purchaser.
>
> How this world *is* given to blundering! We fixed a date for Tom Sawyer to issue; Bliss was behindhand, you were not; the Canadian pirates copied your book, brought it out two months ahead of us, flooded the U.S. with it & *cost* me ten thousand dollars.
>
> Truly yrs
S.L. Clemens [76*]

It was as near to an admission of responsibility and an apology as Clemens was likely to bring himself.

That this is not merely 'a soft-spoken letter [to] mollify him a little' is apparent from his equally candid observations to Conway in a letter of the same date:

> Confound it, I am ever so sorry things didn't turn out as Chatto wished, & as he had a right, no doubt, to expect, but dog'd if I know where the fault lies. I looked sharply after Bliss in the matter of the advance-sheets; & maybe I told him about the other things, & maybe I forgot it. Maybe I only *tried* to tell him, & failed; he never lets you get a word in edgeways. *Dam* business of *all* sorts! — that's my only religious creed. [77*]

Before this letter reached him Conway had formed his own conclusions and had sent Clemens on 4 May a perceptive summary of the affair.[18] Hill quotes only the paragraph in which Conway states categorically that 'Bliss did not do his duty', but the letter has aspects even more interesting. Its tone skilfully blends exposition with placatory banter and reassurance. His own failure to avert the disaster is attributed to a month's absence, at the crucial time, in Italy on doctor's orders: 'But before I left I found that Bliss was sending the advance sheets direct to Chatto (not through me) and I had no reason to dream that there was any misunderstanding between these distinguished business men as to time of publication or electros'. He then, with some dexterity, inculpates Clemens himself under the guise of first complimenting and then teasing him:

> Between ourselves, I rather think that when you were here you made a profound impression upon the Chattonian mind of being a remarkable man for business, specially devoted to it. But he is now aware that you have graduated out of that and do not mingle book-keeping with book-writing . . . Forgive Chatto for my sake: he really is a good fellow, and much the most honest publisher I have found.

Clemens was indeed fortunate in his friends who tried as far as possible to save him from the consequences of his own impetuous enthusiasm and inattention to detail. It was Chatto's forbearance and Conway's loyal mediation (he certainly used his influence with the publisher) that prevented this incident terminating, as it might so easily have done, the promising business connection between Mark Twain and his English publisher. Instead, it consolidated the basis of a lasting working relationship, and the Conways, revisiting the United States in October, were enthusiastically bidden to Hartford, where the Clemenses were 'at home with beds & plates all fixed & ready' and could 'offer an added inducement: a sight of the new baby' (Jean, who had been born in July) [79*].

CHAPTER SIX

A LOSS OF CONFIDENCE

I

The next decade was a relatively prolific period for Mark Twain as a writer but it was one in which his view of the human condition darkened considerably. Between *A Tramp Abroad* in 1880 and *A Connecticut Yankee in King Arthur's Court* in 1889 there is an easily-perceived but significant change in outlook. In that period his main publications were *The Prince and the Pauper* in 1881, *The Stolen White Elephant* in the next year, *Life on the Mississippi* in the year following, and then in 1884 *The Adventures of Huckleberry Finn* (1885 in the United States): five books in five successive years, and five very different books too. His publisher for the books between *A Tramp Abroad* and *Huckleberry Finn* was James R. Osgood of Boston. Then, dissatisfied with Osgood's results, he set up his own publishing house in New York under the management and in the name of his nephew, Charles L. Webster, who had been in Osgood's employ. Webster & Co. published *Huckleberry Finn* and, in 1888, *Mark Twain's Library of Humor*, an anthology edited anonymously for them by William Dean Howells; they also published *A Connecticut Yankee*. All of these books were issued in London by Chatto & Windus, who also brought out, early in the decade, the illustrated *Innocents Abroad* referred to in my second chapter, as well as reprinting several other titles. His English popularity was undimmed.

In 1881 Mark Twain was described as having grossed, from his books, lectures, and plays to date, a total of $250,000, a sum which he maintained would have been $400,000 had he 'published the books himself and paid his publishers a percentage for selling them'.[1] Known as 'publishing on commission', this, of course, was the method Conway had recommended to him in 1875/6, and there is no doubt of its prevalence and popularity. In Britain it had come into favour particularly for local histories, poetry, and scholarly works, but it has been estimated that by 1890 at least three-quarters of the modern fiction issued was published on this basis. Some publishing houses confined their activities exclusively to this, and distributed handbooks recommending it.[2] If Clemens's 1906 dictation is to be trusted (and it is patently inaccurate in its recollections of the sequence of publication of those books), it was on this basis that Osgood published for him. When receipts still failed to come up to Clemens's expectations, the founding of Charles L.Webster & Co. was a natural next step.

Clemens, not unusually, persuaded himself that he had been badly served by his publisher:

> Osgood was one of the dearest and sweetest and loveliest human beings to be found on the planet anywhere, but he knew nothing about subscription publishing and he made a mighty botch of it. He was a sociable creature and we played much billiards and daily and nightly had a good time. And in the meantime his clerks ran our business for us and I think that neither of us inquired into their methods or knew what they were doing.[3]

Osgood's bankruptcy in 1885 lends credence to this and Hamlin Hill's researches indicate a láck of familiarity on Osgood's part with the kind of subscription publishing at which Bliss, for all his shortcomings, was expert, but Hill also suggests that both Webster and Clemens aggravated the situation for the publisher by their intervention.

Yet on the English side the evidence points to the efficiency of Osgood's management: supply of copy and synchronisation of arrangements proceeded more smoothly than at any other period and Osgood seems to have kept matters very much in his own hands, involving Clemens as little as possible. He began in a business-like way by investigating the possibility of obtaining for the author better terms for *The Prince and the Pauper* from a publisher other than Chatto. A letter, signed formally 'Chatto & Windus', went to Clemens accepting this competition 'without fear that your decision will be in our favour'. It reminded him with dignity of their past services to him, especially their 'many desperate struggles to hold the market for "The Tramp Abroad" against threatened unauthorised reprints'. Another note of mild reproach is discernible towards the end of their letter:

> We are quite willing to give for the new volume the same terms as arranged with Mr Conway, viz. a royalty of 2/- upon all sold of the first library Ed. in 2 volumes, 1/9 upon the advertised price of the 7/6 editions, 1/5 upon copies published @ 6/-, 1/2 upon copies published at 5/-, 10*d*. upon copies published at 3/6, 7*d*. upon copies published at 2/6, & 4*d*. upon copies published at 2/-, these royalties being over *one third* of the prices at which we have to sell the books to the booksellers, we defraying the whole cost of production & of advertising out of the balance, leaving as we are sure you will perceive only a very small margin of profit for our own service. Should you desire to publish the book on your own account we should be well satisfied to become your "hirelings" (according to the views ascribed to you in a paragraph in "The World") & so undertake the sale of the book upon a commission of 10 per cent upon the proceeds, but we do not doubt but you would find the royalties we offer more productive. Trusting there

may be no disturbance of the very cordial business relations that
we have had the pleasure of enjoying for so long . . .

Despite the strength of his case, Chatto seems not to have been sure
enough of his powers of persuasion or of his client, for he sent a copy
of this letter to Conway on the same day, asking him to say 'a word in
our favour' when writing to Clemens and repeating his conviction that
'no other house can do better for Mark Twain than we have done for
him'. Osgood himself was in London that summer and called on Chatto,
probably to discuss the matter. It being Saturday, he was unlucky for,
as Chatto explained, 'it is a general half-holiday, but . . . I indulge myself with a whole one'. On his return to Boston Osgood cabled acceptance
of Chatto's terms, confirming this by letter; Clemens also wrote independently, agreeing to take the royalties and adding:

> It is very difficult to determine which offer was the best, yours
> or Routledge's; consequently it was quite easy for me to make
> a choice. – I mean, things being about equal, I greatly prefer to
> remain with publishers who suit me so entirely, & whose energy
> in pushing books has been so amply evidenced.
> Mr Osgood showed me your account of sales on "Tramp" to
> July 1st and he said you had given it to Conway for transmission.
> Conway has forgotten to send it, I suppose. But that is no matter,
> inasmuch as we have it; if the notes had accompanied the state-
> ment, I should feel it best to have Conway killed, on account of
> the delay; but as they were not then due, he has not committed
> a capital offense. [82*]

Conway had not, in fact, forgotten, but the letter, though registered,
had miscarried, as a somewhat injured Conway explained in September.
The notes for £874.16s.9d., eventually reached Hartford in October
and were acknowledged to Chatto with the somewhat disingenuous
observation, 'Conway seems to think that I was likely to change publishers for light inducement; but I have explained his mistake to him'
[84].
This use of Conway as a scapegoat, though it does not mark the end
of their friendship, does coincide with the end of his period as Mark
Twain's English agent: henceforward, Clemens would deal with Chatto
direct or through his American publisher, but without an intermediary
in England. At about this time too Chatto took over from Clemens the
handling of his continental, in addition to his commonwealth, rights,
both for reissues and for translations; but this will be dealt with more
fully in a later chapter.
Remembering the publication problems of *Tom Sawyer* and *A Tramp
Abroad,* Clemens assured Chatto, when *The Prince and the Pauper* was
ready, that 'Osgood will get the pictures & advance sheets to you in

ample time, & there will be no misunderstanding & no trouble about anything'. 'The late Bliss', he added gratuitously, 'was a fool' [84]. On 1 November Chatto was able to report

> All goes smoothly for issuing the volume here by the date arranged with Mr Osgood; expectation is on tip-toe for it and we expect to start with a very large sale; we found the illustrations so import-ant a feature in the book that we concluded it would be better to start at once with the single volume illustrated edition at 7/6.

(The earlier notion of bringing out a two-volume library edition first had been abandoned when the novelty of having electros and text arriving together and in time made this new departure possible.) The specimen page they sent the author delighted him: 'The paper & the print are beautiful, but I believe our engravings come out a little clearer & better than yours do. "However", as George Dolby used to say, "That's a matter of detail" ' [86*]. *The Prince and the Pauper* was published in London on 1 December 1881 and in Boston a few days later, while in between these two publications Clemens ensured his Canadian copyright by a stay in that country long enough to constitute 'temporary residence' [89].

By May 1882 Chatto was able to report the sale of 8,880 copies and to send £1509.0s.1d. in royalties, a result which Clemens acknowledged as 'eminently satisfactory' [91*]. As sales were now 'beginning some-what to flag' Chatto proposed 'to stimulate the demand by . . . supply-ing the larger buyers at a reduced rate' and paying a royalty of 1s.3d. on copies so sold. It was a method he had used successfully with *A Tramp Abroad* and Clemens readily concurred again.

Meanwhile Osgood had offered Chatto advance sheets of *The Stolen White Elephant*; the English publisher was reluctant to reprint pieces already in *An Idle Excursion* but 'afraid there may not be sufficient material for a volume without them'. As American publication had been fixed for June there was, Clemens told him, no time to furnish additional matter 'though I have a sufficiency of it on hand': 'you will still have enough matter for the shilling book at any rate', he added [91*], but Chatto changed his mind after all and decided 'to print the new book just as we receive it and to publish it at about the same price as your edition'. It was advertised at 6/-, but because of the proportion of reprint matter they paid Clemens only 1/- on every copy as against 1s.5d. on the correspondingly priced *The Prince and the Pauper:* it was still a very fair royalty. Again publication went smoothly, 10 June being the date agreed for simultaning.

In August 1882 Osgood was in London and he took the opportunity to offer Chatto Mark Twain's new book, provisionally entitled *Missis-sippi Sketches*. Chatto accepted, offering a royalty of 1s.9d. on a 7s.6d. edition (as for *A Tramp Abroad*) and 1s.3d. on 'those copies sold for export and at a reduced rate'. As an alternative, he suggested a flat rate of 1s.6d. on all copies; he also offered £100 for 'a duplicate set of electros of the illustrations'. By February 1883 the title had been changed to *Life on the Mississippi* and copy was beginning to reach Chatto who proposed 15 May as the date of publication. He confirmed this date on 3 April when he acknowledged receipt of the last copy, allowing himself, unusually, to express the opinion that it 'certainly is a most delightful volume'. A week later he strengthened this: 'I think Clemens is to be congratulated on the production of his best book'.

In one respect Blanck's entries relating to *Life on the Mississippi* seem to be at odds with the records in the Chatto & Windus files. He quotes Merle Johnson and the *Athenaeum* in support of 12 May as the date of English publication, but Chatto's letters speak consistently of 15 May, and that is certainly the date on which the book was registered at Stationers' Hall, the prerequisite essential to obtaining copyright. Blanck's surmise that Dawson's Canadian edition of the book was published simultaneously with the English edition but was modelled on the American edition finds corroboration here, though. Chatto gave explicit instructions to Dawson on the procedure to be followed and himself took precautions against the export to Canada of any copies of the English edition. Chatto also took the unusual step, with this book, of sending a copy of the declaration of copyright to Her Majesty's Customs for protection 'against any foreign editions entering the country'.

The break with Osgood began with Clemens's letter of 21 December 1883:

> The Prince and the Pauper and the Mississippi are the only books of mine which have ever failed . . . I am out $50,000 on this last book – that is to say, the sale which should have been 80,000 (seeing that the Canadians were for the first time out of competition) is only 30,000 . . . [The] publisher who sells less than 50,000 copies of a book for me has merely injured me, he has not benefitted me. [99]

Commenting on this Hill remarks the 'patent illogic' of some of Clemens's expectations of the subscription trade. The sales of this book may also have been adversely affected by the prior appearance of Belford's pirated *Old Times on the Mississippi* and even by the original *Atlantic* articles; many reviewers called attention to this re-utilisation of earlier material.

Any attempt at statistical comparison between American and British sales would be unproductive; differences between the reading publics, in size and in taste, are not quantifiable and the difference in methods of distribution would affect the figures as well. Whether the preliminary canvass that subscription publishing entailed was more advantageous to sales than distribution through booksellers, preceded by newspaper advertisement, is not something that could be reliably assessed. Nevertheless, there is no suggestion at this period, either from Chatto or even from Clemens, that the British sales were showing any decline. Royalties in February 1883 were £610.15s.5d. and in October, after the publication of *Life on the Mississippi*, £902.7s.11d. Thanking Chatto in November, Clemens observed contentedly 'Continue in similar well-doing, and you will continue to prosper both here and hereafter' [98*].

Moreover, Chatto thought that 'the time has almost come when a cheap railway edition at 2/- of "A Tramp Abroad" ought to be brought out, and we expect that in this form it will obtain a very large sale'; however, the cost of production would be so high, because of its size, that he could offer no more than a 3d. royalty on it. Clemens accepted this in a tone very different from that in which he habitually wrote to his American publishers:

> I do not know as much about publishing as you do, but as you think three (3) pence a fair royalty on the two (2) shilling edition of the 'Tramp Abroad' I will take your word for it and we will let it stand accepted at that. [98*]

Neither his English publisher nor his English sales were giving Mark Twain any grounds for complaint. In October 1881 he had described the sales of *A Tramp Abroad* as 'flatteringly large' [84]: its successors seemed to be sustaining his reputation.

II

Of Mark Twain's English popularity in the 1880s there are several random, sometimes trivial, but not uninteresting pieces of evidence. Formal reviews in such journals as the *Athenaeum* and the *Saturday Review* are well represented in Frederick Anderson's *Mark Twain: the Critical Heritage*. Although they are by no means all favourable, they are usually better informed, fuller, and given a greater prominence than those of the previous decade; their authors are often men of some distinction. Thus the *Athenaeum* made *A Tramp Abroad* the subject of its leading review, more than a page in length; its author was almost certainly W.E. Henley.[4] The emphasis is squarely placed on the literary merit of this 'most excellent book': there may be, Henley suggests, in Mark Twain 'something too much of the abstract reporter . . . no doubt there is something too much of the professional jester' but as 'he is in his way a literary artist of exceptional skill . . . he is not often offensive and hardly ever tedious'. Henley instances the 'Blue Jay Yarn' to demonstrate the 'dry, imaginative extravagance of fun' that is Mark Twain's hallmark and claims that 'he shares with Walt Whitman the honour of being the most strictly American writer of what is called American literature'.

Several British critics of this decade, it will be seen were busily trying to define a tradition of American literature and to come to terms with Mark Twain in this context instead of regarding him merely as a funny man. The tendency to take him seriously is evident in other ways too. Conway, for example, relayed to Clemens an enquiry from 'Miss Simcox, a literary lady who writes a good deal in the *Academy*' as to 'whether there is really such a book as *Legends of the Rhine*, alluded to at page four of *A Tramp Abroad*'; he reiterated that 'Miss Edith Simcox is a really clever and cultured lady'. In an earlier letter (4 May 1880) Conway had reported that the book was 'making an excellent impression here, and I am in hope its account of duelling in Germany will raise a first class controversy and agitation'.[5] He may have been taking his cue from the author of the notice in the *Saturday Review* (according to Anderson, this was Leslie Stephen) who, on 17 April, had dwelt at some length on this topic, though generally to point out errors in Mark Twain's account rather than to provoke controversy. This reviewer thought less well than Henley of the book as a whole, but he found things in it that were 'delightfully bright and clever', and he too picked 'The Blue Jay Yarn' for special mention. What irritated him as superfluous for English readers were the 'extracts from exceedingly well-known books about Alpine climbing'. On the other hand, there were doubtless readers like the 'really clever and cultured' Miss Simcox to whose mills such material was grist.

Another testament to Mark Twain's popularity is the abridged version of *Tom Sawyer* that J & R Maxwell of Shoe Lane, London, marketed in 1881 for one penny. Chatto demanded its immediate suppression and such compensation as 'may be deemed equitable by any two well known London publishers'. Agreeing to suppress it 'for peace sake', Maxwell tried to argue the invalidity of Chatto's copyright claim but to no effect. In the office of the chairman of Chatto & Windus to this day hangs a copy of the original contract for *Tom Sawyer*, commemorating the fact that, for all its simplicity, it proved watertight and adequate to its purpose until its expiration. Maxwell's challenge was unsuccessful, but that he made it at all argues his confidence in the book's saleability.

The British reception of *The Prince and the Pauper* gave its author no cause for dissatisfaction. He told his friend Edward H. House:

I received a lot of English notices yesterday, and to my astonishment they are profoundly complimentary; even the London *Times* stoops to flatter. The English sale is one third as great as the American, the same proportion achieved on The Tramp Abroad, which had an exceptionately [sic] great sale for a high priced book. [89*]

The notices had been sent to him by Chatto and in acknowledging them he cheerfully dismisses the two hostile ones which are the only ones reprinted by Anderson in the 'Critical Heritage' volume:

> Your sale of the "Prince and Pauper" has reached a very handsome figure. I shall not be sorry to see it go on prospering. I am very much obliged to you, for sending me all those English notices of the book. They are surprisingly complimentary. I had seen no English notices before, except those from "The Saturday Review" and "The Athenaeum" which were the reverse of complimentary, but it gave me no dis-comfort, because here we consider that neither of these papers would compliment the holy scriptures, if an American had written them. [90*]

Conway's enthusiasm for the book found humorous expression in an undated letter to 'Samuel Newdeparture Clemens' in mock-Tudor language describing the competition in the Conway household over the single copy that all of them wished to read.[6] This may be why Clemens ends his letter to Chatto of 3 March 1882 'Please give my love to Conway' [90*].

III

In August 1882, A.P. Watt, who was establishing a reputation as a literary agent, sought Mark Twain as a client, using a letter of introduction from George Macdonald, the Scottish novelist.[7] Even if Clemens had felt the need of a London agent he would have been put off by Watt's circular listing Bret Harte as one of his authors. The change in Clemens's feelings towards Harte over the years had provoked a bitter diatribe against his consular appointment in Germany in a letter to Howells in 1878 [62]. Watt can hardly be blamed for not knowing of this when evidently Chatto did not either: he sent Clemens a copy of *An Heiress of Red Dog, and Other Tales* in 1879 which occasioned another complaint to Howells about Harte, although this time literary judgment compelled Clemens to modify slightly his strictures on Harte as a writer [64].

If he did not feel flattered by Watt he was no doubt gratified by the attention paid to him in the same year by the Reverend H.R. Haweis. The incumbent of St James, Marylebone, since 1866, Mr Haweis, who came of a musical Surrey family, had achieved a reputation for his church as a musical and cultural centre. He contributed, as a critic of music and letters, to *The Times, The Pall Mall Gazette, The Echo,* and other periodicals, as well as editing Routledge's World Library and, for a year, *Cassell's Magazine.* He was a popular lecturer in the United States as well as in England, and in 1881 had given a series on 'American Humorists' at the Royal Institution. His subjects were Washington Irving, Oliver Wendell Holmes, James Russell Lowell, and Artemus

Ward; only when he repeated the series in 1882 does he appear to have added Bret Harte and Mark Twain. The lectures were published by Chatto & Windus in 1882 as *American Humorists*. G.W. Smalley, Clemens's American friend in London, contributed, in advance of the book's publication, a sceptical comment in his 'London Letter' in the *New York Tribune* of 27 October 1882:

> Mr Haweis is a popular preacher, fond of notoriety, author of sundry books which had admirers when published, and husband of the lady whose serious account of "Beautiful Houses" you reviewed not many months ago. What title he may have to discourse on American Humor we shall see presently.

Mr Haweis obviously felt more at home with his more genteel subjects, but at least he gave Mark Twain serious consideration. 'In freshness and fertility T W A I N resembles poor A R T E M U S, and rises above B R E T H A R T E though he is less intense and pathetic than the latter'. Clemens would have relished the first comments more than the last: he had told Howells of Harte that 'The struggle after the pathetic is more pathetic than the pathos itself' [64], but at least he would have appreciated Haweis's praise of his treatment of the Californian miner: Mark Twain is 'no unscrupulous panegyrist or obsequious idolater of him, like B R E T H A R T E'. The essay is not particularly perceptive: it relies heavily on extensive quotation and paraphrase, is inaccurate in some of its facts, and makes heavy going of some of the humour, especially 'The Jumping Frog' ('the least witty of all his well-known skits'). What Haweis, like many of his English contemporaries, valued was Mark Twain's descriptive powers and his ability to be serious: 'When serious, I believe, he is generally reliable'. 'This is his gift — the long-drawn-out, elaborately spun witticism; the carefully finished, photographically minute picture'.

Mark Twain seems to have been a favourite with the British clergy, for in the same year Mrs Mary Yates Watson, the vicar's wife in the parish of Water Orton outside Birmingham, enterprisingly asked him to donate some books for sale at her bazaar.[8] 'In obedience to your charitable instructions', Chatto told him, a selection of his works had been sent 'amounting at the publishing prices to £4', though his account would only be debited 'as desired at £2'. Chatto hoped that 'the good works initiated by the Water Orton Church Bazaar may be extended by the circulation of these volumes'. Circulation seems to have benefited more than charity in this instance: the vicar's wife sent a touching letter of thanks and disillusion. 'Complimentary tickets were given to *unbuying* and common people who crowded and wrought confusion amongst us. *Heaps* of things were stolen . . . I feel ill and disappointed beyond measure'. Ironically, Clemens's generosity had perhaps contributed to the confusion by distracting Mrs Watson's attention from her responsibilities: 'It was so kind of you to help me and send those nice books – I kept peeping in, and *wanting* to laugh, but the nasty locusts kept prowling around and robbing me of my nice things. The policemen caught two of them'. The irresistible suggestion of a scene from a novel by Trollope or Dickens is strengthened by Mrs Watson's disclosure that she is the mother of eight children and evidently has literary aspirations. 'I have been too busy to bring out any Xmas verses this year but next I will send you some *if* both are alive – I am afraid "The Crown of Life" would be too – too – too sober for your liking'. If the verses were ever sent we may have here the English prototype of Huck Finn's Emmeline Grangerford: the suggestion is tempting but unproven. Another sentiment in her letter is Huck-like and must have appealed to Clemens: 'I think it's a horrid world, and Bazaars are hateful, wicked contrivances of his Satanic Majesty'.

A request for Mark Twain's help against other 'wicked contrivances of his Satanic Majesty' came from Manchester, where in 1882 A. Arthur Reade, a writer and reformer, was compiling an anthology of the views of distinguished men and women on *Study and Stimulants*. Most contributors were confident that alcohol and tobacco did not help, or even positively impaired, intellectual activity. Clemens also declared that 'wine is a clog to the pen, not an inspiration' but his encomium on tobacco ran to two pages (an unusually long piece for this collection). After a sickly childhood, he claimed, smoking had restored his health: 'I began to smoke immoderately when I was eight years old . . . with one hundred cigars a month'. This was increased to two hundred by the time he was twenty, three hundred before he was thirty, and his current quota was certainly not less than that. Abstinence, when he had tried it, had never improved his health: 'it was not possible to improve health that was already perfect'. He had, however, been forced to resume smoking when writing *Roughing It* because abstinence had dried up his inspiration. A. Arthur Reade, clearly nonplussed, assumes, in his 'Conclusion', 'that the prince of American humorists is not joking' and adds solemnly 'I hope that young smokers will not conclude that by following the example of Mark Twain, their brain will become as fertile as his'. The sketch maintains a very skilful balance and others besides Mr Reade must have been uncertain exactly how far Mark Twain's tongue was in his cheek, but to many it must have been doubly welcome in a work of such well-intentioned sobriety.

Clemens's contribution was immediately preceded by one from Turgeniev. The American writers whose views Reade prints were Conway, Howells, H.H. Bancroft, Oliver Wendell Holmes, William Cullen Bryant, and T.W. Higginson. The presence of Mark Twain in company so august is indicative of the serious attention accorded to him in at least some quarters in Britain. Haweis's evaluation of him is one example, and it was at about this time that Thomas Hardy asked

Howells 'Why don't people understand that Mark Twain is not merely a great humorist?'[9]

Always generous with gifts of books, Clemens in 1883 found for *Life on the Mississippi* and *A Tramp Abroad* a recipient more cheerful than Mrs Mary Yates Watson. This was John Bellows of Gloucester, 'author of the admirable little French English dictionary' according to Clemens's note on a letter he had received from him [95].[10]

Again, if the 'unbuying and common people' of Water Orton gratified their taste for Mark Twain by stealing his books, more affluent people did it by appropriating, with acknowledgements, his ideas. In 1884, from Walworth Castle, Darlington, one J. Percy V. Aylmer wrote on behalf of 'a young lady who has compiled one of those atrocities known as "Birthday Books" . . . entirely composed of quotations from your works'; though declining to publish the book themselves, Chatto & Windus had advised her to seek Clemens's permission.[11] The anonymous young lady was Edith Oenone Somerville, later to become well-known as an Irish novelist in collaboration with 'Martin Ross' (a pseudonym for her cousin, Violet Martin). Miss Somerville edited *The Mark Twain Birthday Book* published in 1885 by Remington & Co of Covent Garden, and 'Dedicated by special permission of Mr S.L. Clemens to "Mark Twain"'. It is printed in diary form, giving three days to each double page; the right-hand page is blank except for the dates, the left-hand page has two or three quotations from Mark Twain for each day. The intention is plainly that the quotation, which epitomises a character in one or two sentences, should be either apt or grotesquely inappropriate for the person whose birthday falls on that date. Miss Somerville's own copy is in the Houghton Library of Harvard University. Approximately five inches by three, it has a red cloth cover with a design in black showing a boy fishing, a frog jumping, and a riverboat in the background. The epigraph is taken from *An Idle Excursion*: 'First you won't understand it; by and by things will begin to clear up, and then you wouldn't lay it down to eat'.

Acknowledging the presentation-copy she sent him, Clemens modestly told her she had succeeded where he had failed:

I contracted to compile such a book, but was obliged to get myself released: my books grew suddenly and disastrously barren and empty: I couldn't find the requisite material in them. It was a sharp wound to my self-love. I shall look to you to heal it, and shall hold myself

Gratefully yours
S.L. Clemens [112*]

An interesting postscript to this is the enquiry addressed to Miss Somerville by Chatto & Windus in January 1910, on Clemens's behalf, about the book's original publication. They speak of its having been issued by various firms and being now published by Ward, Lock: the inference is that it was in continuous publication for at least a quarter of a century.

IV

Though she chose most of her quotations from the travel books and *Tom Sawyer,* Miss Somerville was up-to-date enough to include two from *Huckleberry Finn* which had been in print only a matter of months. The history of its English publication, though less chequered than that of its predecessors, shows yet another American publisher to have been little better than Bliss at achieving the desired simultaneity of publication with Chatto. On 1 September 1883 Clemens told Chatto 'I've just finished writing a book; & modesty compels me to say it's a rattling good one, too – "Adventures of Huckleberry Finn" (Tom Sawyer's comrade)' [92]. Chatto at once wrote to Osgood expressing his interest in the book and on 23 October, writing to Clemens on other matters, assured him 'We are all agog for the promised 'Adventures of Huckleberry Finn' and hope you will be able to publish it by next year'; on 27 November he again pressed Osgood for 'early information' about it. Meanwhile Clemens, on 12 November, told Chatto he hoped to be ready 'to talk business and make contracts with you on the new book pretty soon now – probably a month hence' [98*]

He had, however, a number of other irons in the fire at this time: he was obsessed with his latest invention, a table-game to teach children historical facts; he was negotiating the dramatic rights of *The American Claimant*, a play he had written with Howells; he was also keeping a careful eye on his nephew, Charles L. Webster, who, as Osgood's subscription manager, was being initiated into the intricacies of publishing and being used in his spare time as Clemens's business factotum. To the extent that plans for *Huckleberry Finn* existed at all, the notion was to allow Bliss to handle it, but it was also competing with the *Library of Humor* for Clemens's attention. It may have been the 'eager anticipation of Huckleberry Finn' expressed again by Chatto in December that encouraged Clemens, in January 1884, to give it precedence over the *Library* [101], but again dramatic interests supervened (dramatisations of *Tom Sawyer* and of *The Prince and the Pauper*), so that in March he told Chatto that he was 'keeping Huck Finn back till next fall': the reason he gave was the shortage of time for an adequate subscription-canvass for spring publication [103]. In fact he was moving towards the setting up of Webster in a publishing company of his own, and he passed to him Chatto's reply of 18 March, endorsing it 'Good suggestions about early sheets – make note of it, Charley'.[12]

The suggestions should by now have been familiar enough: the supply of early proof sheets would enable the English edition to be set in good time for publication 'a day or two in advance [of the American] in order to secure copyright here' and 'we should ourselves be able to make a much better canvass with the booksellers who of course are the only people we can approach; and also be able to make several better bargains for various continental rights and translations, which have hitherto been missed through not making arrangements in advance'. Self-evident as these points seem (including the reminder that he was not publishing by subscription), Chatto was obviously wise to enumerate them so fully.

Meanwhile Osgood was plaintively enquiring of Clemens 'In a note just received from Chatto & Windus they write "Please give us early information of the progress of MT's 'H.F.' " Shall I reply to this, and if so, how?'[13] In the event Clemens himself told Chatto to expect a letter from Webster as his future publisher; the assurance that he would himself secure Canadian copyright may have been weakened for Chatto not only by previous experience but by the nonchalant statement in the same letter that early sheets could be easily provided 'if we don't forget it' [104]. Webster's letter was rather more business-like in promising the sheets, though they 'will be some time' as the book is to come out 'late in the fall' after a canvass begun early in August; he proposed for the author the same terms as on *The Prince and the Pauper* and *Life on the Mississippi*, and asked Chatto to deal with Tauchnitz's application for continental rights which had reached Clemens.[14]

Chatto concurred, but repeated the request for early copy because they wanted to produce an edition uniform with their *Tom Sawyer* and would thus have to re-set. By June Webster told him 'We are having some little delay and have concluded not to bring out the book before Christmas'. In September, when Chatto was still 'anxiously awaiting early proof sheets', Webster was still vacillating:

> At this early date we cannot state positively when we will bring the book out, whether before the Holidays or not. We shall make a strong effort to bring it out before the Holidays; but we rather fear we shall not be able to, in any event you had better hurry your edition as fast as possible.

There seems less anxiety than might have been expected about a possible repetition of the gap between British and American editions that had jeopardised the success of *Tom Sawyer*.

First proofs went off the same day, but six days later Webster offered Chatto duplicate plates of the entire book for £100. Declining this because, as he had already told Webster once, he proposed re-setting to obtain a uniform edition, Chatto asked for electros of the illustrations only. Again his instructions to Webster were meticulously explicit: he would need a month between receipt of the electros and publication, so Webster should fix a late November publication date and allow Chatto 'at least one day's start'. A price of £50 was agreed in November for the illustrations but the engraving of the Gerhardt bust of Mark Twain, which Webster offered them as a frontispiece was turned down: 'after careful consideration we have concluded that it does not do the author justice'. On 25 November Chatto told Clemens that he and Webster had fixed 'the 10th of December for the publication of your admirable story "Huckleberry Finn" for which I anticipate a grand success' and that he had promised Conway the early copy he had requested; on 12 December he reported to Webster that publication had taken place on the agreed date. Sending Clemens two press cuttings on 7 January 1885, he assured him that '"Huck Finn" is making his way very satisfactorily', and three weeks later he told Webster the same thing. Relations between publisher and author were as warm as ever: Chatto wished Clemens 'very cordially all your heart's desire for 1885' and Clemens reciprocated by inviting Chatto to make for General Grant's *Autobiography*, which Webster & Co. was to publish, an offer 'that will put the book into your hands' [107*]

The publisher's reply is typical:

Accept my best thanks for your great kindness in giving my firm the preference in making an offer for an English Edition of *"General Grant's Autobiography"*. I should work with much enthusiasm in bringing it out and I have no fear that any other publisher is likely to succeed better with it or offer more liberal terms than ourselves.

I hope you will soon be able to favour this country with another visit and a series of readings, you may depend upon it, you are assured of a very big success. We have purchased Routledge's illustrated edition of your *"Gilded Age"* and will include your royalties on the copies we sell of this work in our next a/c.

Two points here need elaboration. Clemens had explained that Webster would visit London in August to discuss the Grant book, so no written tender was called for or, as far as I can trace, submitted. The only other reference to it in the Chatto files is a letter from Webster on 22 August regretting having called too early to see Mr. Chatto and having had to leave London without doing so; he tells Chatto that he has accepted from Sampson & Low the highest bid for the book, but without prejudice to future dealings with Chatto & Windus. To his uncle Webster wrote enthusiastically of the 'splendid contract' he had secured; 'I got several publishers bidding against each other and the competition was sharp', but it is by no means certain that Chatto & Windus were among them.[15]

Their interests, however, were more in Mark Twain as a writer than in Webster and Clemens as publishers. For the rights to and the plates of *The Gilded Age* they had paid Routledge £100, a ten per cent royalty to the author being stipulated in the agreement. What Chatto omitted to mention was that they acquired at the same time for £200 the rights to and plates of *Roughing It*: no royalty was stipulated in that case, perhaps because Routledge had bought it outright in the first place, and Chatto would thus be under no obligation to pay a royalty. This may have been particularly welcome at the time, because in August 1885 he tells Clemens of 'the very depressed state of the book market in this country, which had necessitated our relaxing our terms somewhat in order to keep up the sales of your books'. Nevertheless, as the royalty still grossed £979.17s.0d., he thought Clemens would 'consider the result as satisfactory'.

As will be mentioned later, both publisher and author were somewhat disappointed with the English sales of *Huckleberry Finn*, but they nevertheless agreed in June 1886 on the wisdom of giving it 'a fresh start in a popular form uniform with *A Tramp Abroad*'. As the 'Critical Heritage' volume suggests, the book had not been unfavourably reviewed; Miss Somerville's early acquaintance with it has already been mentioned and another quotation from it indicates its popularity in more radical circles. In 1887 Edward Carpenter, the Socialist reformer, whose admiration for Whitman had led him to publish the Whitmanesque *Towards Democracy* in 1883, used a passage from *Huckleberry Finn* as an epigraph to a chapter in *England's Ideal*. In 1888 Clemens had the satisfaction of learning that Robert Louis Stevenson admired his work, especially this latest novel; and in 1886 the Scottish Society of Literature and Art elected him a corresponding member.[16] In 1886 also Andrew Lang celebrated Mark Twain's fiftieth brithday with a highly complimentary poem in *Longman's Magazine*.

Despite the many anxieties that the mid-80s held for him, Clemens had no cause for complaint at his reputation in Britain, and his confidence in Chatto continued undimmed. He discussed with him the possibilities of another British lecture tour [106] and when his fancy was taken by the Paige typesetter he asked Chatto's advice. The latter sent him a book on the scale of prices currently charged by London compositors and expressed the opinion that 'if a patent type-setter would pay in England and the Continent it would also pay in the Netherlands, where a great deal of printing is done'. Replying, Clemens discussed relaxedly the compositor's measuring of type by *ens* rather than by *ems* as though this was the biggest problem confronting him [113]. Yet it has rightly become a platitude of Mark Twain criticism to comment on the deepening gloom of his views in this decade and the change in his attitude to England.

V

The change seems to have begun in 1879. *En route* for Germany in 1878 the Clemenses had experienced a pang of nostalgia recorded in the notebook entry of 22 April: 'It breaks our hearts, this sunny magnificent morning, to sail along the lovely shores of England & can't go ashore'.[17] Yet when, after a year in Europe, they came to London in July 1879 there seems to have been some disappointment, so that Justin Kaplan observes 'Even England . . . had lost most of its glory and glitter for him; his Anglomania had waned'.[18] This change and the reasons for it are not easy to define or even to document: Clemens seems to have written few letters on this trip and to have fulfilled no public engagements. He dined with Henry James and Whistler, apparently indulging again his spleen against 'the son of a bitch' Harte; it is not inconceivable that James's approach to Chatto with *Confidence* was prompted or encouraged by Mark Twain, for the correspondence dates from shortly after the end of the Clemenses' 1879 visit.

He had been in Conway's company in Paris and probably in London too. An invitation from the American Ambassador in Paris, conveyed by Conway, was accepted with a jest at Conway's expense: 'As a general thing I don't most always believe everything Conway says, but if in an unguarded moment he has slipped up and told the truth this time, I assure you I accept your invitation with a great many thanks' [69*]. Conway told him an anecdote about the man who stole hats from visitors to picture-galleries but confined his attentions to foreigners who would not be long enough in the country to prosecute. Transcribed into his notebook, the story is glossed in a way that, a few years earlier, it would surely not have been: '– a profession which may be said to have been created by the law, since in a country where there was no law, a man would be promptly punished (on the spot) who stole a hat'.[19] This reflection on social justice foreshadows, however faintly, the preoccupations of Hank Morgan or Huckleberry Finn ruminating on the mixed blessings of 'sivilization'.

The book on which he was at the time working and which had been one of the reasons for this visit to Europe was the good-humoured *A Tramp Abroad,* yet his notebooks of the period are filled with entries in a very different key from that. Spurgeon's preaching at the Tabernacle disappointed him and the singing of 'the wooden congregation' prompted the aphoristic observations, 'English sacred music seems to be always the perfection of the ugly. . . . It is a slander to suppose that God can enjoy any congregational singing'. The August climate, as so often, did not help: 'It was so cold I was freezing – the pouring rain made everything gloomy'. The theatre no longer pleased: 'One must have a play-book at English play – the English accent is so different one cannot understand or follow the actors. The same in ordinary conversations which one tries to overhear'. That other notebook entries tried to define such differences in quasi-phonetic ways is hardly surprising in one whose developing interest in the vernacular idiom might be expected to extend to the vernacular of other countries as well. *A Tramp Abroad* and other pieces written at the same time found amusement in the idiosyncrasies of the German language. His comments on English, however, suggest that what he had found novel and delightful in 1872 was now an irritant. Moreover, Clemens's critical standards were becoming sharper, more sophisticated: 'Galleries of pictures where there is much splendid conflagration of color have the effect of nauseating the spectator. Turner soon makes one sick at the stomach – it is partly intense admiration and partly the color'. 'The Slave Ship' especially excited his disapprobation, and again aesthetic judgment may have been unconsciously affected by social theory.

Other notebook entries relate to his reading at that period and are similarly intemperate, especially in their discussion of eighteenth-century English fiction 'No drearier reading than *Tom Jones* by Fielding'; 'Been reading that disgusting *Tom Jones* – the same old paltry stuff and poverty of invention . . . *Roderick Random* over again'. His quarrel with these books is literary rather than moral: he objects to people who praise them while attacking *The Mystery of Mechanicsville* for 'their argument fits both – "the memory of such a society should not be preserved – it has no right to a place in literature" – it defiles literature'. He goes on to contrast his own *1601* as 'a piece of the finest kind of literary art', untroubled apparently by the society of which that preserved the memory.[20]

Kaplan draws attention to his notebook fulminations about the 'bestialities' of European life and culture, and notes the incongruity of his participation, at the same time, in the activities of the Stomach Club in Paris. The incongruity is perhaps more apparent than real. The proceedings of the Stomach Club were private, and in addressing them he chose jocularly to celebrate what is sometimes known as 'solitary vice'.[21] His views – by no means unique – may be rationalised as a condemnation of that which is socially harmful and corrupting to others (a category in which he includes *Tom Jones*) and a recognition of the liberty of the individual to pursue privately activities not socially harmful. A previous speaker, he told the Stomach Club, 'has taught you that all forms of the "social evil" are bad. I would teach you that some of these forms are more to be avoided than others'. I do not believe that he was speaking wholly in jest, for, detached from its immediate subject, the 'moral' is applicable to the books he was to write over the next few years. The Shepherdson/Grangerford feud, the suffering imposed on Jim by slavery, and the unscrupulous duplicity of the King and the Dauphin were 'some of these forms' that Huck was to recognise empirically as 'more to be avoided than others'; so was the mob-justice that threatened Colonel Sherburn and that was visited on the confidence-tricksters – 'Human beings can be awful cruel to one another'. Sherburn's shooting of Boggs is not condoned, but it is presented as less socially destructive than the other forms.

This moral relativism is ethically questionable from many standpoints but it does represent the view Clemens was coming to adopt in the 1880s. 'All right, then, I'll *go* to Hell', Huck decided, persuading himself that the 'fugitive and cloistered virtue' of the individual's salvation was less important than his responsibility to other individuals and, by extension, to the community. Hank Morgan's entrepreneurial know-how was to be channelled into an attempt to produce a society better for *all* its members than the elitist system of King Arthur's court, and his desperation at the mob was occasioned by their reluctance, their blind inability, to recognise that it would be better. Ironically Mark Twain saw this particular issue in terms more absolutist than we are now disposed to, which is one of the difficulties that we have with that book, but its basic theme is surely social progress.

VI

In much the same way, because it was his experiences in Europe and England in 1878-79 that developed this social philanthropy in Clemens, he misled himself into localising it into a conflict between the Old World and the New. The society depicted in *Tom Jones* was bad; it was also English; therefore American society was better. From such solipsistic thinking, as well as from simpler causes, derives that homesickness in 1879 to which Kaplan points. Yet this was still not finding serious expression in his published works. *Life on the Mississippi*, in 1883, for example, contains the wellknown bravura passage on Sir Walter Scott: 'He did measureless harm; more real and lasting harm, perhaps, than any other individual that ever wrote . . . Sir Walter had so large a hand in making Southern character, as it existed before the war, that he is in great measure responsible for the war'. This is quite different, however, from the notebook castigations of *Tom Jones* though, like them, this is concerned with the influence of literature on conduct. Hyperbole here is under much stricter control for a particular effect. The subject of attack is 'the Walter Scott Middle-Age sham civilisation', much as in Browning's 'The Flight of the Duchess' or Edwin Arlington Robinson's 'Miniver Cheevy', though in the South the infection is more widespread: it is not the Old World as a whole that is at fault.

A similar sense of perspective is sustained, perhaps even more surprisingly, in Chapters 27 and 40 where Mark Twain is discussing English travellers' accounts of the United States. In July 1882, Osgood reports in a letter the despatch to him of 'a lot of books relating to travels in the U.S. by English people in the first half of this century; twentyfive volumes in all. They include Mrs Trollope, Basil Hall and Marryatt [sic] etc. etc.'[22] Such reading should have sent soaring the nascent flames of Anglophobia, but instead the references to these authors in *Life on the Mississippi* are unexpectedly urbane, and understanding. Not even in the privacy of the notebooks are they criticised, yet comparisons between America and Europe multiply there.

'Write an Englishman's Tour in America' is a suggestion of 1878:[23] it might have led to an interesting variation on the 'telling book on England' he had contemplated in 1872. In 1890 the idea recurs in the notebooks as *'Impressions of America*: Being a Diary [stolen from an Englishman] of a visiting Englishman found in a room in a hotel (Sojourn of 2 weeks). Information obtained from two sources — personal observation and other flitting Englishmen'.[24] Though by then, as is well known, Matthew Arnold's animadversions on American civilization had sharpened Clemens's anger, the idea of the book ante-dates this by some years. In 1883, for example, a notebook entry distinguishes an Englishman as 'A person who does things because they have been done before' and an American as 'A person who does things because they haven't been done before'.[25] In 1885 he notes his inability to find humour in *Pickwick Papers* and adds 'Dif. bet. Eng & Am humor, E is conscious, Am is ostensibly unconscious. English methods of explaining jokes with italics parentheses etc.'[26] An entry in 1882 on the subject of snobbery outlines the anecdote he was to use nine years later in 'The Shrine of St. Wagner' about the English family who had seen the Prince of Wales fifty times already, were patiently waiting to see him again, but quite understood why Clemens told them Americans would not wait so long to see President Grant if they had seen him once: 'They said "Of corse [sic] not" (he being only a President)'. That the notebook entry identifies the family as the Routledges is of less conse-quence than the fact that it ends with the generalisation 'The world *is* full of snobs'.[27]

Mark Twain's indignation at this time was by no means exclusively focused on England. The notebooks are far more rabid on the subject of the French, and in some respects his Anglophilia was as strong as ever. In Switzerland in 1878 he reflected on the greater courtesy shown to him in banks in New York and London whereas 'Here I am utterly unknown & must stand around & wait with Tom, Dick and Harry'. Even the accidental mention of his name gains him from English and Americans instant good offices and 'such heart-warming cordiality'. Piously he concludes 'I am spoiled by . . . 10 years petting — I needed to come to a country where I was unknown to get the tuck taken out of my self-complacency'.[28]

The tuck, however, was taken out of rather more than that, but not in a way that was helpful to him as a writer.

In January 1879 he told Howells

I wish I *could* give those sharp satires on European life which you mention, but of course a man can't write successful satire except he be in a calm judicial good humor . . . – in truth I don't ever seem to be in a good enough humour with ANYthing to *satirize* it; no, I want to stand up before it and curse it, and foam at the mouth – or take a club and pound it to rags and pulp.[63]

When, a month later, in Paris, Conway asked him what he was working on, his answer ostensibly refers to *A Tramp Abroad* but its formulation suggests a deeper and more metaphysical application: 'Well, it's about this: A man sets out from home on a long journey to do some particular thing. But he does everything except what he set out to do'.[29] In some ways it is his whole career that is epitomised here, and he may partially have sensed that. It was not merely with England that he was out of love: he was disenchanted with Europe, with the vanity of human fame, with the pretensions and affectations of civilized society, and also with himself. What before he had been able to laugh at as a humorist, a connoisseur of human littleness, he could no longer treat so lightly. These inadequacies were holding man back from the better society of which he was capable, and Mark Twain's impulse was to resort either to imprecations or to violence in his frustration. Yet to do so was to succumb to the very way of the world that he was condemning, and the recognition of this only increased his anger at himself and at the world: he was doing everything except what he set out to do. Herein, I believe, lies the key to his work in the 1880s.

Three theories dominate that work and blacken its humour: the dualism of human nature; the effect of heredity, training and environment; and man's inhumanity to man. The vision becomes progressively darker as the decade lengthens, and what darkens it is far more significant and deeper-seated than mere Anglophobia, though there are times when it suits his purpose to use that as a stalking-horse. To the most spectacular of such occasions we shall come in the next chapter: first we need to pursue a little further the image of the man doing everything except what he set out to do.

VII

Assuming that he set out to write humorous books, we are struck by the fitful way in which, in the '80s, he pursued that aim. The frequency of the times when, in his own phrase, 'the tank ran dry' and work in progress was laid aside increased with the years. In the case of *Huckleberry Finn* we have seen him distracted from publication by other interests. There was the preoccupation with the promotion of the history game. Then came the return to the lecture platform, undertaken reluctantly in 1884 with George Washington Cable. 'I take to the platform tonight', he wrote to Chatto on 5 November, 'after an eight or ten years' absence from it. This trip's my *last* – for ever & ever' [105*].

Yet in December he could speak of himself as 'having a jolly good time' and could ask Chatto's advice on another season in London. The tone, however, is unusually hesitant and diffident:

> Tell me, shall I come over and try it in London in the Spring or Summer in a small hall somewhere in the West end? I am tempted to venture it. Would I "draw" do you think? Won't you ask some of the knowing ones and drop me a line? Would the people come to hear me? [106]

Chatto replied that he was 'especially glad' to hear of the project:

> I have not the slightest doubt of the success of the venture and several competent judges to whom I have hinted the matter are equally sanguine. You would have the choice of several very comfortable Halls in Piccadilly besides the Egyptian Hall which I think would perhaps be the most suitable.

Nothing came of the project: his American tour was exhausting, and the more equable Cable, as his letters show, was troubled by the unevenness both of Clemens's platform performances and his off-platform temper. His irascibility, his often petty and jealous animosity towards his companion, his depression have all been fully described elsewhere.[30]

Clemens the lecturer had to contend also with Clemens the would-be playwright and was shortly to be superseded by Clemens the publisher, convinced that in Grant's *Autobiography* he had a goldmine that his particular talent could exploit. Thus it was not he who went to England as a lecturer but Webster who was sent as a salesman while his principal busied himself at home.

When *Huckleberry Finn* eventually appeared and made less impact on the British market than was hoped, his reaction is especially interesting. If American sales of a book had flagged, he would have fulminated against Bliss or Osgood or Webster for criminal negligence. He does not blame his English publisher; he does not even, as an Anglophobe would have done, blame the English public; he blames the book, and in terms especially unexpected in view of the importance now attached to the novel as a landmark in the vernacular tradition. His comment to Chatto is:

> It is true that Huck Finn has not treated you kindly, but it must be because the English people do not understand that dialect; for here, where the people do understand it, the book has sold more than 60,000 copies, at my usual high prices – $2.75 to $4.50 a copy. Times have been harder here than anywhere else in the book-reading world, I suppose – in fact they have been unspeakably bad – so it was doubtless not your hard times, but that unchristian dialect that modified the sale. I am afraid the same thing has wrought against Tauchnitz, for his clientele are mainly

traveling Englishmen and native Germans. That dialect would give
these latter the belly-ache every time.*

As if to emphasise his realisation that Chatto is not to blame he adds
a note expressing his personal disappointment that they will not be
publishing Grant's *Memoirs*: 'It's like going out of the family' [108*].
There are no other publishers of whom or to whom he would have used
that phrase.

No Anglophobe, and no writer convinced of the merits of his book,
could have accepted the English sales so phlegmatically. The unease
went deeper. To Joel Chandler Harris in November 1885 he expressed
his cordial thanks 'for the good word about Huck, that abused child of
mine who has had so much unfair mud flung at him. Somehow I can't
help believing in him, and it's a great refreshment to my faith to have
a man back me up who has been where such boys live, and knows what
he is talking about' [109]. That his faith needed such refreshment and
backing up is not adequately explained by such grotesque incidents as
the book's removal from the Concord library by a committee decision.
When in the following year he wrote to Edith Somerville of the 'sharp
wound to my self-love' and the discovery that 'my books grew suddenly
and disastrously barren and empty' he may, not wholly consciously,
have been referring to something much deeper than his inability to cull
choice extracts for a birthday book [112]. In the 1880s Samuel Langhorne Clemens was losing confidence in Mark Twain. It was this,
probably more than cupidity or a misplaced commercial enthusiasm,
that diverted his attention into the next and potentially most disastrous
distraction, the automatic type-setter.

CHAPTER 7

A CONNECTICUT YANKEE
IN ENGLAND

I

In May 1887 a humble but distinctly articulate young admirer wrote to Mark Twain from the Manchester suburb of Withington:

Dear Mr Mark Twain,
    My brother Jack and I have read the Adventures of Tom Saw-yer, the Adventures of Huck Finn, Life on the Mississippi, and The Prince and the Pauper, and think them splendid, especially The Prince and the Pauper I think. We have been thinking it would be a delicious History of England, if you wrote it, and made a few variations, of course, like you did in The Prince and the Pauper. It would not matter about you making it true if you made it interesting. We should like you to write it so much, please do.

I am your loving reader,
Kate L. Corbett (*aet*. 9)[1]

Had the letter been written a year earlier we could have claimed that *A Connecticut Yankee at King Arthur's Court* was Manchester-inspired, but we know that he had already begun on the manuscript of that book before this suggestion reached him. Whether he ever told his precocious little correspondent just what 'delicious' and 'interesting' variations to English history he was contemplating at that time remains unknown, as does Miss Corbett's opinion of the book if she read it; but her letter, besides emphasising his popularity, suggests the possibility that not all British opinion was implacably opposed to American fictional liberties with British history. *A Connecticut Yankee* has understandably come to be recognised as the most perplexing book in the whole Mark Twain canon: two long-standing assumptions that need to be challenged in coming to terms with it are that it was unwelcome in Britain and that it was the product of Anglophobia on Clemens's part. The former I shall hope to set in a new perspective in what follows; the latter is tenable only if the book can be accepted as having merely a minimal relation to the author's other activities during its gestation.

Six months after Miss Corbett's letter another young English girl made Mark Twain's acquaintance, this time in person and in Hartford. This was Sydney, grand-daughter of Charles Dickens. The novelist's son – also a Charles and his father's successor as proprietor of the magazine *All the Year Round* – was, in the autumn of 1887, following his father's example by touring the United States giving readings from Dickens's novels, which he is reputed to have done excellently. Exactly twenty years earlier Clemens had heard the elder Dickens read at the Steinway Hall; it had been his first outing with Olivia Langdon, and this may have been one reason for their inviting the son and his family to visit them. Hindsight, knowing the financial problems ahead of Clemens at this time – the collapse of his publishing house and of the Paige Typesetting Machine venture – might find a kinship of spirit between him and this Englishman of whom the *Dictionary of National Biography* records 'In all his business enterprises he fell short of success'.

They were themselves aware probably only of kindred senses of humour. Dickens, accepting the invitation, wrote of his 'modest pride in the British Bradshaw as the choicest collection of conundrums, without answers, in the world', but Bradshaw was, he found, surpassed by 'the complicated ingenuity' of American railway guides; he had little confidence that he would reach Hartford. This may have put Clemens in mind of his own joke about public transport, for 'Punch, Brothers, Punch' was revived for the Dickenses' benefit. After the visit Sydney, as an autograph hunter, wrote to propose exchanging a signed photograph of her father for one of Mark Twain; she added that Dickens thought this 'might possibly soothe the laceration to his spirit which these dreadful verses, of which you are aware, have so frequently inflicted' and Dickens himself wrote a postscript: ' "Punch, Brother, Punch with" – no, no, it is too much. But I forgive you!' Obviously the lines had taken 'instant and entire possession' of the Dickenses as they did of the narrator and his companion in 'A Literary Nightmare', of Conway and of Professor Clifford, and of so many unknown and unnamed readers since.[2]

II

There is no record of other topics of conversation. Had it been the elder Dickens, international copyright would certainly have been one, for the subject was as dear to him as it was to Clemens, and we know it was much in the latter's mind at this time. It may well have arisen in a light-hearted way, for Mark Twain had just completed his 'Petition to the Queen of England' (it is dated 6 November, the day on which he probably received Dickens's acceptance of his invitation) and he may well have read it to them. They would have enjoyed its mockery of the bureaucracy that the elder Dickens had so often castigated in his novels, but the piece and its background have an especial relevance to this study.

In 1882 Clemens, reporting the growth of his English sales, had observed with satisfaction:

I comfort myself that while the rest of our tribe are growling over international copyright, I am the recipient of a most gaudy English income, from three books which cannot be pirated. [89*]

The gaudiness of this income had come to the notice of Her Majesty's Inspectors of Inland Revenue who wrote to Chatto in the summer of 1887 proposing to tax it. A statement prepared by Chatto in that year, probably at Conway's request, shows that, in the ten years from June 1877 to June 1887, they had paid Clemens in royalties a total of £7,872 4s. 4d. To the Commissioners of Inland Revenue, however, Chatto explained a little disingenuously that, as these payments were in the nature of honoraria, he could not say what proportion of them might be legitimately deemed to represent a taxable profit. Informed of this ' "brush" with the Commissioners', Clemens replied to Chatto with cheerful honesty:

You know what the sum is which you have paid me for the years 1885-6 and 1886-7. Therefore, please regard said sum in its entirety as "profits" and pay the tax upon it to the Revenue Office and charge my account; and from all future profits (payments of royalty), subtract and pay my tax before sending my money to me.
   This is the swiftest and fairest and simplest plan that occurs to me. [119*]

The documents, he explained, he had retained 'because I might want to print some nonsense on the subject some time when I've got an idle hour' [118*].

The idle hour was not long in coming, and the result was the 'Petition'. A delightful piece in itself, it also deserves consideration in conjunction with *A Connecticut Yankee*. The rambling inconsequentiality of its opening recalls Swift's 'Petition of Mrs Harris', but Mark Twain's use of prose, where Swift had needed irregular doggerel verse, to suggest ordinary speech testifies at once to that command of a vernacular idiom for which he is so justly praised. Here he uses it to singularly good effect and with real subtlety. He explains where he lives, and how he has received a letter from a Mr. Bright (Mark Twain retained the actual name of his correspondent); he admits to not knowing the Queen personally, although he once saw the Prince of Wales from an omnibus going in the opposite direction; and he then appears to collect himself:

However, I have wandered a little away from what I started about. It was this way. Young Bright wrote my London publishers, Chatto & Windus – their place is the one on the left as you come down Piccadilly, about a block and a half above where the minstrel show is – he wrote them that he wanted them to pay income tax on the royalties of some foreign authors, namely, "Miss De La Ramé (Ouida), Dr. Oliver Wendell Holmes, Mr. Francis Bret Harte, and Mr. Mark Twain". Well, Mr. Chatto diverted him from the others, and tried to divert him from me, but in this case he failed. So then young Bright wrote to me. And not only that, but he sent me a printed document the size of a newspaper, for me to sign all over in different places. Well, it was that kind of a document that the more you study it the more it undermines you and makes everything seem uncertain to you; and so, while in that condition and not really responsible for my acts, I wrote Mr. Chatto to pay the tax and charge to me.

Had he intended mere burlesque he might have reminded the Queen (as he himself had been reminded by a London acquaintance in the previous year) that the publishers 'are styled here by would-be humourists 'Shutters and Windows'"[3] but that would have destroyed the carefully sustained balance of the passage. Their proximity to the minstrel show (with which Her Majesty's familiarity is taken for granted) sets the publishers in a light not wholly serious; and the assumption that the felicitously-named Bright is 'young' and therefore over-zealous also helps to minimise the gravity of his grounds for complaint. The hyperbole ('a document the size of a newspaper') and the colloquial 'It was this way' and 'Well, . . .' establish the easy spontaneity with which the fictitious petitioner states his case. Clemens the tax-payer has shifted into Mark Twain the humorist and is now shifting again into Hank Morgan conversing with King Arthur's modern counterpart. Even if this was the 'dry interval' in the actual writing of the *Yankee* he is certainly rehearsing the role here and in the following passage where he observes that the tax is levied 'in pursuance of the Acts of Parliament for granting to Her Majesty Duties and Profits':

I had not noticed that before. My idea had been that it was for the government, and so I wrote *to* the government; but now I saw that it was a private matter, a family matter, and that the proceeds went to yourself, not the government. I would always rather treat with principals and I am glad I noticed that clause.

The business-like preference for dealing with principals is pure Hank Morgan, but even more significant is the paragraph that has gone before:

Of course, my idea was that it was for only one year, and that the tax would be only about one per cent, or along there somewhere, but last night I met Professor Sloane of Princeton – you may not know him, but you have probably seen him every now and then, for he goes to England a good deal, a large man and very handsome and absorbed in thought, and if you have noticed such a man on platforms after the train is gone, that is the one, he generally gets left, like all those specialists and other scholars who know everything but how to apply it – and he said that it was a *back* tax for *three* years, and not one per cent, but two and a half.

The Professor's unwordliness that is stressed in this adroitly-managed digression is not essential to the story nor is it really borne out by the very practical advice he is represented as giving, but it characterises him at once as the antithesis of the Yankee who, as Clemens was to tell Dan Beard his illustrator, 'has neither the refinement nor the weakness of a college education'[4] but who boasts of knowing how to apply his knowledge: 'Why, I could make anything a body wanted — anything in the world, it didn't make any difference what'.

But if the shadow of the Yankee hangs over the 'Petition', it is a genial Yankee devoid of the anti-institutional egalitarianism of the later book and without any of its bitterness. Small wonder that, as an American who was in England at the time told Clemens later, it 'went the rounds of the English press and created a great deal of amusement'.[5] Five years later, collecting pieces for a new book, Clemens remembered its original publication in *Harper's Magazine* for December 1887 and complained that, though it was 'a real good *Letter to Queen Victoria*', Harpers had not given it the prominence it deserved: 'The idiots put it in the Drawer, of course — it's all the sense they've got' [170]. Prominent or not, it was seen by Chatto as early as 25 November, and he was 'greatly delighted' with it. 'We are sorry', he told its author, 'we did not have a copy of it in time that we might have sent the Inland Revenue instead of the cheque for £47. 19*s*. 4*d*. which we reluctantly paid on your account'.

Meanwhile the Commissioners were having their own little joke by sending Clemens as a receipt a document 'nearly a yard square' on which he had to pay postage. His letter to Chatto about this illustrates perfectly Clemens's flair for humorous correspondence and the easy intimacy between the two men. He begs Chatto to dissuade the Revenue Office from sending any more receipts 'for the postage is something perfectly demoralising. *If* they feel obliged to print a receipt on a horse-blanket, why don't they hire a ship and send it over at their own expense?' He proposes a compromise solution for the future: 'You go and work in on the good side of those revenue people and get them to take the profits and give me the tax. Then I will come over and we will divide the swag and have a good time' [120].

Chatto, however, found the whole thing less easy to accept. He delayed payment of the tax until a reminder had been received from the Collector, and Mark Twain's tax form for 1888 remains to this day in the firm's safe — as blank as the day it was issued. Folded in with it is a newspaper cutting relating to the 'Petition': it is rubber-stamped 'Government Received 1 Dec. 87'. Evidently Chatto could not resist the temptation of bringing it to the attention of 'young Bright', who, it is to be hoped, at least read it before returning it to the sender. This sense of humour in Chatto obviously endeared him to Clemens, but so did his magnanimity and his dislike of bureaucracy. More than once Chatto offered the services of the firm's lawyer, Mr. W.H. Christmas, who was willing to act for 'simply the bare costs out of pocket' if

Clemens would challenge his liability to tax either retrospectively or in the future. More than once Clemens declined the offer with gratitude, 'but some day we'll measure our strength with the Imperial Government and see what comes of it' [121*]. A final sentence in the light-hearted letter already quoted strikes a sincere note in giving his reason: 'The country that allows me copyright has the right to tax me' [120]. Anglophobia could never have produced the 'Petition', and Clemens's temperament was far too volatile for him to have accepted taxation so readily and with such resignation and logic if he had any serious disposition towards Anglophobia. Yet at the same time as all this he was working intermittently on *A Connecticut Yankee*.

III

Chatto first became aware of Mark Twain's Arthurian interests in January 1887; he wrote eagerly on the 24th:

> I have just seen a report of your discourse delivered at the meeting of the Military Service Institute Governor's Island, giving an outline of your still uncompleted new book "*The Autobiography of Sir Robert Smith of Camelot*"; and as might be expected, this has so stimulated my appetite for the remainder that I lose no time in writing to ask if you can kindly favour me with any further particulars concerning the volume, and if you are sufficiently advanced with it to enable me to make any announcement or preparation in connection with the issue of an English edition of it.

Clemens's reply was encouraging and equally courteous:

> That was only the opening chapter of the book – the only one yet written. The rest was a thin skeleton of what the rest of the book proposes to be after it shall have been written. I think maybe I shall go to work on it again next summer – and then it will be submitted to you first of all foreign publishers. [114*]

Chatto does not identify the report he has read, but if it was that in the New York *Sun* he would have known that the story was to include the mowing-down of knights with a Gatling gun and the commercialisation of the Round Table into a joint stock company, yet he was evidently not apprehensive.

Resuming work on it in the summer as promised, Clemens ran into difficulties. 'I want relief of mind,' he complained to Webster on 3 August:

> the fun, which was abounding in the Yankee at Arthur's Court up to three days ago, has slumped into funereal seriousness, and this will not do – it will not answer at all. The very title of the book requires fun, and it must be furnished. But it can't be done, I see, while this cloud hangs over the workshop. . . . everything that *can* worry me does it; and I get up and spend from 1 o'clock

till 3 a.m. pretty regularly every night, thinking – not pleasantly.
[116]

Yet only twelve days later, on the crest of another wave, he was 'swelled
up' by the discovery that he was 'making an uncommonly bully book',
had written three hundred pages already and would easily finish it by
the end of the year. His satisfaction was such that he saw it as likely to
sell 100,000 copies and would not market it 'until I can see at least an
80,000 copy sale ahead'. This calculation was based on the assumption
that 'Huck Finn was a 50,000 copy book' [117] : as he was writing to
Webster and Webster's assistant, Fred Hall, who would know the sales,
he is unlikely to have distorted this figure, but it casts serious doubts on
the 'more than 60,000 copies' which he had quoted two years earlier to
Chatto as the American sales to that date.

Sending him his royalties in August 1887 Chatto told him how glad he
would be 'to be able to announce your new book . . . which (from the
specimen of the opening chapters which we have heard of) we believe
will prove a great success'. Clemens acknowledged the royalties with
satisfaction, but his plans for the book had already been pushed back:

> It's quite a good result, for an "off year". We will boost it up,
> presently – next March (15th). Not with Smith of Camelot, for
> that won't be ready for a year yet. [118*]

'Quite a good result for an "off year"' had by now become almost a
stock phrase for him to use in acknowledging his royalties. Every year
was an 'off year', and from Chatto's occasional use of the phrase when
sending the drafts one suspects that it had become something of a joke
between the two men. The 'boosting up' was presumably to be done by
the *Library of Humor* which he offers Chatto in the same letter and
which was in fact not to do as well as he hoped, but that is a separate
subject. It is, however, this letter which mentions 'printing some nonsense' about the brush with the Inland Revenue authorities.

Almost a year elapsed and Chatto once more prodded his recalcitrant author: 'I hope you will soon tell the story of Smith of Camelot
to Edison's phonograph & let us have it'. A number of notebook entries
indicate that Clemens was considering a humorous piece about the
phonograph (which had been patented ten years earlier) at about this
time. Whether Chatto's reference to the instrument suggested this to
him or whether it alludes to something in a letter from Clemens to
Chatto now lost is uncertain. It was not until three years later that, racked
with rheumatism, he asked Howells to investigate for him the possibility
of using a phonograph for dictation [143]. Annotating the letter Smith
and Gibson see the idea as 'apparently suggested to Clemens by Colonel
Sellers's scheme, in . . . *The American Claimant*', but it may well have
been prompted by this random and half-humorous comment of his
English publisher.

Far from accepting the suggestion at the time, however, Clemens's reply merely postponed the book still further:

> I had a sort of half-way notion that I might possibly finish the Yankee at King Arthur's Court this summer, but I began too late, & so I don't suppose I shall finish it till next summer. We go home to Hartford a week hence; & if at that time I find I am two-thirds done, I mean to try to persuade myself to do that other third before spring. [129]

These hopes were evidently not fulfilled, for on 6 May 1889, Chatto, writing to Webster & Co. on a totally different subject, concluded with a request for 'any further particulars of Mr Clemens' proposed new book "Mr. Smith of Camelot", which we hope may be published this season'. Fred Hall referred the enquiry to Clemens and one of them must have written encouragingly to England, for Chatto, remitting the royalties on 3 July observed:

> There are many enquiries for the "Yankee at the Court of King Arthur" which I suppose is the same as "Mr Smith of Camelot" with a stronger title. I am glad to learn that it is approaching completion, and I hope you will soon be able to let us have some proofs in order that we may get to work in the preparation of the English edition.

IV

Mark Twain's reply to this straightforward and goodnatured request is one of the most remarkable and least explicable letters in his entire correspondence with Andrew Chatto. Since its publication by Paine in 1917 it has given rise to more misconceptions about their relationship and about the book itself than any other single factor, and the problem is complicated still further by discrepancies between the text of the letter as Paine prints it and the text received by Chatto. I reproduce here the wording of Clemens's autograph original which still survives in the Chatto & Windus files:

Hartford, July 16/89

Dear Mr. Chatto,

Your statement and drafts came yesterday for £364, for which I thank you and endorse your opinion that its a very good return for an off year.

I have revised the "Yankee" twice; Stedman has critically read it and pointed out to me some needed emendations; Mrs Clemens has read it and made me strike out many passages and soften others; I have read chapters of it in public several times where Englishmen were present, and have profited by their suggestions. Next week I shall make a *final* revision. After that, if it still isn't blemishless I can't help it, and ain't going to try.

Now mind you, I have taken all this pains because I wanted to say a Yankee mechanic's say against monarchy and its several natural props, and yet make a book which you would be willing to print exactly as it comes to you, without altering a word.

We are spoken of (by *Englishmen!*) as a thin-skinned people. It is you that are thin-skinned. An Englishman may write with the most brutal frankness about any man or any institution among us, and we re-publish him without dreaming of altering a line or a word. But England cannot stand that kind of a book, written about herself. It is England that is thin-skinned. It causeth me to smile, when I recal [sic] the modifications of my language which have been made in my English Editions to fit it for the sensitive English palate.

Now as I say, I have taken laborious pains to so trim this book of offence that you'll not lack the nerve to print it just as it stands. I'm going to get the proofs to you just as early as I can. I want you to read it carefully. If you can publish it without altering a single word or omitting one, go ahead. Otherwise, please hand it to J.R. Osgood in time for him to have it published at my expense. This is important, for the reason that the book was not written for America, it was written for England. So many Englishmen have done their sincerest best to teach us something for our betterment, that it seems to me high time that some of us should substantially recognize the good intent by trying to pry up the English nation to a little higher level of manhood in turn.

Sincerely yours,
S.L. Clemens [130*]

In the Mark Twain Papers at Berkeley an unsigned typescript on Charles L. Webster & Co. notepaper is substantially identical to this except in very minor details ($364 instead of £364, in the first paragraph, for instance), so the responsibility for the editing of the published version is indisputably Paine's.

Paine produces a much more formal letter which opens uncharacteristically, dispenses with preliminaries, and achieves an immediate and defensive aggressiveness:[6]

> Gentlemen, — Concerning the Yankee, I have already revised the story twice; and it has been read critically by W.D. Howells and Edmund Clarence Stedman, and my wife has caused me to strike out several passages which have been brought to her attention, and to soften others. Furthermore, I have read chapters of the book in public . . .

Paine does not date the letter and implies that it was written after the book's American publication, which is plainly wrong. We have Howells's own statement, in a letter to Clemens, that he did not begin reading the book until 18 September,[7] so Paine's introduction of a reference to him here is also wrong. Paine does not print the two sentences at the end of this paragraph ('Next week . . . ain't going to try'); this, like his omission of the opening paragraph, his spelling out of the contractions 'you'll' and 'I'm' in the final paragraph, and his ending 'Very truly yours', increases the cold formality of the letter. In the final sentence of the fourth paragraph both typescript and Paine have 'read'; 'recal', spelt thus, occurs elsewhere in Clemens's correspondence too, but the difference is not crucial. In the same sentence Paine prints 'them' for 'it', thus suggesting that it is the English editions that have been adapted where Clemens only claims that the language has been altered; in the typescript 'it' is in type and 'them' substituted in pencil, but in the original at Chatto & Windus Clemens certainly wrote 'it'.

Obviously some of Paine's changes are more significant than others; the reasons why he made them at all can only be conjectured — perhaps to strengthen the letter by giving it a more unified tone — and are less important than the implications of the letter itself, for despite the discrepancies between the two versions, it is still substantially the same letter and still very strange. Introducing it, Paine comments:

> The *Yankee* did not find a very hearty welcome in England. English readers did not fancy any burlesque of their Arthurian tales, or American strictures on their institutions. Mark Twain's publishers had feared this, and asked that the story be especially edited for the English edition. Clemens, however, would not listen to any suggestion of the sort.

It is a legitimate inference from either text of the letter, but it is obviously not supported by the facts.

The date and the opening reference to the receipt of the royalties confirm that Chatto's letter of 3 July (already quoted) was the latest in the series: in that and in all his other references to the book the publisher had expressed nothing but enthusiasm for it — certainly no fears or reservations. Two ideas are now introduced for the first time which one would have expected Clemens to have raised with Chatto before this: first, that the English editions of earlier books had been doctored to suit 'the sensitive English palate'; second, that *A Connecticut Yankee* 'was not written for America, it was written for England'. The first is demonstrably untrue, the second is at best suspect. The over-riding necessity to secure copyright by 'simultaning' had, as has been shewn, always imposed on the British publisher a production-schedule so tight and so hand-to-mouth that any serious editing would have been impracticable, even if it had been contemplated — and we find no evidence that it had. Textual variations between the English and the American editions of *Tom Sawyer* were, as we have seen, fortuitous, and the language of the English text was in many instances more colloquial than the American. There had been no attempt at 'modifications' to 'that unchristian dialect' in *Huckleberry Finn*, although Clemens seems subsequently almost to have wished that there had. His quarrel with Hotten had been over the attribution of specific pieces to him, not over any modifications to language; Routledge had allowed him to authorise the texts used, and any changes introduced into the English *Innocents Abroad* were made by Mark Twain, not required by Routledge. The whole accusation is as strikingly at variance with the correspondence and the relationship between Clemens and Chatto since 1876 as is the remarkable suggestion that Chatto might 'lack the nerve to print it just as it stands'. Nothing in their previous correspondence prepares us for this or justifies the truculence of Clemens's attitude here. The reiterated insistence on the sacredness of the author's text (it occurs five times in this letter) had never before been raised in that correspondence nor had it needed to be.

Paine's editing obscures some very curious shifts of tone within the letter itself (in the version that reached Chatto) that are clearly significant but are difficult to explain. The amiability of the opening paragraph with its use of the 'off-year' joke could hardly have led the publisher to expect what followed. The emphasis on revisions meticulously carried out at the suggestion of Stedman, Olivia, and the anonymous Englishmen does not wholly accord with the self-confident brashness of the 'Yankee mechanic's' vernacular 'I can't help it, and ain't going to try'. Even if one hears in that not brashness so much as weariness with the whole process of revision, there is still an inconsistency of tone. The vernacular also contrasts with a rhetoric somewhat out of place in a letter, so that one would hardly have blamed Chatto had he reproached Clemens, as Queen Victoria reproached Gladstone, for 'addressing us as though we were a public meeting'. Alternatively, he might have suggested that, like the Player Queen, Mark Twain seemed to 'protest too much'.

In fact he did neither. He did not reply until 8 August, by which time a date of publication had been proposed, and his only comment was dignified and restrained: 'I am very pleased to learn that the Yankee at the Court of King Arthur is to be published on December 10th next. I do not think there is any possibility of your writing anything I should not be pleased to publish'. To have been no more perturbed than this by Clemens's outburst, or at least to resist the temptation to retaliate, argues, on Chatto's part, a shrewd knowledge of and liking for his correspondent rather than indifference or pusillanimity. In one respect, however, Clemens may have been less than delighted by Chatto's quiet reassurance, for he had in the interim caused Webster & Co. to write, on 5 August, an even more specific letter to London:[8]

We enclose a form of Preface for the English Edition of Mr Clemens' new book. This will differ materially from the Preface of the Am. Edition. We will send you two sets of sheets and would like if possible, to have you make arrangements with Baron Tauchnitz. There will probably be some portions of the book which you may not care to publish, although we think such passages are very rare. Mr Clemens suggests that at the end of Chapter XXVI what he says in regard to 'royal grants' you may wish to leave out: we will mark this portion in the proofs we send you. In reading over the proofs, please advise us of such portions as you wish to leave out and we will communicate with Mr Clemens regarding same.

    We understand of course, that the book is a satire on English Royalty and Nobility, but as we have said it is a pleasant one, and one with the exception of an occasional passage, that no one should take offence at. All these changes should be made before the plates are cast as it would be quite difficult to do so afterwards . . .

From this it is even clearer than from Clemens's letter that no proofs had been despatched to Chatto, so that he could not possibly have 'asked that the story be especially edited for the English edition'. This letter tends to minimise the iconoclastic nature of the book that Clemens had emphasized; the chapter reference should be to XXV rather than XXVI; the instructions as to when the changes should be made are hardly necessary; and the preface, instead of being enclosed, had to be sent on the next day. An explanation of why a different form of Preface was considered necessary would have been interesting but is not forthcoming. The Preface to the English edition consists of only one unsigned paragraph; the American edition follows this with a second, discussing the Divine Right of Kings, and the name MARK TWAIN. However, in the Berg Collection of the New York Public Library there is a proof of the one-paragraph text with 'Proof of Chatto's Preface' written on it. It is date-stamped 18 August 1889, and at the bottom are the words 'All right. SLC' in Clemens's holograph. Apparently he is approving the version sent to England two weeks earlier. The most likely reason for dropping the second paragraph might be that its facetiousness, especially in the closing sentences, could encourage the English reader, for whom the book purported to be specially written, to underestimate its seriousness of purpose even before beginning on it.

    Chatto did not demur at the Preface, nor did he propose any cuts, but totally ignored both the general and the specific suggestions Webster & Co. had made. Thus, far from the English publishers being apprehensive about the book, the only suggestions for toning it down came from the author himself and, at his instigation, from his American publisher. It is as though Mark Twain positively *wanted* cuts to be made and would have been happier still had Chatto declined to publish the book at all. Behind the hectoring tone of his letter, so unusual in his correspondence with Chatto, behind its factual inaccuracies and the injustice of it allegations, there lies, I believe, a very troubled mind. Whatever praise Stedman or others had bestowed or might bestow on the book, Mark Twain himself knew only too well with how much difficulty he had written it; 'if it still isn't blemishless I can't help it, and ain't going to try' tacitly admits as much. He must also have known that, as Henry Nash Smith and others have demonstrated, the inner logic of his story had taken command and defeated the optimistic faith in democracy it was supposed to have celebrated. He must have realised that it was a scathing condemnation, not of 'monarchy and its several natural props', not of British institutions and 'English manhood', but of human nature and the faith in human nature on which Western democracy is ultimately based. To insist that it is the English alone who are under attack is to divert attention (Mark Twain's as much as anyone else's) from the condemnation of American civilisation that the book also involves. If the British could be induced to take umbrage at it, the diversionary tactic would be even more effective, the author's criticism would be vindicated, and he would be recognised as a man with a serious message. The paranoiac insistence on the sacrosanctity of the text, not one word of which is to be changed, is similarly evidence of a belief in the importance of what he has revealed; the pretence that only the non-democratic and thin-skinned English would wish to tamper with it disguises conveniently the full import of the revelation.

Melville, having completed *Moby-Dick*, told Hawthorne 'I have written a wicked book, and feel spotless as the lamb'. Mark Twain believed that he too had written a wicked book but, always a victim of that conscience against which he inveighed in *Huckleberry Finn* and in this book itself, could not bring himself to feel spotless. The letter to Chatto is a desperate attempt to transfer that guilt to other shoulders and, in so doing, to change its nature. What Poe would have recognised as the imp of the perverse in Mark Twain would have liked nothing better than the outright banning of the book in England: the tone in which he could then have said 'I told you so!' would have sounded conveniently like Anglophobia rather than the deeper and more genuine misanthropy that he was still trying to deny even to himself. Aghast at the subversive implications of his fable, he feels that if it is attacked (especially by the British) he is proved right but his misanthropy will be increased; if it is not attacked, then he has failed in his attempt to attract serious attention, and his despair at his imperceptive fellow human beings is intensified.

V

Meanwhile Chatto was becoming uncomfortably aware of a more immediate problem: the by now familiar one of getting copy from the Americans in time to meet the publication deadline. On 29 July Webster & Co. had notified him that they hoped to bring it out on 10 December but as Dan Beard could not complete the two hundred and fifty illustrations before November he had undertaken to work on them chapter by chapter; page proofs and electros of the illustrations would be sent to London, and six or eight copies of the American edition for them to bind up with their own title-page to secure copyright. Chatto knew enough about Webster & Co's inevitable production difficulties and of Clemens's unreliability in such matters to write separately to Websters on the same day that he wrote the reply to Clemens already quoted. The explicit and meticulous detail of this letter (of which the following is only an extract) and its emphasis on a procedure that should by this date have become routine argues little confidence in the American house, and even that little was to be severely strained:

> As the time appears to be likely to be very close, it will be necessary for you to commence sending us at once, and at every earliest opportunity, proofs, and impressions (however rough) of both text and plates, as fast as you receive them, and also to give us ample notice of any unforeseen delay in sending us copy and electros that can postpone the date of our publication. *Especially will it be necessary for you to bear in mind that the English copyright will be lost in this country by first publication in America.*

Websters promised on 19 August to commence shipping proofs and electrocuts immediately. Two days later Clemens sent Chatto the formal agreement for the book and suggested 6 December for British publication, 8 December for Canadian, and 10 December for American; he was to receive a royalty of 1s. 9d. on every copy of a 7s. 6d. edition [133]. (He had told Hall in July 'I want the same terms which Chatto has paid me these last four years'.)[9] The note is brief and hurried, but makes no mention of the July eruption. Early in September he was still correcting proofs and telling Hall not to send them to Chatto till he had finished [135].

By 16 September Chatto had received proofs of the text only to page 113 and only proofs of some illustrations instead of electros of them all; on 13 November, three weeks before the publication date, he was still short of some material:

> Please to send us, by return, copy for the title page and preliminary matter to Twain's *Yankee*.
>   We are disappointed at the slowness with which proofs and blocks are reaching us – We ought to have had the whole of book and illustrations in our hands by this date, in order to publish by the date originally fixed. Even then, the time would have been short for so heavy a book. Please to send us everything outstanding at once.

Time would have been even shorter, Chatto might have added, for any editing or cutting, even if he had wished to undertake it. By 22 November he had received all proofs of the texts, but was still 'anxiously awaiting' electros of the remaining illustrations; he urged Clemens not to allow publication of the American edition 'before we have received a perfect copy of the book that we can register'. This did not reach London until 5 December, the day before the agreed date of publication, but by then Chatto had been advised that 'to use American-printed copies for the purpose of registration might not be quite safe'. Accordingly, he notified the author with evident satisfaction, 'we have therefor by working night and day, managed to have our own printed copies ready for this purpose'. He had deposited a copy at the British Museum and registered it at Stationers' Hall on the promised date 'although the bulk of the copies of our edition will not be ready for delivery to the general public before the 13th of this month'. Three days later he told Tauchnitz 'There is already a great enquiry for the book which leads us to expect a still greater popularity for it than for any of the author's recent works'.

During these months Clemens had been particularly concerned with the illustrations. In July he instructed Hall to give Beard an absolutely free hand, whether the picture was humorous or serious [131]. He wrote ecstatically to Beard about the drawings in August [134]; in October he accepted Beard's criticism that his reference to a turkey was anachronistic as that was an American bird unknown in England until centuries later, and he agreed to the substitution of a goose;[10] in November he was again congratulating Beard [136], and in December telling a correspondent 'to my mind, the illustrations are better than the book — which is a good deal for me to say, I reckon' [138]. This may not have been complimentary hyperbole so much as further evidence of the doubts and reservations about the book that he had not fully identified to himself. It was, of course, a work for which he had done an unusual amount of preparatory reading, much of it in British sources as Howard Baetzhold has very fully demonstrated:[11] what disconcerted Mark Twain was the realisation of how that material had been transmuted by his creative imagination even more than by his conscious will, but he would not repudiate the result.

Interestingly, in August he had found it necessary to defend the sacrosanctity of his text against domestic depredations, telling Hall 'The proof-reader must follow my punctuation *absolutely*. I will not allow even the slightest departure from it' [132]. That he was always touchy on this score is evident in his later exchanges with Chatto over *Following the Equator*, but in 1889 it is part and parcel of his general sensitivity over *A Connecticut Yankee*. The impressions that English publishers were afraid of the book did, in fact, gain some currency at the time by the publication in the Canadian press of the following paragraph; the spitefulness of its tone may owe something to the contemporary Canadian hostility to Americans being able to obtain Canadian copyright so easily, but whether its final statement was prompted by malicious invention or by rumour remains unclear:

Mark Twain Coming to Canada
The American angry, however, with monarchists
in general and English people in particular

Mark Twain is coming to Canada for the purpose of obtaining a copyright upon his new book, "The Yankee at the Court of King Arthur". Judging from the chapters published in one of the American magazines the book is not a very funny one; the humor being very forced. There is a great deal of irreverence toward religion displayed in the work, and it is because all respectable English publishers have refused to publish it without striking these parts out that Mark Twain is so angry.

A cutting of this was sent to Clemens in February 1890 by a Canadian writer, H.H. Collins, with a profuse apology for having attacked the book in the Canadian press 'a short time ago' on the basis of this paragraph which he now recognises as 'altogether misleading': if Clemens wishes to publish a counter-attack 'it is no more than I deserve — but I trust to your generosity and my personal unimportance'. On the envelope in which the letter arrived Clemens had scribbled 'Seems to kind of *want* it':[12] it is a phrase with which Chatto might appropriately have endorsed the letters from Clemens and Webster & Co. in July and August. The equanimity and quiet humour with which he did in fact close this particular subject on 30 December 1889 must have left Mark Twain with mixed feelings and a sense of anti-climax:

Dear Mr Clemens
      The enclosed cuttings from the Pall Mall Gazette concerning your new book will amuse you. From the two early copies of our English edition you will see that not a word of yours has been cut out or altered, except as regards keeping the title to your original wording "*A Yankee at the Court of King Arthur*" which is shorter and I think more easily grasped by the British public. I have sent copies to Tauchnitz (but I think he stands in more awe of the German Emperor than we do of our royal family) and to some other continental publishers for translation. I have had a reply from a Russian publisher for whom Siberia seems to have no terrors.

Very faithfully yours,
Andrew Chatto

Paine's allegations, in short, seem to lack any substance, and it is both regrettable and strange that they and the letter they introduce should for so long have been accepted unchallenged at their face value as evidence both of Clemens's Anglophobia and Chatto's interference with Mark Twain's text. These misconceptions could have been cleared up long ago by a simple comparison of the English and American

editions, even without sophisticated collating machinery and without
reference to the correspondence adduced here for the first time. Critical
analysis of *A Connecticut Yankee* has shewn on internal evidence its
misgivings about nineteenth-century America: it is a pity to perpetuate
the fictions that England and the English were its primary and justified
targets, and that Andrew Chatto, who did so much for Mark Twain's
English reputation, asked for it to be modified.

One further point needs to be made. The cuttings from the *Pall Mall
Gazette* which Chatto thought would amuse Mark Twain were in all
probability from the issues of 21 and 23 December. There were three
items in these two numbers: one, on 23 December, was a front-page
'Interview with Mark Twain' at Hartford on 3 December that concluded
on page 2 over the initials R.D. Clemens, it appears, had treated R.D.
to a diatribe against monarchy echoing many phrases from the August
letter to Chatto. He had then inveighed against English publishers and
newspapers as cowards, complaining of what had happened to the
Yankee:

> "I have modified and modified my book until I really couldn't
> cut it any more; and now Mr. Chatto, who is the most courageous
> of them, will have to cut it more. I am anxious to see my fate. I
> have got the preface, and as only the first part remains I presume
> he has cut it. Yes, cut off more than half my preface" said Mr
> Clemens, in sorrowful tones; "and all because of a little playful
> reference of mine to the divine right of kings".

Urging Chatto & Windus to reverse their decision, R.D. solemnly prints
the omitted paragraph, though one phrase is dropped, probably inadver-
tently.

Other features of the interview, such as Mark Twain's claim that the
completed manuscript had been lying in a drawer for three years until
the time was ripe to publish it, make it quite clear that he was putting
on a little performance for R.D.'s benefit and that R.D. had swallowed
the bait. Evidently it was in this spirit that Chatto read it and sent it to
amuse Clemens, with no comment whatever on its allegations against
him. Perhaps he subscribed to the modern belief that there is no such
thing as bad publicity; more probably he knew Mark Twain's sense of
humour, and perhaps remembered how much notice Mark Twain had
attracted in 1872 by his rather more justified attack on Hotten in the
Spectator. For whatever reason Clemens and Webster had cut the Preface for the English edition, Chatto was not disposed to remonstrate
with them at the time nor to complain when the author used it now
for purpose of advertisement.

The *Pall Mall Gazette* of 21 December had provided a foretaste of
the criticism the *Yankee* would arouse. On its front page an unsigned
article had begun with a tribute to Mark Twain as 'far and away the first

of American humorists' who 'can get a laugh out of a grindstone or a civil engineer'. It had then proceeded to 'deprecate the abuse of his high gift' and 'his undoubted genius' which he was using 'to vulgarize and defile the Arthurian legend' glorified by Tennyson. Cervantes was one thing: this was something different; the writer admits to having been amused by it, 'But is nothing to be safe from the Yankee humourist?' Immediately a correspondent sprang to the book's defence and on 23 December, at the foot of the column adjacent to R.D.'s interview, announced that, as an admirer of Tennyson and Malory, he had found his reverence and delight 'no whit impaired by the Yankee's effusions':

> Rather did I read this book with a sense of deep emotion and sympathy, born of the earnest purpose which underlies the fooling and which is in no way interfered with by the fooling. The masses have no place in the Arthurian legends: in the Connecticut's narrative their wrongs and their sufferings are detailed; while the character of the King is, in my humble judgment, ennobled and made grander than Tennyson had left it.

If Chatto's other enclosures amused Mark Twain, this one must have gratified him by its sympathetic insight into the book's seriousness. Here were identified for him at the outset the two poles between which British criticism of the book would oscillate.

A response that many readers in this country must have felt, involuntarily or out of prejudice, was summed up on 28 February 1890, again in the *Pall Mall Gazette*, by the Hon. Reginald Brett in a rather blinkered commentary: 'In fact, Mark Twain might have begun his "object lessons" at home. He might generously leave to us for a short while longer our ideals'. Too thin-skinned an English reader was liable in his indignation to overlook the fact that if Mark Twain's object lesson did not begin at home in the United States it certainly ended there. Perhaps, after all, Mark Twain's strategy in the 1880s was cunningly and successfully designed to obscure precisely that fact.

In March 1910, a little more than a month before his death, he reread the book 'for the first time in more than 30 years' (as he claimed, with some exaggeration) and pronounced himself 'prodigiously pleased with it – a most gratifying surprise' [333*]. The reasons for his pleasure are not specified, and we can only speculate on them: it is not inconceivable that he was surprised to see how well the book anticipated the disillusion with 'the damned human race' to which he had by that time come, but for which his original audience was certainly not prepared.

CHAPTER 8

THE EARLY '90s

I

That *A Connecticut Yankee* encountered hostility in Britain is as indisputable as it is unsurprising. The frequency with which the reviewers quoted from and referred to Tennyson indicates Mark Twain's temerity in choosing this particular subject at this time: it was not firmly-held monarchical principles that were affronted so much as respect for the Laureate's Victorianisation of the Arthurian matter. Whether intended as a diatribe against 'monarchy and its several natural props' or as a more fundamental indictment of what he was later to call 'the damned human race', the book was received as merely a lapse of taste. Its author was not recognised as an iconoclast but only as a humorist who had rather tiresomely failed for once to amuse.

Such a reaction should not necessarily be attributed to the imperceptiveness of the English: there is a confusion of effect in the book that has teased many critics and is perhaps incapable of wholly satisfactory resolution. The book 'written for England' that the controversial letter of July adumbrates would, to make its point, need to be either socio-political criticism or satire. Its fictional form and its reliance on humour preclude the first; it falls short of the second, despite the fertility of its imagination and the sharpness of some of its thrusts, because of Clemens's failure adequately to establish the moral basis of his work.

Discussing this in 'Mark Twain the Great Victorian' I drew a contrast with Byron, Clemens's interest in whom can be seen as early as *The Innocents Abroad*. The reference to a gondola as 'an inky, rusty old canoe with a sable hearse-body clapped on to the middle of it' is, I suggested, a verbal echo of 'Beppo' where a gondola

> glides along the water looking blackly,
> Just like a coffin clapt in a canoe.

More recently Clemens's debt to Byron has been more fully documented, but I still find one of his comments revealing in its attempt to identify himself with the poet: 'Byron despised the race because he despised himself. I feel as Byron did and for the same reason'.[1] If you despise the race you do not write 'The Vision of Judgement' though you may write *A Connecticut Yankee*. Beneath Byron's contempt there for monarchs, hypocrites, and poetasters runs a deep and passionate belief in liberty and in the potential of man when he really achieves freedom:

it is this that gives the poem its satiric unity and focus. The true satirist knows and makes clear what he is for, even though our first and clearest impressions will usually be of what he is against.

In *A Connecticut Yankee* it is difficult to be sure of either. The attack on monarchy is weakened by the attractiveness of Arthur in some situations; the celebration of democracy is subverted by the autocratic conduct of 'The Boss' (and the inescapable Tammany associations of the soubriquet introduce a new non-English dimension, even if the name 'Morgan' was not deliberately chosen for its associations with American business enterprise); the denunciation of oppression is contradicted by the description of a mob so contemptibly supine and unintelligent as positively to invite exploitation; the virtues of 'Yankee know-how' and the new technocracy are undermined by the holocaust with which the novel ends. True satire is not defeatist: it depends on a belief in the possibility of change, which is antithetical to Mark Twain's declaration 'There is no such thing as nature; what we call by that misleading name is merely heredity and training. We have no thoughts of our own; they are transmitted to us, trained into us'.[2] The Darwinism on which Mark Twain is obviously drawing had postulated the evolution of species, but he seems to be denying even that possibility. If so, there is no hope for us, no point in indignation and anger, no need for satire to engender those emotions.

The absence of a clearly defined moral position from which sustained satire is alone possible becomes evident even in small and local instances: Dowley the smith is boasting of himself as a selfmade man and pointing as proof to the luxuries with which his house is furnished. Here surely is a perennial human weakness ideal as an object for satire; here is an Arthurian Babbitt whose 'conspicuous consumption' clearly awaits the irony of a Veblen. A chapter title promises us 'Dowley's Humiliation,' and indeed Dowley is humiliated; but the way in which it is done deserves comment. The Yankee arranges a display of even more conspicuous consumption and thus defeats Dowley at his own game: the underlying moral issue is evaded as surely as it is in the next chapter when the Yankee outsmarts Dowley in a discussion on political economy not by the application of better principles but by the fortuitous advantage of being able to bring a nineteenth-century knowledge to a sixth-century problem. He is smarter than Dowley, has a greater expertise, but is not significantly better. He is the product of a more technological society but his mastery over that technology is seriously limited, not by 'monarchy and its several natural props', but by human inadequacy. Yet how consciously the author has realised this is very much open to question.

It is not surprising if, faced with these confusions, Victorian readers, deciding they were not amused, resorted to the simpler response of hostility, but the nature and the extent of that hostility has been as much over-stated as has the Anglophobia that is supposed to have prompted the book. That there were aspects of England, past and present, of which Mark Twain was critical in this book is not in dispute; had the criticism been better articulated and less ambiguously organised, it might have produced the hostile response that he seemed to want; that it was not better presented is indicative of the schism within Samuel Clemens that prevented his condemning England without tacitly admitting the deficiencies of his own country and the fallibility of mankind.

II

Chatto does not seem to have been as disappointed at its sales as he was at those of *Huckleberry Finn*. In January 1890 he drily reported to Clemens 'The Russian who thought he would like to publish *"The Yankee"* now begs to be excused. Baron Tauchnitz seems to entertain views of a similar kind' (Tauchnitz did, in fact, take up his option on it); but in April Chatto described it as 'selling well' in England, and in August the royalty payment was accompanied by a detailed statement of sales to 1 July. This itemises home sales as 8,211 in cloth, 867 in sheepskin, 291 in seal, and 595 in half-morocco, a total of 9,964 which, had he not been away for the summer when the draft arrived, Clemens would doubtless have acknowledged as 'quite a good return for an off-year'. In a summary rendered a few years later in a different form Chatto & Windus put at £734 the royalties earned for its author by *A Connecticut Yankee* in the calendar year 1890; it was almost exactly twice the amount earned in the same period by all his other English editions marketed by them.

Certainly the book did nothing to impair relations between Clemens and his English publisher: if anything they became at this time even closer and more cordial as their business interests became more diversified. Although, as was suggested in the last chapter, Chatto's primary interest was in books by Mark Twain, he had always been willing to help Webster & Co in their other publishing ventures. Between the publication of *Huckleberry Finn* and *A Connecticut Yankee* several such transactions had taken place which at this point, taking a short chronological step backwards, we ought briefly to summarise.

Mark Twain's Library of Humor was mentioned only in passing. In October 1887, offering to simultane on 15 March 1888 if Webster could provide sheets sufficiently in advance, Chatto offered the same terms as for *Huckleberry Finn*. Webster, however, was not ready to fix a date as he was still negotiating publication rights with some of the authors represented; he was also not prepared to agree the English royalties, intimating that on this book the royalties would be paid to the house and not to Clemens. Then in December Webster asked Chatto, as though for the first time, what terms he would propose 'if arrangements are made with you for handling the [book] '.

This was understandably too much for the more business-like Chatto, who promptly sent Clemens a summary of the correspondence and asked for his instructions. At about this time Mark Twain's notebooks were becoming repositories for vigorous diatribes against Webster, often written in direct speech. Webster's health was failing, and the firm's financial problems were worsening, but Chatto's goodwill was crucial, so Clemens took matters into his own hands. He sent a letter of apology on 8 January [121] and eight days later assured Chatto that electros for the illustrations were in hand and proofs of the text would soon be ready for despatch. His confidence in Chatto is obvious:

> The chapter in the book about Colonel Sellers (by me) is from the "Gilded Age" – of which Routledge holds the English copyright. Knock it out. Examine for *other* contraband matter – I don't know of any myself – & put stuff from my books in place of it if you want to.
>
> I have told Mr Hall that you will acccount to *me* – there is no occasion to account to my firm. [122*]

Acknowledging this, Chatto confirmed that royalties would be as for *Huckleberry Finn* and *The Prince and the Pauper*, and reminded Clemens that they had acquired from Routledge the rights to *The Gilded Age* and were already paying him royalties on it. Webster returned the agreement for countersignature on 6 February, but admitted that the book was not yet set up.

Webster himself retired that month, so that it was Clemens who, on 14 February, told Chatto the electros were on their way to him and that the text, in paged galleys, would follow; publication would probably be deferred till 25 April [123] . In fact the dates agreed early in March were London 20 April, Canada 21 April, United States 23 April [124, 125] . There followed the customary hand-to-mouth process of printing the texts as proof – inevitably delayed – dribbled through; by 19 March Chatto estimated he had received 'only about half the whole of the volume which is reckoned at over 700 pages', and it was not until 16 April that proofs of the last fifty-four pages reached him. Nevertheless he achieved technical publication on the due date, although he had even then not received adequate instructions for the locating of some of the illustrations in the text, and when, in mid-May, copies of the American edition arrived he found that he had never been sent copy for Mark Twain's prefatory letter and the Introduction. Even then the trouble was not over for in June he had to complain to Clemens at being billed by Webster & Co. for the plates presumably supplied to the Canadian publisher; Clemens's scribbled 'Hellfire!' on the envelope seems mild in the circumstances.[3] His letter instructing the firm to apologise urgently to Chatto ('you cannot be too prompt in repairing this injury') is published in Hamlin Hill's volume [127]; he also wrote personally to apologise ('these stupidities make a body long for blood') and to ask Chatto's help with the publication of General Sheridan's *Personal Memoirs* ('& it seems to me these chuckleheaded bills are not a pleasant preparation for that' [128*]). 'It affords me great pleasure', Chatto courteously replied, 'to be able to co-operate with you', and in September he confirmed his formal acceptance of their offer of the English market for that book.

In the same letter he regretted that *The Library of Humor* 'has not sold as well as a new and original book entirely by yourself'. Tauchnitz had been very sceptical of its suitability for the European market and it had not even gone well in the United States. Clemens tried to shrug off his disappointment by telling Chatto: 'I imagined that a Library of Humor would go well – but I know better, now. On it we have scored an amusingly distinct failure here. I shan't meddle any more in that direction' [129].

Webster & Co were, however, already committed to meddle in one somewhat similar direction, and that venture was to prove even less successful. To it, indeed, Mark Twain was later to attribute the firm's commercial collapse.[4] Just as Howells had edited the *Library of Humor* (though anonymously), Edmund Clarence Stedman had, with Ellen Mackay Hutchinson, edited a *Library of American Literature*. Clemens's initial reaction to both books was lukewarm. Although he later blamed on Webster the lack of success with the Howells volume, his own dilatoriness (as Webster's son justifiably points out in *Mark Twain Business-man*) certainly did not help. 'I think well of the Stedman book', he told Webster in March 1887, 'but I can't somehow bring myself to think *very* well of it' [115]. None the less, they proceeded with it. Webster sent Chatto a prospectus in February 1888 when returning the contract for the *Library of Humor*. Chatto asked to be sent a specimen volume when one was available.

> We think it likely to be a work eminently suitable to the class of books we publish. As it appears to be a costly work to produce we think the most suitable form for us to handle it will be for you to quote a price at which you can supply us with copies in sheets.

Although he usually preferred to have the text reset in England, this anthology was planned to run to ten volumes (which actually became eleven) so Chatto's caution is understandable. He may also have been remembering the fact that Stedman's critical work, *The Victorian Poets*, which he had published in 1875, had not been conspicuously successful: at the end of the year he had had to report to Stedman the sale of only 180 copies out of 'the first small edition of 250'. Chatto described himself as 'so favourably impressed' with the book as to have

spent more than £25 on advertisements and to have distributed more
than thirty free copies so as 'to give it a really good start in this country';
though the sales were 'a great disappointment' he was hopeful that it
would 'make its way as it gets better known'. In 1878 he had declined
Stedman's *American Lyrics and Idylls:* 'we find business is so dull that
we cannot venture on making a proposal for it'. Nevertheless, he had
remained on friendly personal terms with Stedman to whom he occa-
sionally sent copies of Swinburne's work. In 1882, for example, he
accompanied *Mary Stuart* with 'a new volume of poems by Robert
Buchanan whose publishers our firm have now become': imagination
begins to play with the possibility of a random meeting, in Chatto's
office, between Swinburne and the author of 'The Fleshly School of
Poetry'. That the letter ends with 'best respects' from Mrs Chatto and
himself to 'yourself & wife' indicates that, like the Clemenses, the
Stedmans were on visiting terms with the Chattos. (The publisher's
generous hospitality to his authors becomes increasingly evident as this
narrative continues.)

All this throws some light, incidentally, on the otherwise unexpected
mention of Stedman, in the controversial letter of July 1889, as one of
those who have read and advised on *A Connecticut Yankee*. He and
Clemens had come into contact with each other in the 1880s through
their interest in the American Copyright League and its concerns, but
he was not a friend to whom Clemens regularly turned for critical
advice; indeed Clemens's later letters to Hall speak of Stedman very
contemptuously. The *Library of American Literature* project would at
this time, however, have brought them into closer collaboration and
suggested Stedman as a reader of the *Yankee* manuscript; the knowledge
of Chatto's friendship with and evident respect for him would give point
to specifying Stedman's approval of the book.

The intemperate injustice of that letter, as has been seen, Chatto
seems to have been able to accept, regarding it perhaps as poetic licence.
The inefficiencies of Webster & Co. he found less tolerable, if we can
judge from the marked terseness with which, in January 1890, he complained at being asked again for money that he had already paid them.
Yet the amount of help and advice he gave Fred Hall, who took charge
after Webster's retirement in 1888, increased and continued. It was not
as though the business they gave Chatto, apart from Mark Twain's own
works, was actually or potentially lucrative. He was, for example, sceptical
of their proposal in the spring of 1889 to bring out a cookery book
'suitable for both American and European markets': English and Continental cookery books sold well, but he reported 'a strong feeling here
that on account of the different conditions of the food supply in the
two countries, no work can be made to satisfy the requirements' of
both Europe and the United States.

In the summer of 1889 Webster & Co. revived their idea of securing the autobiography of H. M. Stanley, the African explorer. Webster claimed that Stanley had, in writing, promised him this in 1886, but the letters for that year published by Hamlin Hill make that seem unlikely. In July 1889 Clemens reopened the correspondence with a letter which he asked Chatto to forward, as Stanley's whereabouts were uncertain.[5] Chatto asked Sir Francis de Winton to send it to Stanley but the explorer did not reply. Then in November a paragraph in *The Times* gave Chatto the idea of seeking Stanley's address from Sir William Mackinnon and telegraphing to Stanley in Zanzibar the gist of Clemens's letter at 7*s*. 9*d*. a word ('to send it in extenso would cost about £35'). From de Winton Chatto also learnt that the publication in America of John Rose Troup's *With Stanley's Rear Guard* was to be legally contested (it was suppressed in England). This information he promptly passed on to Webster & Co., knowing that they were in negotiation for a parallel work, Herbert Ward's *My Life With Stanley's Rear Guard*, which in fact they published two years later. The further correspondence between Chatto and Hall over this is not relevant to the bid for Stanley's autobiography, but it is worth mentioning that it interlocks chronologically with the letters from Clemens and from Webster & Co. about the 'cuts' in the English *Yankee*.

By December Chatto had discovered that Stanley had already arranged for the English publication of a book on his African travels and was expecting to secure £40,000 for it. Ironically the publisher was to be Sampson & Low, Chatto's successful rivals for Grant's *Memoirs*, but this did not reduce his efforts on behalf of Webster & Co. for the American rights. When, in January 1890, Hall came to London to negotiate with Sampson & Low, he found that Chatto, who had called on them several times in this connection, was a very useful ally; telling Clemens that he had asked for advice on a draft of a letter to the rival publisher, Hall observed:

> I hesitated somewhat about letting Mr. Chatto so entirely into our confidence, but he seemed so much interested in our behalf that I thought it safe. His advice of course was valuable as he is a shrewd business man and understands the book trade.[6]

By March 1890 Chatto was able to acknowledge receipt of 'the magnificent set of volumes of your "*Library of American Literature*"', and to order twenty-five sets 'which I hope you will be able to invoice to us at half the price'. In September he reported that review copies had gone to *The Times, The Daily News, The Athenaeum, The Pall Mall Gazette, The Review of Reviews* and *The Speaker*; he had also sent complimentaries to Gladstone and to William Sharp, the Scottish journalist (Andrew Lang's championing of Mark Twain might have made him a more obvious recipient) and ordered a further twenty-five sets. Replying, Hall offered the inducement of a further five percent discount on future sets

(60% as against the previous 55%) and urged that sales be pushed as hard as possible. Worried about the heavy expenditure on this project, Clemens in a notebook entry at this period speculated about selling a share to Stanley or to Chatto. Nothing seems to have come of this and indeed there would have been very little advantage in it for the English firm.

IV

It was not only as a publisher that Chatto was acting on Clemens's behalf in 1890. At the beginning of the year he was approached by a Mrs Beringer who was interested in adapting *The Prince and the Pauper* for the stage as a vehicle for her teen-age daughter, Vera. On his own initiative Chatto secured an agreement whereby Clemens was to receive two and a half per cent of the takings and the two adaptors five per cent. There was, he thought, every likelihood of a box-office success. 'I hope you will be pleased with this arrangement', he wrote on 14 January, 'for had anyone chosen to dramatise the story here without requiring our sanction, it would have been a very difficult matter to have interfered with them'.

Coincidentally a dramatisation of *The Prince and the Pauper* by two other adaptors, Daniel Frohman and Abby Sage Richardson, had opened in Philadelphia on Christmas Eve 1889 and was transferring to New York on 20 January.[7] Chatto may well have known of this, but what he could not have known was that an old friend of Clemens, Edward H. House, claimed that he had been given dramatic rights to this book by the author several years earlier; on 11 January 1890 he had applied for an injunction in New York to prevent further performances of the Frohman version. Mark Twain, who had in 1884 copyrighted his own not very effective dramatisation of the story [102], disliked Frohman's greatly, but apparently alerted Chatto to the problems of the situation, for on 12 February the publisher cabled him to restrain Frohman from proceeding with an application for English rights. In a draft of a letter to his lawyer, Daniel Whitford, about this, Clemens decided 'not to put Chatto into an embarrassing position' by interfering with the London contract which Chatto would have made 'with no interest in view but my protection' and with no time for prior consultation [140*].

In New York the House case dragged on for seven weeks until, on 8 March, Judge Daly granted an interim injunction. House's lawyers, Morgan & Ives, promptly wrote to Chatto in the hope of preventing the London production also. Chatto read Judge Daly's ruling and told Clemens that he was 'unable to agree with that learned lawyer in his conclusion that there was a definite contract' between House and the novelist. Writing as 'Chatto & Windus' he coolly informed Morgan & Ives 'that in virtue of the first publication of the work in this Country our Mr. Andrew Chatto is the registered proprietor of the English

Copyright of it, and is therefore the only person who can authorise the dramatization of it in this Country' – a statement which, in its confidence, contrasts markedly with his description of the position when first writing about it to Clemens.

Whatever the legal niceties, Morgan & Ives seem to have accepted Chatto's view of the situation, for the London production opened three days after Chatto's letter; when it closed, it was from natural causes, not from legal action. In New York Clemens had got a lot of bad publicity from the House hearing; it was not entirely undeserved, but the case was in fact a tangled, acrimonious and unpleasant affair that dragged on for years. Chatto's bold and decisive reply to Morgan & Ives at least saved Clemens from anything on that scale in this country. It is an interesting interpretation of the benefits accruing from the 'prior publication' that secured English copyright for an American book, but whether a court of law would have upheld Chatto or House is a matter for speculation.

The production opened at the Gaiety on 12 April, and in the audience was the faithful Conway. As soon as he got home he wrote an ecstatic letter to 'My dear old friend' to assure him of 'its wondrous success'. As in the American production, the roles of Tom and the Prince were doubled by the young leading lady. Conway rhapsodised over the fifteen-year-old Vera Beringer's performance which had moved the audience to tears in the moments of pathos and to enthusiastic applause at the end. 'Indeed the acting was all fine'; 'The whole prison scene was perfectly mounted. Teniers couldn't have arranged it better'; Mrs Beringer had 'followed the story well,, and got the drama into just 2½ hours'. Conway wished that Clemens could 'only have come in astral body from Hartford' to take a curtain-call. He also

> could not repress some regrets that the adapting triumph was not that of our dear Mrs Richardson, of whose toil on the story I had some knowledge before I left. It is a public calamity that there should be such a snarl over the thing in America.

The letter then turns to other gossip, including the news that, at dinner the previous night, 'I heard you both glowingly talked of by Charles Dickens, who appears to have enjoyed Hartford more than any other place in America'. Clemens may have been rather less pleased at Conway's laconic comment 'Your King Arthur book is a pretty book' and at the rapidity with which he moves from the book itself to an anecdote of presenting a copy of it to a boy, George Washington, the youngest member of the English family from which the first President was descended. Had Conway been happier about *A Connecticut Yankee* he would almost certainly have said so more effusively, but in all other respects the letter suggests the same easy intimacy between them as ever.[8]

It is to be hoped that Clemens knew him well enough to treat Conway's enthusiasm with caution, for *The Prince and the Pauper* was not destined for the success he predicted. With the August royalties Chatto sent Clemens his apologies for the smallness of Mrs Beringer's gross takings, which was 'a great disappointment'. Although she was determined to try another production of the piece, in fact in September 1891 she sold her rights in it to Joseph Hutton, with Clemens's percentage remaining the same. Another potential source of much-needed money for Clemens, beset by the problems of the Paige typesetter, had dried up.

V

By now Percy Spalding, who had been with the house since 1876, begins to play a more prominent, or at least a more identifiable, part in the correspondence. It was Spalding who, in response to a request from Hall, took out subscriptions for him to *The Athenaeum* and *The Speaker*, describing them as 'the best representatives of literary opinion & criticism in this country'. In December 1890 Hall suggested that Webster & Co. should make a formal arrangement to publish Chatto & Windus books in the United States. Clemens told him to discuss it with 'the good Chatto' [142], and by April 1891 Hall reported the receipt of offers 'by almost every steamer'. Though he thought not one in four was suitable for the American market, he was still hopeful of a title by Walter Besant or 'some other well-known English author' becoming available.

Connections between the firms became closer. Spalding had to ask Hall, in February 1891, whether Clemens really knew the Captain Mallinson who had obtained credit from Chatto & Windus some months earlier on the strength of his friendship with Clemens, but whose note had now been returned dishonoured. When, in return, Hall enquired about a Dublin firm who had been recommended to them Spalding bluntly warned him that they were 'Not safe to be trusted for a penny'. Chatto & Windus were, of course, still obtaining books for Mark Twain (in February 1891, for example, sending to Germany for a copy of Sebastian Kneipp's *My Water Cure*) and handling his continental rights to his entire satisfaction, as he told Bram Stoker in March [145]. They were, however, in Chatto's words, hoping 'soon to hear from you particulars of a new book by you upon which we may "spread" ourselves'.

Clearly they had no fear that the *Yankee* had done his reputation any harm. It had not, for example, deterred John A. Stewart from including a very sympathetic essay on him (along with essays on Lowell, Holmes, Whittier and Howells) in his *Letters to Living Authors* in 1890. W.T. Stead's choice of the *Yankee* as the book of the month for February in the *Review of Reviews* had, he observed, 'brought down upon my head very severe animadversions from not a few of my friends', but it brought him also a letter from the author [141] which he promptly printed in *Portraits and Autographs: an Album for the People* in the same year (the comment just quoted is from that volume, where he goes on to extol Mark Twain as 'one of the benefactors of mankind'). A new book of distinction would have boosted both reputation and royalties, but unfortunately nothing of that nature was forthcoming.

In Europe in the summer of 1891 Clemens had thoughts of re-mining the vein that had produced *A Tramp Abroad*. Seeing press references to this but hearing nothing from the author, Spalding wrote anxiously to Hall for Clemens's European address: 'you know Mr. Chatto & I will be only too pleased to go over to him if he would like to see either of us on any matter of business'. (Clemens was to take up that offer in 1894 very gratefully.) A month later Spalding expressed his pleasure that 'we may shortly expect another book, also your European letters for publication in book form here'; he sent him a royalty cheque for £389. 5s. 0d. and copies of Sir Edwin Arnold's *The Wonderful Adventures of Phra the Phoenician* and Sara Jeanette Duncan's *An American Girl in London*; he explained that the short stories published by Kipling in America as *Mine Own People* would shortly appear in Britain under a different title, and promised Clemens a copy. The cheque Clemens returned, asking instead for letters of credit on which his European bankers could draw 'because the bank might break (any bank can do that) but your house will go on forever'. The books were particularly welcome 'as we came away rather constipated for reading matter' [149*]. Chatto promptly offered to supply any titles from 'our catalogue of fiction comprising nearly 600 books', but this was not what Clemens wanted.

> In my present (or approaching) labors, I can make use of almost any *facts* that fall in my way — history, travel, biography, statistics — nothing in the domain of fact will come amiss — but I can weave-in fiction enough of my own, you see. [150*]

A week later the request was repeated:

> You sent me your list of novels, but I musn't read novels when I am preparing for work. You publish a great library of didictic [sic] works if I remember rightly: won't you send me that list? I laid out some of the books I needed, but I think half of them have been left at home. [151*]

The vagueness about the exact nature of his needs and his work cannot have been encouraging to Chatto, who followed the despatch of his general catalogue with an enquiry about the book on Colonel Sellers that he had seen rumoured in the press. They were preparing their lists for autumn and spring 'in which we should wish your book to take a foremost place' if title, publication date and numbers of illustrations could be specified: the earlier copy could arrive, the better they could 'prepare for an effective "*boom*" which we are very desirous of carrying out with it'. Clemens confirmed the title as *The American Claimant* but added 'Your other questions oversize my information; but I have sent the letter home and Mr Hall will answer you'. In response to a cordial invitation from Chatto he promised to visit England 'a year hence' before returning home [153*]. Meanwhile he continued on the continent, urging Chatto in October not to divulge his address, and asking for a Wirt foutain pen as he had lost his [154, 155]. Three days after Clemens wrote from Berlin the pen was despatched from London; so was the news that *The Prince and the Pauper*, rewritten by Joseph Hutton, was opening that night (12 October) at the Vaudeville Theatre. The Wirt pen was pressed urgently into service translating the German children's story *Der Struwwelpeter* in 'three days and nights' [157, 158], but plans to publish it came to nothing.

Chatto & Windus repeated their interest in bringing out his European letters as a companion volume to *A Tramp Abroad*; he sent the second letter in December with the promise of others [161] but nothing came of this project either. There is a frenetic lack of concentration about Mark Twain's work at this time which was certainly occasioned in part by ill-health, especially rheumatism in his arm; he was also justifiably worried about his business ventures and his need to raise capital. He was shortly to revive once more the idea of the children's history game, and once more to abandon it.

Had he put more effort into *The American Claimant* it might materially have improved his fortunes. The subject was a topical one, for 'American claimants' were becoming a source of real anxiety to British landowners. In 1882, for example, one Warwickshire family urged their vicar, in replying to an enquiry he had received from a namesake of theirs in New York, to represent their estate as less valuable than it was, lest the enquirer prove to be a claimant. From a preliminary canvass Chatto was able to hold out to Mark Twain reassuring expectations of 'a very fine and successful sale' for the book which were, in the event, not really fulfilled. Clemens, having arranged serialisation with McClure in America before book publication, was looking for a similar arrangement in England. Conveniently Chatto was planning to bring out, under the editorship of Jerome K. Jerome and Luke Sharp, 'a brilliant new sixpenny magazine "*The Idler*" ', and offered to begin the serialisation in the opening number, in February. The twelfth instalment would thus appear in January 1893; alternatively, if it suited Webster & Co. better, *The Idler* could complete by November, so as to permit October publication in book form. *McClure's*, however, expected to complete in April, so Chatto, by making up copies from the *Idler* type, effected nominal publication on 2 May to secure British copyright until the book was properly issued in the autumn. Throughout the summer the usual series of letters went from Chatto & Windus to Hall, plaintively asking for the electros and for information as to where they were to be located in the text. Copy came back in the usual instalments, little and late, but this time Clemens was in Europe and unwell, so the story is not, as before, complicated or enlivened by his well-meant personal interventions. He was quite content to leave the details to Hall [156, 163, 165]. One minor unsolved mystery is why Hall should have placed the order for five thousand copies of *The Idler* that Chatto acknowledged on 2 January 1892; if they were for re-sale in the United States *McClure's* would surely have had grounds for complaint.

Beset by financial worries, rheumatism, and, at the beginning of the year, congestion of the lungs, Mark Twain made little progress in 1892 with creative work. In April he told Hall 'I do not expect to be able to write any literature this year. The moment I take up a pen my rheumatism returns' [167]. Dissatisfied with his letters from Europe currently appearing in *The Illustrated London News*, he had told Chatto in January not to publish them in book form until he had added to them later in the year [164]. Chatto assured Hall that the magazine publication would guarantee British copyright; the American system of filing the title and making formal publication of the book was not operative in Britain, where an actual copy of the book had to be deposited or sold before it could be protected. In the event, nothing more was to happen to this idea.

Anxious as Chatto was for a new book by Mark Twain, he turned down as a mere piece of book-making one offered him in April 1892 by Webster & Co. They had made no attempt at simultaning this, but sent it to him with two books by other authors (one of these, a Whitman selection, he declined because 'We already publish a very carefully edited volume of selections made by W.M. Rossetti which we think will satisfy the English market'; the other title was already being published by Cassell). *Merry Tales by Mark Twain*, he found, contained only four pieces not included in volumes previously published by him: these were 'The Campaign that Failed', 'Luck', 'The Captain's Story' and 'Meisterschaft'. If any uncollected pieces could be added to these – he instanced 'Telepathy' – he would be glad to publish such a volume. *Merry Tales*, however, might 'by disappointing readers who may expect something not previously collected, lessen the sales of his other works'; nor, he thought, would it benefit Mark Twain's interests if Hall tried to place it with another British publisher. Although the volume contained only seven pieces in all, the decision was probably sound; these July royalties of £314. 0s. 9d. were, he told Clemens, 'shewing still a steady sale of the books on which the first of novelty has abated'.

By now he had evidently cornered the market, for in February 1892 Routledge, reminding him that he had acquired *The Gilded Age* electros in 1885, asked whether he would now like to buy the stereos of the two-shilling edition of it for £30 and a two-volume edition of the *Sketches* for the same figure. Chatto promptly offered him £100 if to those he would add stereos and copyrights of the two-volume *Roughing It* which sold at one shilling a volume. To this Edmund Routledge replied with equal promptness 'You can have as I promised before the vols. of Twain, but Roughing It we don't wish to sell at all'. Chatto accordingly paid £60 for the other titles, receiving with them a typed copy of the original *Gilded Age* contract.

To Mark Twain's various interests, he continued to minister willingly and efficiently. In November 1891 he sent him the facsimile of the warrant to execute King Charles I which was published by them, and received an enthusiastic acknowledgement in which Clemens predictably called attention to the signature of his ancestor on it [159]. When Olivia decided that Christmas to give her husband a copy of the picture of the judges at the trial she asked Chatto & Windus to acquire one for her, at not more than £3; they obtained two, with which she was delighted: a modern engraving at £3 and, for £1, a smaller one which they thought historically more accurate [160, 162].

By now Mark Twain was turning his attention to Joan of Arc and again it was Chatto's advice that he sought. In December 1891 Chatto recommended the '5 good-sized volumes published in Paris in the years 1841-9 by Quickery' as providing 'just the sort of *minute contemporary evidence*' Clemens recalled having seen in 'an old English book' which Chatto could not identify. He could not trace an English translation of Quickery, but he enclosed 'Lord Stanhope's article reprinted from the Quarterly Review, & Mr Tuckey's life in the new Plutarch series', as well as listing, with publishers and prices, Bray's *John of Arc and the Times of Charles III,* Cathy's *Footsteps of Joan of Arc,* Parr's *Life and Death of Joan of Arc* and 'De Quincey's Joan of Arc in his 'Miscellanies"'. In October 1892 he sent Clemens a transcript of the *Encyclopaedia Britannica* note on the literature of Joan of Arc with the assurance 'we shall be only too happy to take any amount of trouble to take further particulars'.

Next month, Mark Twain's attention having shifted to *Pudd'nhead Wilson,* they found and sent him a book on finger-prints which he promised to devour: 'I don't know how you could have done me a greater favor' [169*]. By now they were supplying him with books not at trade price but at one-third discount. They also looked up in the Oxford University Calendar a young gentleman who had written to Clemens; there being no other information available they concluded 'It looks as though it is a polite way of asking for an autograph'. Disposed at another time to attribute his rheumatism to the stiffness of the Wirt pen they had bought him, he thought of ordering a different one [166], and no doubt they would have found one to suit him. At the end of one letter Chatto jauntily wished him 'as the Irish say, "More power to your elbow" — the lame one'; the house could hardly have done more to contribute to that power, and it is easy to see why, in August 1893, Clemens should call them 'a credit to your light-disseminating and civilization-ameliorating profession' [176*].

VI

Eventful and disastrous as the next few years were to be for Mark Twain and for his family, they can, from the more specialised viewpoint of this narrative, be quickly summarised. *The £1,000,000 Bank Note and Other Stories* was published in England in April 1893; Clemens's instruction to Hall seven months earlier that Chatto must be enabled to 'simultane' had been obeyed [168]. 'A Petition to the Queen of England' was collected in this volume, as was the piece on telepathy suggested by Chatto, but the four new pieces in *Merry Tales* were not collected in England until 1900 with *The Man That Corrupted Hadleyburg*.

By the summer of 1893 Mark Twain had at last satisfied himself with the revisions of *Puddn'head Wilson* and had turned his attention once more to *Joan of Arc*; Lord Gower's book on the subject, which Chatto sent him in April, attracted particularly warm expressions of thanks from Olivia and later from Clemens [171, 173]. Notifying him in August that the annual royalties came to £734. 9*s*. 4*d*., Chatto asked about *Pudd'nhead Wilson's* progress:

> Our expectation is on tip-toe for the new story on which you have been so severe a task master to yourself, and we are all agog to lend a hand in the rewarding of such industry & perseverance. Can we make a start with it? We tremble when we think that even now you may not be satisfied with it. We might arrange for the English Serial use of it on your behalf if you could favour us with your views on the subject, and let us have a duplicate typewritten copy.

They repeated the request on 18 August: 'Can we do anything for you as regards placing the serial issue of your story while you are away at the World's Fair?' This crossed with Clemens's letter containing the handsome tribute to them already quoted, but neither instructions nor text were forthcoming and in October they cabled Webster & Co. for proofs.

The storm-clouds were by now gathering around Webster & Co., as well as around the Paige type-setter, with such rapidity that nobody found the time to tell Chatto of the situation. If the storm cleared, it would have been unwise to have alarmed him; time enough to tell him if it did not clear. In any case, no decision had been taken on the book publication of *Pudd'nhead Wilson* or of *Tom Sawyer Abroad*, so there was nothing to tell him on that score, although the failure to take up his offer to arrange English serialisation is more surprising. Clemens's mind was probably alternating between shorter and longer term solutions to his problems than the publication of these books. In August he had told Hall how desperately he was awaiting 'Brer Chatto's' cheque [175]; its size was the immediate cause of his ecstatic tribute [176], but his respect was not based solely on his royalties. A notebook entry of about this period is even more interesting in its suggestion that he was contemplating Webster & Co. becoming Chatto & Windus's New York house. Nothing in the letter-books indicates that any approach was ever made to them, however, though a sale to Chatto (if that is really what he had in mind) would have solved one pressing financial problem for Clemens very well. Moreover, if not selling Grant's *Memoirs* to Chatto had been 'like going out of the family', becoming Chatto's New York house would have been like keeping Webster & Co. in the family, for his dealings with Chatto had always been conducted on the friendliest basis.

Perhaps the idea was never broached because Clemens was still hoping that Webster & Co. could survive on its own. Perhaps he realized that a New York house was hardly a commercial proposition for any London publisher at that time. Perhaps he knew Andrew Chatto well enough to recognize that the project would not attract him. Astute business man that Chatto was, his concept of the firm and of his own role in it was essentially patriarchal. He still wrote most of the correspondence in his own hand; he was his own reader where fiction was concerned and elsewhere too; when the crucial sale of a title to Mudie's Library had to be negotiated, it was Chatto who called a hansom cab and went to conduct the affair himself. Had either of his sons followed him permanently in the business, it would have been perfectly described as a family firm. That they did not do so — except for a comparatively short period — may have been because, in becoming so successful a self-made man, he had not sufficiently learnt to delegate responsibility to others. An ardent amateur yachtsman, he probably believed in the advantages of only one man at the tiller. For all his interest in and first-hand acquaintance with America, the benign figure that Frank Swinnerton remembers with such affection was too set in the ways of London to want to acquire a New York outpost that he could not personally command and in whose staff he had such little reason for confidence. That the idea should have occurred to Mark Twain at all, however, is a tribute to Chatto that, for all his modesty, the publisher would have appreciated, for his self-reliance was not of the arrogant kind.

The harassed Hall seems to have replied to Chatto's enquiries about *Pudd'nhead Wilson* and *Tom Sawyer Abroad* by suggesting that he could obtain the texts of both from the London publishing house of Fisher Unwin; the most likely explanation of this is that they imported *St. Nicholas* and the *Century*, in which magazines the stories were running as serials, though it seems strange that the usually well-informed Chatto should not have known of this. (His letters to Clemens in the previous August show that he knew serialisation was intended.) In January 1894 he told Hall that he had visited Fisher Unwin who were unable to supply all the instalments; he also expressed surprise that Hall was charging $450 plus the cost of production to supply electros of the illustrations to the two stories, and suggested the desirability of a reduction. By some means, however, he brought out *Tom Sawyer Abroad* in April 1894, the month in which Webster & Co. was declared bankrupt. When Clemens returned to America for the summer a series of letters [177 to 180] warmly acknowledges Chatto's help to Olivia in negotiating cheques in France.

Various ideas were considered for the American book publication of *Pudd'nhead Wilson* but none was communicated to Chatto. The most promising suggestion was to go back to Bliss's American Publishing Company, who still marketed Mark Twain's earlier books, and let them bring it out by subscription. In August 1894 a bewildered Chatto asked the author for news of the book: the English edition, he explained, had 'long since been printed off' for simultaning in September, but the illustrations were still lacking. Clemens at once remonstrated explosively about these delays with his friend and advisor, Henry Huttleston Rogers, the oil magnate, who was trying to see what could be salvaged from the wrecks of Paige and Webster for him [181]. An official receiver had been appointed for Webster & Co., one Bainbridge Colby; he eventually got the blocks to Chatto late in October, but only in a damaged condition and with, apparently, instructions to delay publication still further. To secure copyright, Chatto told Clemens, it would be essential to publish on 15 November 'but in deference to Mr Colby's imperative cable we shall not issue the book until December 1st, although the chances for its sale would have been better had we been allowed to publish it on the earlier date'. It still preceded the American publication, but as it had been set from the *Century* serialisation it did not include 'Those Extraordinary Twins'. Only when he received a copy of Bliss's edition did Chatto become aware of the omission; he wrote at once to Clemens very much regretting it and hoping that it might be rectified in an English reprint some time.

By the beginning of 1895 the full magnitude of the financial disaster was becoming apparent to a very stunned Clemens in Paris. Drastic remedies were under consideration: even the Hartford house had to be let, and calculations of possible sources of income were giving him insomnia. His income from Chatto & Windus royalties he estimated at $2,000 a year, as against $1,500 from 'the Hartford books' [183]. Even though the American figure excludes the Webster & Co. publications, royalties on which would go to meeting the firm's debts, the English income compares very favourably with it. In calculating it he may have drawn on a summary supplied by the firm of the amounts paid to him in royalties for the years 1890-94 inclusive. It survives on the verso of a sheet of the firm's notepaper (now owned by the Berg collection in New York) but with no covering letter.

The explanation may be that it was delivered by hand, for either Chatto or Spalding went to Paris at Clemens's request at the turn of the year. The publication of a Uniform Edition of his works had occurred to Mark Twain as another means of raising money. Discussing it with Rogers in a letter of 3 January 1895, he adds the laconic post-script 'I sent for my London publisher and he gave me help and in-formation on the Uniform' [182]. There is unfortunately no reference to this meeting in the correspondence (a cable summons to Chatto seems likely) and no other record of it, but a letter from Chatto on 9 January was probably a sequel to it. He tells Clemens that he has ordered from Sheffield the Wade & Butcher razors that he could not obtain in London; and he encloses, as requested, though emphasising that it is not for publication, details of the cost of manufacturing ten thousand copies of the 3s. 6d. edition of *Pudd'nhead Wilson*. This itemised and annotated statement merits reproduction as a piece of economic history:

Composition 8 sheets of 32 pages & small type	21. 19. 6
Stereotyping 8 sheets @ 30/- per sheet	12. . .
Working 10,000 copies in sheets of 64 pages 80 reams	20. . .
Working title and illustrations 8 pages	7. 15. .
*Paper 80 reams 140 lbs. @ 3d. per lb.	140. . .
Paper 20 reams for plates	14. . .
Stereotypes of illustrations – per Webster & Co.	18. 9. 4
Binding Block	5. . .
Binding @ 5d. per volume 10,000	208. 6. 8
Advertising to date (it will take much more to work off the whole 10,000 copies)	80. . .
	527. 10. 6

Costs one shilling and three quarters of a penny per copy
1. 0¾
<u>   7</u>   author's royalty
1. 7¾   (The nett receipts from a 3s. 6d. volume less wholesale discounts and commissions may be taken at 1/10½. Although nominally published at 3s./6d. all retail booksellers sell to the public at 9d. for the shilling – this book is sold everywhere for 2s./8d.)

* the paper therefore costs almost three pence and three farthings per copy.

The surprisingly low margin of profit implied for the publisher (2¾d. on a 3s. 6d. book) presumably reflects Chatto's confidence in a quick sale of this sizeable edition. It does not look as though *A Connecticut Yankee* had given him any doubts about Mark Twain as a commercial proposition.

How Clemens intended to utilise this information is not clear, for it seems to have no bearing on the Uniform Edition. He, Rogers, or Colby may have wanted to cross-check Bliss's costing of the American

Pudd'nhead Wilson, but that would not explain why he also asked for, and was given, a similar statement in respect of another Chatto publication, W. Clark Russell's *Round the Galley Fire.* He may have wanted evidence to support his retention of Chatto & Windus as his English publisher when his publishing arrangements in America were in the melting-pot. In May 1895 when the publication of *Joan of Arc* was under discussion, a change of English publisher may have been mooted: Clemens told Chatto, 'I am very glad you have arranged for Joan, and that I am to remain with you and not go wandering among strangers'; there is, however, no suggestion that this was a decision in which he had been involved at all [186*].

The phrase that he uses has its poignancy, for he and his family were going back to Elmira, New York, for the summer, prior to his return to the lecture-platform and to international travel, when they would be wandering 'among strangers' indeed. They sailed on the *New York*, to which vessel, at Southampton, Chatto had despatched two overcoats that he had had made for Clemens in London. The publisher by now was really a friend of the family and a friend in need: of them, in the summer of 1895, Clemens seemed to have all too few.

CHAPTER 9

ROUND THE WORLD
AND BACK TO LONDON

I

'Apparently I've *got* to mount the lecture platform next fall or starve' [184] : with this realisation, in February 1895, Clemens launched the plans that were to culminate in his exhausting world tour begun later that year and finished in the following summer. From it came his last travel book, published in England as *More Tramps Abroad* and in the United States as *Following the Equator.*

Back in Elmira, New York, in June 1895, after his European exile, his health began to improve ('There is more Clemens than carbuncle now'). He also found that his American publisher, Frank Bliss, was 'plucking up quite a spirit' with an offer of $10,000 for a book on the world tour. To the author this seemed a more attractive proposition than the *Century's* of $12,000 for a dozen articles. In a letter to Rogers he committed himself to the book but without prejudice to the possibility of magazine publication in whole or in part [188]; to Bliss, however, he declined to make any firm commitment until he had given the matter more thought [189].

Meanwhile the financial situation was made slightly less acute by a cheque from Chatto for $2319.60; this represented royalties of £492. 13s. 4d. from which sundry expenses had been deducted before conversion at a rate of 49⅜. When he knew they planned to leave Elmira on 1 July Chatto had offered to make up the account for the year earlier than usual to ensure its safe receipt; he had in fact done so by 6 June, and it was graciously acknowledged by Olivia [187].

In the event, it was 14 July when the Clemenses left Elmira for Cleveland, Ohio, on the first stage of the journey that would take them across the American continent, to Australia, India and Ceylon, Africa and eventually back to Southampton. This, rather than Elmira, Clemens regarded as his real starting point, perhaps with an unusually literal-minded desire to demonstrate, since he was writing the book in England, that he had completed the circumnavigatory circle. It is perhaps also indicative of the extent to which he now considered himself a citizen of the world, rather than of America; indicative, even, of the alienation from America that personal bereavement and grief had brought him to by the time he wrote the book.

Lionised though he was throughout the trip, and successful as his platform appearances were, it was one of the most gruelling and least enjoyable periods of his life. The magnitude of his debts and his determination to clear them gave a frenetic desperation to what might otherwise have been an interesting and novel experience. Relaxing it could never have been, with its taxing combination of travel, lectures, social engagements, and note-taking for the book; even without his money worries, he would have found it a strain to be funny in public for twelve months when in private he was racked with carbuncles, colds, and other indispositions. Financial necessity dictated a programme so punitive as to seem expiatory: twenty-two lecture appearances in America and Canada, followed by about a hundred and ten abroad. It earned him, it has been estimated, $30,000 profit with which to clear between a third and a half of the debt. It undoubtedly enhanced still further his reputation, but at a very considerable personal cost.

The Sydney *Daily Telegraph* hailed his advent as 'a blest relief' and promised him 'a royal reception'. 'There is,' it declared, 'probably no other man living, except perhaps Mr Gladstone, so universally known or whom so many people in every civilised country have to thank for having brought new interests into their lives, and given them something to think and talk about'; but, it continued, he 'is no feather-headed jester': *A Connecticut Yankee* and *Pudd'nhead Wilson* contained 'abundant proofs that the writer has a better grasp of some of the great problems of the world than many of the specialists who have dealt with them'. The comparison with Mr Gladstone, though unexpected, was evidently not casual.

Such panegyrics were some consolation to the peripatetic Clemenses who, in India in March 1896, heard rumours of another and promptly asked Chatto to send a copy of it to Natal to await them [190]. This was in *Punch* of 4 January 1896: 'A pleasing notice of Mr Clemens & his works', Chatto called it, when complying with their request, but in fact it concentrates on *Huckleberry Finn*. The anonymous writer describes sharing his eleven-year-old nephew's enjoyment of this 'great book' which has 'enough in it to fit out twenty ordinary books with laughter' and is equally rich in scenic description, character presentation, observation and sympathy, even tragedy. The Sydney *Telegraph's* conjunction of Mark Twain with Gladstone pales beside this writer's praise of 'this Homeric book — for Homeric it is in the true sense, as no other English book is, that I know of'. To one reader at least 'that unchristian dialect' had proved no obstacle.

Despatching this in April, Chatto was able to report that proofs of *Joan of Arc* were arriving and that it would be published early in May. The English publication of this book was apparently accomplished more smoothly than that of any of its predecessors, for there is no other correspondence relating to it, and Blanck records the *Athenaeum* as listing it on 16 May. That Clemens had abandoned his earlier intention

of publishing it anonymously is a measure of his returning confidence
in himself as a writer and a reflection of the public readiness to take
him as more than merely a humorist. Andrew Lang's review, which
appeared as early as 18 May in the *St James's Gazette*, made precisely
this point:

> Mark hath been accused of mocking at serious things; in this book
> he does not mock at what is sacred . . . The colour is modern, the
> taste in humour and dialogue is Mississippian; the historic sense of
> time and manners is absent. But the book is honest, spirited, and
> stirring.

Lang's praise was significant for he had himself just published a romance
about Joan of Arc, and he began the review by referring to a letter from
Clemens in India on the coincidence. He points out inaccuracies and
anachronisms in Mark Twain's version and finds Joan 'too much like an
argumentative young "school-ma'am" '; but he is delighted by Mark
Twain's attribution of humour to her (indeed Lang makes her sound
like Shaw's Joan in this respect). He is also sympathetic to the use of
the page as narrator, drawing parallels with Tom and Huck. Mark Twain's
'heart is in it' and it will extend the Americans' admiration for Joan. He
also makes, but does not develop, the point that 'Mark's is American
humour throughout, and not so very remote from the medieval'.
Clearly the sins of the *Yankee* were forgiven him.

Sir Walter Besant was unctuously ecstatic in his column in *The
Queen*, the weekly ladies' magazine for which he wrote regularly. 'A
most amazing book' with 'that power of "grip" which this writer
possesses in so eminent a degree', it presents 'a Joan of Arc more noble
more spiritual, of a loftier type than we could have conceived possible
in the author of "Huckleberry Finn"'. Mark Twain has shown himself
to have 'a nature or a soul . . . lifted high above the common run', and
Besant recommends this 'most moving portraiture' to his genteel
audience. In the adjacent columns Mrs Lynn Linton was deploring
'Vulgarities' in a tone of comparably impeccable loftiness.

Besant's notice did not appear until September. Advertising the book
in the *Athenaeum* on 4 July Chatto was able to quote enthusiastic comments from four daily papers. The *Daily Chronicle* decided Mark Twain
was 'far more than a mere man of letters . . . he is a great writer'; the
Morning Leader was also very favourably impressed; the *Daily News*
praised the book's 'wisdom, insight and reverence' and its 'tenderest,
deepest pathos'; while the *Glasgow Herald* 'doubted whether even the
Church's decree of beatification was as significant a compliment as is
this tribute from the pen of Mark Twain'. *The Speaker* was laudatory
on more literary grounds, finding it 'not only the best thing he has ever
done, but one of the best things done by anybody in fiction for a long
time past'; they praised the 'delicacy' and 'pathetic reticence' of the

closing scenes, and could not blame the Scottish reviewer who had taken
it as a genuine historical document, for the book was 'so amazing in its
realism, its vividness and force that, like one of Shakespeare's plays, it
compels acceptance'.

The *Athenaeum*, which had often championed Mark Twain in the
past, was much less favourable. In a short notice they decided it was
'rather long winded and didactic' though 'undoubtedly full of enthusiasm'; 'children might do worse than take their ideas of the Maid's
wonderful career from this account, as long as it was carefully explained
to them that the style is not to be imitated'. The successors of little
Kate L. Corbett, who had so enjoyed Mark Twain's earlier works, were
evidently expected to be more sophisticated and less spontaneous in
their response. 'The verisimilitude of the narrative', pontificated the
Athenaeum, 'is rather spoilt by the Americanisms which intrude too
frequently in the book'. The *Daily Chronicle* was prepared to make
allowance for this: the scope of the book was such that 'all the irritating
anachronisms are speedily forgotten'. For the *Morning Leader* 'his
language has undergone a startling change' for the better. Besant had an
interesting view of this: the mundane characters 'seem all, more or less,
connected with Tom Sawyer and Huckleberry Finn . . . They are not in
the least like the peasants and soldiers of the time. That matters nothing
— nothing at all', for the author 'carried away wholly by his vision . . .
could not listen to the talk of the cottage and the barrack room, and
filled in their discourse afterwards with the assistance of Tom and
Huckleberry'. The *Chronicle* compared Mark Twain to Balzac, the *Glasgow Herald* to Lang, and *The Speaker* thought the book 'infinitely
better' than Lang's. The previous number of *The Speaker* had reviewed
Mrs Oliphant's *Jeanne d'Arc: Her Life and Death* sympathetically,
though finding it 'slightly too impassioned'; the issue after the one reviewing Mark Twain noticed J.H. Skrine's dramatic poem *Joan the Maid*,
so there was sufficient competition. When Clemens eventually saw these
reviews in August and September 1896, after the world tour, they must
have given him pleasure; unfortunately that pleasure was diminished by
the personal tragedy that had by then overwhelmed him.

II

Back in England on 31 July 1896 Clemens at once telegraphed Chatto
to forward any mail to the Southwestern Hotel, Southampton [191].
On the same day Chatto sent him some letters from Harpers, six copies
of *Joan of Arc*, a royalty cheque for £446. 7s. 9d. and a letter expressing
his pleasure 'that you and Mrs Clemens are once more back in the old
country'; if they intended 'residing for some time in the neighbourhood
of the Isle of Wight' instead of coming to London, 'it will afford me
much pleasure', Chatto assured him, 'to wait on you'. A week later,
however, Clemens's daughter Clara wrote to ask for mail to be directed

to Highfield House, Portsmouth Road, Guildford [192]. Once there, she wrote again, presumably at her father's dictation, to explain that 'he is unable to use his right hand owing to a cut in the left, his leg was also injured trying to walk to the village the other day, & his hair is falling out fast. These he considers causes enough for shoving all his affairs onto the shoulders of another': they would, however, 'all be very glad indeed' to see Chatto if he would come on the following Monday [193*]. (He had written on 12 August to accept, on any day convenient to them, 'your kind invitation to a chop or a steak, when I might take your instructions regarding "Tom Sawyer, Detective" & make a suggestion for a new issue of your other books at 3/6 per volume'.)

If the afflictions Clara mentions were being humorously overstated at her father's dictation, another and a more terribly real one was about to shatter the family's much-needed peace. Clara's elder sister Susy and younger sister Jean had not accompanied them round the world but were now expected to join them in England. Instead, news came that Susy was ill. On 14 August Clemens telegraphed Chatto that they might return to America the next day [194], but in the event it was Olivia and Clara who went, leaving the anxious father in Guildford. A telegram from the firm had considerately told him that, although Chatto was out of town, the message would be passed on, so he now sent a card urging the publisher to come as arranged. On the Monday Clemens assuaged his loneliness by writing to his wife. Nothing had been heard, he told her, from Chatto, who was presumably on holiday. Then a postscript announces with evident delight 'Chatto has come' [195].

The only record of the visit is Chatto's note, pencilled on the copy of his last letter, of their having agreed on the usual 7d. royalty on all copies of the 3s. 6d. edition; but the company of an old and sympathetic friend on that melancholy occasion must have been a great comfort to Clemens. In this situation after his trip round the world he might have been pardoned for recalling the lines in 'The Ancient Mariner': '. . . this man hath penance done/And penance more shall do'. The next day a cable told him that his much-loved twenty-four-year-old daughter was dead of meningitis: Olivia and Clara were still on the way to America.

That same day, ignorant, of course, of this news, Chatto wrote to report having opened a bank account for him and having put off an interview-seeking representative of the *Daily Chronicle*: 'I told him of your determination not to be interviewed unless you were taking to the lecture platform' – a possibility that they had presumably discussed the day before. He sent him some reviews of *Joan of Arc* (including Lang's), 'the two books by Edward Garrett which you wished to obtain', together with Froude's *Oceana* and Max O'Rell's *John Bull & Co*. It was in all probability Chatto to whom Clemens sent, on 19 August, a notice of Susy's death for publication. All that survives is a distraught postscript, the cancellation (reproduced in the extract given below) suggesting that, even in his distress, he was mindful of the importunate newspaperman who, Chatto had told him, 'has begged me to again submit to you the desire of his paper to be remembered by you':

> Will you hand the enclosed half sheet to ~~the Chronicle~~ any newspaper you please, no *copy* it & give them the copy, so that they will not know it came from me. I have many personal friends in England, & they should know of my disaster. [196*]

The letter of condolence Chatto was sure to have sent would have been on private notepaper and not copied in the firm's letter books, but Clemens knew that he could call on his help. Chatto must have gone down to Guildford at least once more, when Mrs Clemens and her daughters rejoined Clemens on 9 September bringing a 'sheaf of letters' from H.H. Rogers. Acknowledging these and paying tribute to Rogers's 'heroic achievement', Clemens comments with decisive finality 'Chatto said that a better arrangement could not have been invented' [197]. With Chatto they also discussed their desire to settle for several months in London; it was probably he or Spalding who made reservations for them at Ford's Hotel in Manchester Street to which they moved temporarily on 11 September.

Telling Rogers that they were leaving Guildford, Clemens asked that mail should be directed to him care of Chatto & Windus, 214 Piccadilly. In fact the publishers had left that address on 1 September. They had been at various places in Piccadilly ever since Hotten had set himself up in 1855 at 151b and later moved across the road to 74-75. Chatto had moved to 214 in 1880, and now they went about a mile east to 'larger and more convenient premises' at 110-111 St Martin's Lane. Chatto had withheld this information from the Clemenses, probably lest they felt guilty at taking up his time at such a juncture with their domestic concerns. Forwarding mail to him on his first day at Ford's, however, Chatto urged him to favour them with a call at their 'new place of business', near St Martin's Church and the National Gallery. One such visit Clemens recorded in his notebook not because of business transacted but because St. Martin's clock chiming the half hour reminded him how often on his world tour he had heard that 'old, old & familiar' tune – 'heard it to weariness from every church clock in Australia, & now & then in India & Africa'.[1]

Chatto in the same letter offered further advice on residential areas. Although the Northern heights of London were 'supposed to be more bracing', they were as foggy and damp as other parts, and inaccessible as well; he recommended Kensington as 'certainly very healthy' and as offering a good choice of flats: Ellis of Brompton Road would be a reliable agent to consult. Percy Spalding then took the matter in hand as well as undertaking the printing of an 'In Memoriam' for Susy. Suitable houses, he reported, could be rented for five, six or seven guineas a week, and on 26 September he was able to telegraph Mrs Clemens that the tenancy of a house in Tedworth Square, Chelsea, would be available from 3 October until at least the following July. Spalding duly negotiated the contract and the Clemenses duly moved in, for a rent of five and a half guineas a week – half a guinea more than Clemens had told Rogers they could afford [198].

In addition to the need for money, the need to come to terms with his bereavement now impelled Mark Twain into an intensive period of writing; neither impetus, however, was conducive to the frame of mind in which good work was likely to be achieved. The first chapter of the travel book, provisionally entitled *Round the World,* was written on 24 October; a week later he authorised Chatto to tell enquirers that he was 'entirely out of the lecture field' [201*]. His nose was now firmly to the grindstone. He continued to use Chatto & Windus as his address, although Rogers was given permission to write to 23 Tedworth Square if he wished [199]. Bliss was not given the private address until the following May, and then only on condition that he gave it to no one else [231].

III

The book on which Mark Twain was engaged was the only one of his works to be written entirely in England, and the history of its publication is curious. Bibliographers such as Merle Johnson and Jacob Blanck describe it as though the same text was issued in America as *Following the Equator* and in England as *More Tramps Abroad*. Differences in title between English and American editions were not unprecedented (the *Yankee* was a case in point), but here we are dealing with differences far more fundamental than that. It is not merely that the American book was what Johnson rightly calls 'a sumptuous volume with numerous illustrations by the best artists of the period' while *More Tramps Abroad* was less lavishly produced, having only three full-page illustrations and one in the text. *Following the Equator* is divided into sixty-nine chapters, *More Tramps Abroad* into seventy-two (the Conclusion is common to both). As each chapter is headed with a maxim from Pudd'nhead Wilson's Calendar, the English version might be expected to contain three maxims more than the American, but the facts are more complicated than that, and in all there are eleven maxims which appear in only one of the two books. Nor would it be accurate to say simply that the English version contains three chapters more than the American, for the discrepancy is caused by the two texts being divided differently at several places. Again, each book omits substantial passages that are included in the other, there are also occasional differences of wording and paragraphing, and *More Tramps Abroad* is significantly longer than *Following the Equator.* Yet oddly all this went unremarked until 1965 when I first called attention to it.[2]

Mark Twain's heart was never in this book. At some points he incorporated   straight into his manuscript whole pages torn from his notebooks or from printed books by other writers. Yet, perfunctory as they seem at times, the copious quotations are not mere padding: they do reflect his own interests and reinforce his opinions in ways perhaps intended to differentiate the book from its more humorous predecessors. Chatto & Windus were inevitably pressed into service to provide the material he needed: F.G. Aflalo's *Sketch of the Natural History of Australia* [203]; 'Olive Schreiner's (& her husband's) little book (political) – forgotten the name of it' [212*] (it was duly identified at St. Martin's Lane); 'Garratt's book, reviewed this morning, "Story of an African Crisis" ' [232*]; these are mentioned in letters, as are 'Prof. Drummond's Natural Law in the Spiritual World. The Ascent of Man. Pax Vobiscum – and The Greatest Thing in the World' [228*]; no doubt there were others as well. It was Chatto & Windus who were asked to trace the poem by Alfred Austin on the Jameson raid, and who provided other newspaper cuttings on that subject.

There was no shortage of material, as he explained to Bliss on 19 January:

> The new book must be like Roughing It, I take it – 550 pages. I think the actual number of words in R.I. is 180,000. I have written 130,000 & could finish by March 1st; but I expect (as usual) to write a good deal more than necessary, so that I can scratch out as much as I want to. [215]

A month later he told Howells of his indifference to everything but work, adding: 'I have finished my book, but I go on as if the end were indefinitely away – as indeed it is. There is no hurry – at any rate there is no limit' [219]. In this spirit he continued to tinker with the book, writing to Bliss on 19 March:

> I finished the book (in the rough) March 1st, then spent a week gutting it. I gutted a third of it out, & then began a careful revising & editing of the remaining two-thirds. I shall complete this revision in two or three days. I set the type-writer to work on the first 10,000 words a couple of days ago.
>
> When she finishes the first 100,000 words I will carefully revise that & it will then be ready for you.
>
> I must do all this extraordinary revising because the book has to come into comparison with the Innocents & so I must do my best to bring it chock up to the mark.

He gives 1 June as his expected date of completion and adds a postscript 'If I get the book to suit me thoroughly, I shall know the title to give it' [223].

The title was in fact to prove more troublesome than he foresaw. A week later he asked Bliss whether it should be *Imitating the Equator* or the title he had given Rogers the previous November, *Another Innocent Abroad*. He was, at this point, 'more than satisfied with it', and added 'I wouldn't trade it for any book I have ever written – & I am not an easy person to please'; editing was proceeding more quickly than the typing of the copy that was to go to Bliss, but he had decided to end with India: South Africa he would reserve for a later book 'if there is material enough in that rather uninteresting country' [224*]. The decision is probably more indicative of his real feelings about the book than his professed satisfaction with it; that revising it did not take him till June as estimated is also more likely to have been due to his lack of patience than to rigorous dedication. The notebook writes it off as finished on 13 April, and on the 14th Clemens confirmed this in sending to his friend, J.Y.W. MacAlister, a chapter which, he said 'the Madame' had 'edited . . . out of it' on the grounds of indelicacy [227]. Livy had been reading the manuscript as it came from the author's pen and her editorial role in relation to this book has been discussed already by other scholars. However, Bliss and Rogers thought that South Africa should be included; Mrs Clemens concurred; Mark Twain blustered, but capitulated, and reluctantly took up his pen again. He had, he told Rogers, discarded as too ambiguous a title *An Old Innocence Abroad* [230].

If he did not ask Chatto's views on the inclusion of South Africa, it was not only because the combined opinions of Bliss, Rogers and Mrs Clemens could not be gainsaid. In February he had told Rogers that he wanted 'to strike Chatto for a new and better arrangement, for I have a good bid from another London publisher' [220]. Following his usual preference for an intermediary in such negotiations (on previous occasions it had been Conway and Osgood), he was using Bram Stoker, Henry Irving's manager, whose *Dracula* was to be published the same year [229]. While this was in progress tact or embarrassment may have kept him from personal approach to Chatto on other matters. As usual, however, Chatto was not to be outbid: he offered a twenty-five per cent royalty, half-yearly instead of annual payments, and an option on an edition de luxe later, of which the lion's share of the profits would go to the author; the author would, however, be free to issue such an edition through another publisher if he preferred. A formal contract to this effect was exchanged on 17 May; by now the book was called *A Tramp Abroad Again*.

A letter to Rogers on the following day [232a] says, rather oddly, that he *thinks* he will stay with Chatto; he had, however, communicated this decision to Bliss a fortnight earlier, suggesting that Bliss ought to come to London to see, among other things, whether Chatto would concede him the Australasian and South African markets for a subscription canvass. 'I had concluded, weeks ago, that your interest in the book was a little pale', Clemens wrote, and congratulated him on its reawakening [231]. The author's expectation was that the book would be finished by the middle of May; the accuracy of the forecast and the speed of his composition are both illustrated by the notebook entry of 18 May: 'Finished the book *again*. Addition of 30,000 words.'

It was not until 15 June that he was ready to submit the manuscript to Chatto, and on that date he sent the first forty chapters (I-XXXVII inclusive in the American numbering) comprising 1,024 pages.[4] He enclosed, describing it as the result of collaboration with friends, a holograph title-page: *More Tramps Abroad* [234]. The idea of a different title for the American version may well have come from Bliss on his visit in June. Chatto in subsequent letters to Bliss refers to the American title as *The Latest Innocent Abroad*; Blanck quotes a *Publishers' Weekly* reference to it as *The Surviving Innocent Abroad,* and it was only on 27 July that Clemens, finally deciding on a title that did not refer to his earlier works, succinctly cabled Bliss 'Following Equator' [244]. Bliss had probably taken back with him the typescript of the first forty chapters. The second batch of manuscript went to Chatto on 28 June. At Clemens's request [236] the typescript of this was mailed to Rogers on 30 June, but a note in the margin of page 406 (now partially obscured by the binding) suggests that Bliss did not receive it until 28 July, though Rogers had acknowledged receipt of it to Chatto on the 8th. The final instalment was despatched by Chatto on the 6th. This piecemeal and delayed delivery of the copy may partially explain the discrepancies between the two editions.

Chatto as usual read the manuscript himself and on 1 July discussed with the author some cuts that might advantageously be made. On the same day he sent Bliss a note of these, but having no copy of the typescript he was obliged to give the page numbers of the manuscript, while apologetically recognising that these would be of limited use to Bliss. All but two of the cuts, however, (they will be described in more detail later) occurred in the section that Bliss had presumably taken home with him, and Chatto's descriptive comments should have helped him to locate them. Writing independently to Bliss the next day Clemens told him that he and Chatto had 'ripped out a whole raft of reprint matter from the Australian part of the book'; he thought this had improved the book and added that Chatto was sending on details 'so that you can leave it out, too, if you like' [238]. Evidently he was not personally bothered about ensuring uniformity in the two editions, and it is possible that he never knew how widely they differed, for in April 1899 he told Howells:

> I wrote my last travel book in hell; but I let on, the best I could, that it was an excursion through heaven. Some day I will read it, & if its lying cheerfulness fools me, then I shall believe it fooled the reader. How I did loathe that journey around the world! — except the sea-part and India. [288]

Even if he never read the book again thereafter, he still had to read it in proof. This he did at Weggis, on Lake Lucerne, whither he and his family had moved early in July, giving up the Tedworth Square tenancy. Chap. LXIV of *More Tramps Abroad* (LXI of *Following the Equator*) is headed by the maxim 'In the first place God made idiots. This was for practice. Then He made School Boards'. This had originated in a notebook entry in 1893/4, with the difference that there the Almighty's masterpiece had been not School Boards but proof-readers. At Weggis he must have felt himself a prophet confirmed. On 19 July, finding that the printer had not spelt out his contractions and abbreviations and foreseeing 'enormous trouble', he told Chatto 'I hope to God you will kill him (But don't tell him I said so)' [239*]. A note accompanying a fragment of this letter rightly records that 'Mr Clemens had a real affection for his London publishers, Chatto & Windus'. The complaint was passed on to Spottiswoode, the printer, two days later in more temperate form, but on 22 July Mark Twain was in eruption again.

This time the cause was the printer's liberties with his punctuation; he told Chatto to cable Bliss for sheets instead of trying to work from his manuscript which 'is perfectly lousy with errors and foolishness which are not in Bliss's copy.' In postscripts added over the next two days he confessed to some uncertainty as to whether or not he had intended to retain some footnotes and an appendix, and warned them that he had probably used one maxim twice [240-242]. On 25 July he composed a little masterpiece of invective against the proof-reader, which ends: 'The damned half-developed foetus! But this is the Sabbath Day, & I must not continue in this worldly vein' [243]. These letters begin, as is his custom when complaining, 'Dear C & W'; the next, on 30 July, is in a very different key and is addressed to Andrew Chatto personally, apologising for the misunderstandings that have arisen. Chatto had replied by return of post to the diatribe of 25 July, assuring him that his punctuation would be faithfully preserved and explaining that he understood Clemens to require proofs in a hurry as the basis for a lecture; he had accordingly despatched first proofs, and not the revises which Clemens had thought he was reading and which he would in future receive. For this Clemens thanked him ('I would rather suffer any death than read a first proof') [245] and by 9 August was proclaiming that the next 'batches of sheets are divine. It is no vexation to read them' [247].

A more serious problem was Chatto's discovery that not all the chapters were furnished with maxims. By 21 July he had noticed the deficiency in Chapters XXI and XXIII (English), and by 26 July in Chapter XXV. Twain was apologetic, but could offer no immediate help:

> I am dreadfully sorry about the maxims, but you will have to get them from Bliss. They were written at odd times during the year

on fragments of paper; & when the book was finished I put them in the fire, not thinking they could be needed again. [245]

Accordingly, on 3 August, Chatto wrote to Bliss for the maxims of Chapters XVI, XXI, XXIII and XL. On 12 and 16 August he repeated the request, and on 1 September was obliged to tell Clemens that Bliss 'seems to have been unable to identify the chapter numbers with his own copy'. Of the maxims he had eventually sent, only that for Chapter XXI was of any use – the others had already been used in other chapters. A maxim had earlier been provided for Chapter VII (English) by adapting slightly two sentences from the text of Chapter V; similarly, despite his letter to Bliss, Chatto had for some reason already decided to transfer to Chapter XVI a maxim he had found in the manuscript for Chapter XL. He now asked Clemens to produce new maxims for Chapters XXIII, XXXV and XL, which presumably Clemens did. Bliss's difficulty in identifying the chapters required suggests that he had already made the changes in chapter division. The typescript shows that this was frequently done by cutting the pages with scissors and pasting them together differently, so that the original chapter numbers may well have been lost in the process.

Bliss was singularly uncooperative throughout the summer. In England he had suggested the end of November or the beginning of December as a suitable time for publication, and on 1 July Chatto asked him to fix a date, but on the 21st Chatto told Clemens that he was 'waiting to hear from Bliss the exact & earliest day when he can register the U.S. copyright'. He continued to wait. Despite reminders from Chatto on 16 August and 1 September Bliss remained silent on this point. On 30 September Chatto cabled him, asking him to agree to publish not later than 4 November, and followed this by a letter suggesting that, if not ready to publish, he might at least 'go through the usual formalities to protect American copyright' rather than hold up any longer the English publication. Johnson's entry claims that Bliss had already done this on 10 September, but he still did not tell Chatto, who now found himself obliged to delay not only his own publication but also that of the Tauchnitz edition and of a German translation by Robert Lutz, for both of which contracts had already been signed.

On 5 October Bliss wrote to Chatto & Windus that he could not publish before mid-November and still could give no precise date: 'I ought to have had 6 to 8 months to do the illustrations instead of 3 but we are doing the best we can.'[5] On 9 November Chatto cabled him 'Urgently desirable publish Twain November 18 cable confirmation', to receive the peremptory reply on the 10th 'Publish twelfth'. On 11 November Chatto told Lutz and Tauchnitz that the twelfth was the publication date, and on the twelfth he duly registered it at Stationers' Hall and deposited a copy at the British Museum. (The accession date stamped in that copy confirms this.) Reporting publication to Bliss on 19

November, he not surprisingly refused him permission to import *Following the Equator* into Australia and Canada: not only would Her Majesty's Customs prevent it in defence of Chatto & Windus's copyright, but 'copies for these two countries have already been shipped, & we are glad to say the book has been well taken up, especially in Australia'.

Beyond making some suggestions for canvassing the book Clemens appears to have left Bliss very much to his own devices. Having read Chatto's proofs he was unlikely to ask for Bliss's; at his request Chatto regularly sent Bliss corrected revises as they became available, and this no doubt seemed to the author sufficient. Bliss can have taken very little notice of the revises, for he submitted the typescript to a good deal of further editing, some of it distinctly cavalier and arbitrary, as a comparison of the two books shows.

IV

As early as 19 March Twain was thinking of this, in the American edition at least, as an illustrated book, and was suggesting to Bliss that if A.B. Frost ('the best humorous artist that I know of') was 'not *too* expensive' he should be commissioned to do three or four full-page pictures [223]. He thought of the book as more than mere entertainment, for when in Chapter XXII (American) he retold the Ceylonese legend of Hanuman carrying the mountains he inserted a note to Bliss asking for 'a serious picture, by a poet, not by a humorist.' (This was in fact illustrated by Frederick Dielman.) By 3 May the inclusion of photographs was being considered, and one inducement that Clemens extended to tempt Bliss to London was the opportunity of helping in the selection of these. Bliss's obvious lack of enthusiasm for *Following the Equator* may have led him to the belief that lavish illustrations might help to sell it. Pictures (many of them full-page) were commissioned from several of the most celebrated artists of the day, including Dan Beard who had illustrated the *Yankee*; and, as Johnson notes, the entire book was 'printed on "plate" paper for the proper display of the illustrations'. Photographs from various sources were also used, as well as sketch maps and diagrams; many of them were inserted in the letterpress, and some of the less important cuts may well have been made to accommodate the text to the page more attractively.

Evidently space was an important consideration with the American edition, for it is noticeably shorter than *More Tramps Abroad*. At one point in the typescript a marginal note, probably by Bliss, reads: 'from here on to end of chapter *can* be left out to save space if we want to'. Curiously, this refers to the lengthy description of the plague, from Kinglake's *Eothen,* which the American Chapter XLII retains but which Chatto persuaded Clemens to omit from the English text. Only on three other occasions does *Following the Equator* retain material not used in *More*

Tramps Abroad. In Chapter XXXII, when Twain is describing his voyage on 17 November in the *Flora*, the American text retains four and a half paragraphs from 'The *Flora* is about the equivalent of a cattle-scow' to 'If the *Flora* had gone down that night . . . .' In *More Tramps Abroad* this is replaced by the single laconic sentence 'The vessel was extravagantly overcrowded', a change probably due less to the British propensity for understatement than to Andrew Chatto's desire to avoid a possible lawsuit. He was particularly worried by Twain's allegation that 'when the Union Company find it inconvenient to keep a contract and lucrative to break it' they use inferior vessels and overcrowd them; he has pencilled on the manuscript as an *aide-memoire* 'Inconve to kp a con' and the offending passage is cancelled. That he was not trying to suppress legitimate criticism of the shipping line, however, is clear from the passages which follow this, where he allows Twain's more factual and legally unexceptional statements to stand unchanged. Similar considerations led Chatto to recommend the removal from the opening chapter of a potentially libellous passage in which Twain impugned the impartiality of Courts of Directors investigating the captain's responsibility for accidents at sea; in this instance Bliss followed Chatto's example. The American Chapter IX retains several pages which Chatto and Twain had 'ripped out' of the English Chapter X; this is the discussion of climate that occurs between '. . . the hens laid fried eggs' and 'Captain Sturt, the great explorer . . . .' Again, the English chapter ends 'I have not seen a proper dust-storm' while the American adds another two sentences of summary; in an initialled note in the manuscript Clemens had suggested cutting these but had not actually cancelled them. The comparisons between the Australian and the American climates in the deleted passage may have seemed to Bliss of sufficient interest to his readers to justify their retention.

More usually Bliss's tendency is to omit, though his reasons can often only be conjectured, especially as many of the omitted passages are not struck through in the typescript. Such cuts may have been made at proof stage and may be connected with the fact that each chapter begins on a fresh page, whereas in the English book this convention is not observed; a high proportion of Bliss's cuts do occur at the end of a chapter, but the nature and the length of the passages omitted suggest that other considerations may have operated as well. Thus he may have felt that American readers would not want the quotation from the patriotic poem by the Poet Laureate, Alfred Austin, with which Twain closed Chapter LXVI (American), but Chatto's retention of this was far from chauvinistic, for Twain's comments on it are scathing in their irony. Bliss may have been right in assuming that his audience was less interested than Chatto's — and than Twain himself — in the celebrated case of the Tichborne Claimant, for in his Chapter XV he omits, entirely on his own authority, two passages which, in the English edition, take up in all nearly five pages. In Chapter XXIX (American) Bliss cuts out just over two pages of the English text in which Twain is quoting from Laurie's *The Story of Australasia*; commentary on Laurie's style leads Twain to the statement 'It often happens that people frame phrases which have no meaning to a grammar, and yet convey a clear meaning to the world', and his discussion of this, though not profound, is too good to be sacrificed. Moreover, Bliss resumes the text, after the cut, with Twain's final quotation from Laurie, 'The voyage thence up the Derwent Frith . . .'; he prints it in quotation marks but gives no indication of its source and omits the praise for Laurie's 'capable and sympathetic eye for scenery' with which Twain had just qualified his strictures on Laurie's style. Other changes seem equally arbitrary and need not be itemised here; more interesting are the major changes for which some reason may be seen.

In Chapter XXI (American) a slip of paper is bound into the typescript, and on it is written:

A wearisome chapter on *aboriginals*
Fr. B.   All dead now.

Even without this statement Frank Bliss's lack of sympathy with Clemens's interest in natives could be deduced from the number of cuts which excise matter of this sort. At the end of this chapter *More Tramps Abroad* continues for two pages beyond the American chapter's finishing point in order to re-tell a story from Mrs Praed about Donga Billy, an aborigine trouble-maker who had challenged her father to single combat, his primitive weapons and 'frank and fearless courage' against the white man's pistol. The outcome is predictable: Donga Billy is 'gathered to his fathers' but not before he has wounded his adversary with a boomerang and speared his horse. Twain makes no comment on this beyond the praise of Mrs Praed's literary powers with which the next chapter opens: the duel is so much a miniature version of the holocaust with which the *Yankee* ends that his sensibility may have been less outraged by it than that of a more modern reader. The incident must, however, be read in conjunction with the remark with which the American chapter ends: 'There are many humorous things in the world; among them the white man's notion that he is less savage than the other savages'. But Bliss found this wearisome, and if he cut out this instance of the white man's ruthlessness he reduced another passage in which Twain describes a more humane and enlightened approach. This was in Chapter XXVII (American) which conflates two chapters of *More Tramps Abroad* and in so doing loses over half a page of the English text; in this passage Twain had described in some detail Robinson's bloodless victory over the natives, and had earlier discussed the government's attitude to Robinson's policy, but this too Bliss had cut out. At page 285 of the typescript a marginal note, again partially obscured by the binding, reads 'follow Eng Edition on this Robinson matter. Fr. B'; in fact, far from following the English edition, the American here condenses and in some places re-arranges it considerably.

Another anecdote that apparently wearied Bliss occurred immediately after the point at which Chapter XVI (American) ends. Here, in two pages of the English text, Twain tells the story of Buckley the escaped convict who for thirty-two years lived among the Australian aborigines as one of them, becoming 'an important and influential man in the tribe' before returning to civilisation. This theme of the outcast was much in Twain's mind at this time. In Chapter VIII the manuscript contains a long quotation from Tennyson that he had intended including for its description of a wilderness; he struck it out but significantly the poem from which it comes is 'Enoch Arden'. Throughout the book Twain is preoccupied with the narrowness of the line that divides civilisation from savagery, the good citizen from the convict, the honest man from the rogue; and also he is deeply concerned with man's inhumanity to man. The 'whole raft of reprint matter' that he and Chatto ripped out was wisely excluded, but its original inclusion betokens no flagging inspiration or loss of inventive power on Twain's part: it is rather as though he were seeking almost desperately for some independent verification of his own view of man. What Bliss found wearisome Clemens found fascinating, but his interest is philosophical rather than anthropological. The stories of the aborigines that he took from Mrs Praed and Laurie bolstered to some extent his failing belief in an Adamic innocence: the manuscript shows two abandoned attempts at equating Australia before Captain Cook with the Garden of Eden.

From the Australian writer Marcus Clarke he wanted to borrow some extended stories of the cruelty practised in the original Australian penal settlements, stories which often exhibited the convicts in a far better light than their jailers. *The Selected Works of Marcus Clarke* were apparently not available in England, and some of the passages he wanted could therefore not be copied, but other books were available. *The Lost Tasmanian Race* by James Bonwick F.R.G.S. furnished him with information about the white man's annihilation of the natives, and he incorporated in his manuscript a number of printed pages torn from the copy he had used. These are of especial interest for the marginalia evidently scribbled while he was reading it and not intended for publication; they include 'Traded upon their poverty & hunger', 'Assassins', and, on punitive reprisals, 'The Savage's own idea – kill anybody you can get if you can't get the right one'. The most revealing of all is his comment on Bonwick's anecdote of Spanish cruelty towards American Indians: 'I don't need to arraign the civilized races – I can use his own words'. Nevertheless he did originally end Chapter XXVIII (English) with a passage that began 'The Chapter is an indictment of the Human

Race. Not of the English, not of the Spaniards, not of any particular group, tribe or division, but of the Race. Apparently Civilization is merely Suppressed Savagery'. He expanded this by alluding to Bonwick's story of a white man who had killed a native woman for sport; he repeated Bonwick's 'solemn, unworded, but sufficiently plain suggestion that on that very day, as a judgement upon that white fiend, God drowned that white fiend's *wife & child*'. In the tone of voice characteristic of *The Mysterious Stranger* he immediately followed this with the question 'What had *they* done?' Chatto reduced the amount of quotation from Bonwick and cut the final paragraph just described; Bliss more ruthlessly printed none of this Bonwick material at all. In Chapter XXVII he goes straight from 'the extermination was complete: not a native was left' to 'It was a strife of years, and decades of years' without even a paragraph break: *More Tramps Abroad* here has over two pages of quotation from Bonwick and comment by Twain before starting a new chapter (XXIX), 'The strife went on, for years and decades of years' (another minor verbal difference between the two texts).

Other marginalia on the Bonwick pages indicate that Clemens was not unaware of parallels with his own country. Admitting in *More Tramps Abroad* that 'The incidents read like plagiarisms of our own early-day Indian tales, but not always. Very far from it', he blamed 'that satanic convict element of the white population' for Australian atrocities, and added somewhat equivocally 'Our ancestors stopped with killing; they did not deal in torture'. Twain's bitterness about the treatment of 'our black brother' by 'our blood-brother from over the way' (both phrases are his) would have found in America an audience more sympathetically responsive than in Britain, yet the American version omits all this, while Chatto, who might have pleaded pressure of space as an excuse for suppressing it, allowed it to stand unaltered, and also retained similar anti-British material in the South African section of the book. It makes nonsense of the suggestion that Twain's books had to be specially toned down to suit the sensibilities of the English public.

Only on two occasions does Chatto seem to have edited the text of this book with this in mind, and they are both minor. In Chapter VII manuscript, typescript, and *Following the Equator* all give 1858 as the date when Fiji was ceded to England; in *More Tramps Abroad* the date is silently corrected to 1874. The second occasion is in Chapter XXII (American) when, speaking of the aborigine's throwing power, Twain credits one of them with having thrown a cricket ball 119 yards and adds 'This is said to beat the English professional record by 13 yards'. On the manuscript Andrew Chatto has pencilled 'Qy. See Whittaker's Almanac' and the English edition reads, perhaps disingenuously, 'This is said to be within a dozen yards of the professional record'. Evidently the publishers took seriously their responsibility for factual accuracy but not for Twain's opinions on British imperialism. Nor were they interested in censoring his more pessimistic views on life as Bliss was on at least one occasion: in his long reflective passage inspired by the lignified caterpillar in Dunedin (Chapter XXX in the American text) Twain had developed his comments on the unperfected tapeworm for twenty-one lines beyond the point at which Bliss cut it short, but Chatto printed it in its entirety. His theme is the elaborate process by which Nature contrives 'to get at man without his being able to provide against the scheme', and he fulminates against the suffering inflicted upon human and animal life when no law of nature has been violated by them: 'But Nature is always doing that. It is her trade'. This is directly in line with his deleted criticism of the injustice of the oblique punishment visited upon 'that white fiend' and with the many sardonic comments on the simple faith of missionaries that Olivia persuaded him to tone down or eliminate. Something of this tone survives in *Following the Equator* and more in *More Tramps Abroad*, but in the book that Twain originally wrote it was far more pronounced.

The history of the publishing of these two books would suggest that by 1897 Twain seemed a more valuable asset to Chatto than he did to Bliss. The manuscript is so heavily corrected in places that a willingness to set from it at all when a typescript was in existence argues unusual respect for the author, although it must be remembered that the typewriter was at this time sufficient of a novelty for some compositors still to prefer working from manuscript. As late as 1899, for example, Chatto advised another of his authors, Justin McCarthy, 'Typewriting the MS would seem to be a somewhat needless expense'. (If 'typing' was not current as a verb, neither was 'typist' as a noun: 'typewriter' — as some of Clemens's references make clear — was as likely to mean the operator as the machine.) In this case, when the last batch of copy went to the printers on 6 July it was accompanied by a note in Andrew Chatto's hand: 'Original MS of Mark Twain's *More Tramps Abroad* pages 1247 to end 1764. Please take the greatest care of it & return to Chatto & Windus with 3 proofs of each sheet'. How much care was taken of it may be seen not only from its fine state of preservation but, more significantly, from the commendable fidelity with which it was followed by the compositors whose names survive, pencilled across the first page of the sections for which each was responsible. There can be no doubt of the patience and zeal with which Chatto looked after his author's interests in the promotion of a book which he must have known was no masterpiece; nor of the trouble to which he went to ensure the accuracy of his author's text. Bliss, on the other hand, seems to have been so cavalier in his attitude throughout, and so unscrupulous in the textual changes he took it upon himself to make, that there is every reason to adopt *More Tramps Abroad* as the authentic and authorised text of this work, and *Following the Equator* as an abridged variant of it.

V

Chatto's confidence in the book's selling-power without the adventitious embellishments of the American edition was justified. On 16 November, four days after publication, he was already reprinting. Over 7,000 copies had been ordered, deliveries were delayed until 25 November, and he needed 2,500 copies of the reprint urgently. The half-yearly cheque in January 1898 was for £1,095. 9s. 10d. and was accompanied by the news that '"More Tramps Abroad" made a good start, enabling us to put in hand another edition, & we feel hopeful this will soon be exhausted'; Mrs Clemens replied that she and her husband 'were both greatly pleased with the excellent showing of the statement and the consequent size of the check' [259]. By the spring the fourth edition was on the market (the catalogue bound in at the end of the volume is dated March 1898) and the summer royalty cheque came to just over £900. Obviously the reading public was not being deterred by the lukewarmness or even hostility of reviews such as those reproduced in the Critical Heritage volume. If, like one reviewer, they were encouraged by the English title to expect something in the vein of *A Tramp Abroad*, they may have been a little disappointed; *Joan of Arc*, however, had proved that there was an English audience ready to respect Mark Twain as a serious and thoughtful writer even more than as a humorist. That much had also been made clear to him by an enthusiastic letter from a Jessie MacDonald of Edinburgh — 'an insignificant little school-teacher in a far-off country' she called herself — that reached him in July 1897. A reader of his books since her schooldays, she wrote now to thank him 'for all, I think, that you have ever published' (and she included the *Yankee* by name). Realising that she spoke for many, she thanked him not only 'because you have made us laugh, although that is much': 'You have stirred us with scorn of meanness and shams, you have raised our eyes to what is beautiful and noble in Nature and in mankind'.[6] She was doubtless an avid reader of *The Queen*, but her expression of enthusiasm deserves respect.

When *More Tramps Abroad* was published, readers like Miss MacDonald would not have found everything in it entirely to their liking, but they would have responded to the sincerity of its criticisms. Moreover, it was their Empire about which he was writing and in the year of the Queen's Diamond Jubilee attention was especially focused on her dominions. For the same reason the English reader may have been more tolerant of the high proportion of reprint matter in the book. Paine was not wholly wrong in saying of the *Yankee* that 'English readers did not fancy any burlesque . . . or American strictures on their institutions', but *More Tramps Abroad* may have won back, by the documentation and seriousness of its strictures, some who could not accept the buffoonery and ambivalence of the Arthurian tale. (It must be added that Mark Twain himself seems to have become less censorious of royalty, for a notebook entry of 1897 speaks of the Prince of Wales as the hardest-worked of all working men and the one who ought to strike for an eight-hour day.)

Generally the reception of this book must have restored to Mark Twain something of his 1872 faith in 'so reserved and dignified a people as the English' and no doubt contributed to his championing of England and English values from this time, on which other scholars have so rightly commented. The gaudiness of his English income from *More Tramps Abroad* must have been especially welcome to the impoverished Clemenses, and he had ideas for increasing it still further. When Bliss suggested using the chapter-heading maxims as a calendar he demurred, he told Chatto, because 'that would give them but one year of life'; having observed that 'On the Continent, *anything* that's a post-card sells', he proposed that Chatto should issue them individually on postcards. Together with the maxims in *Pudd'nhead Wilson* a series of about sixty was immediately available: 'If they "go" I will furnish new batches every few months' [267*]. This did not commend itself to Chatto as a viable business proposition, any more than did Clemens's notion that copies of *Following the Equator* should be imported for the English market; Chatto rightly felt that 'there might be some confusion & disappointment among buyers in obtaining the same book under another title'.[7] Neither of them was concerned with (or even aware of) the textual differences; it was the illustrations that Mark Twain thought might sell it in England. He had been disappointed that *More Tramps Abroad* was unillustrated. Wishing to present a copy to Princess Charlotte of Saxe-Meinigen, he had hoped to surprise her 'with the beauty of the pictures in the book – & by gracious Chatto didn't put any in'. It was Bliss, therefore, to whom he turned for a copy tastefully bound in crushed Levant: 'I think the world of those illustrations' he told him. Nevertheless 'It needn't cost a fancy price, and I don't want it to' [257, 265].

When *More Tramps Abroad* had been on the market a few weeks he found himself in trouble with a relative of one of the British authors he had quoted; his handling of the incident emphasises the importance he attached to one aspect of the book at least. In Chapter L, in the course of a long indictment of the Thugs, he had referred to one as 'the mighty hunter . . . the Gordon Cumming of his day'. This he footnoted with a passage ascribed to Cumming: it describes his having brewed and drunk coffee while detachedly watching the suffering of an elephant he had wounded before eventually despatching him with another shot. As the original letter has not survived, the exact nature of the relative's complaint is less clear than is Mark Twain's gleeful solution of the problem. He decided, by lengthening the quotation, 'to get the whole hideous thing in', and proposed a new footnote to occupy the same

space as the one removed but cross-referenced to an appendix giving
the extract in its entirety. That way, he felt sure, 'Every reader will look
it up and devour it' [267*]. Agreeing that 'This should satisfy the sensitive relative's craving for accuracy', Chatto did not discuss the possibility
of the relative being the C.F. Gordon Cumming, four of whose travel
books were currently in the Chatto & Windus list. He did, however,
check the whole matter meticulously before correcting the text. He reminded Mark Twain that in the manuscript there had been inserted 'a
leaf (page 251) torn from a printed book with the headline "The
Africander"'; it was, he found, only 'a fairly accurate quotation' of
Cumming's own words in *Five Years of a Hunter's Life in the Far Interior of South Africa* (1850). The fourth edition of *More Tramps
Abroad* contains the expanded and corrected passages, by comparison
with which, Clemens noted, *The Africander's* wording 'is really feeble'.

Neither version needs or receives any comment from Mark Twain,
but his condemnation of man's inhumanity is self-evident. He may have
regained his faith in the English, but after what had happened to him
in the preceding decade a restoration of his faith in human nature
would have been too much to expect. Towards the pessimism of his
final works like *The Mysterious Stranger* he had been moving inexorably
since *Huckleberry Finn*. What he insisted on retaining in *More Tramps
Abroad,* as well as what he removed from the manuscript, shows how
far he was along the road to Eseldorf.

CHAPTER 10

ABORTIVE SCHEMES
AND COMPLETE EDITIONS

I

Before continuing this narrative beyond *More Tramps Abroad* a little more has to be said about the Clemenses' stay in London while that book was being written. One consequence of that visit is the paucity of information about the English publication of *Tom Sawyer, Detective.* On his visit to Guildford in August 1896 Chatto had begun the arrangements for this orally with the author and they were presumably continued in this way. No attempt was made to 'simultane' with Harper & Co., who were publishing it in New York, or even to bring into line the contents of the two volumes. Harper published by 6 December, reprinting *Tom Sawyer Abroad* and other stories along with 'Tom Sawyer, Detective'. The English volume appeared not more than a day or two later, the British library copy being accessioned on 10 December. Simultaning was less important than usual because most of the pieces had been previously published in periodicals.

The English volume was enterprising in that it included (according to Blanck) five pieces collected for the first time. These were 'Adam's Diary', 'How to Tell a Story', 'Mental Telegraphy Again', 'What Paul Bourget Thinks of Us', and 'A Little Note to M. Paul Bourget'. The last item seems to have been written specially for this volume in that Chatto, on 29 October 1896, acknowledged receipt of 'the MS Max O'Rell article' (the 'Little Note' is concerned with a somewhat vituperative reply by 'Max O'Rell' to Mark Twain's previous Paul Bourget piece; Mark Twain pretends to believe it to be by Bourget himself under a pseudonym, but in fact 'Max O'Rell' was another Frenchman, Leon Paul Blouet). Later, when proofs of the 'Little Note' came back from Clemens, Chatto promised that a revise would be sent 'with a note from us to Mr John Henry Harper in accordance with your request', presumably so that it could be later collected in a Harper volume. Another request from Clemens acknowledged by Chatto was for the removal of a note preceding 'Tom Sawyer, Detective' itself (the note, which American editions retain, vouching for the authenticity of the incident of the story). The only other story included in this volume was 'The Californian's Tale' which had appeared in the New York Authors Club *Liber Scriptorum* in 1893. Though Chatto told Clemens he was very glad to have that 'to make up the size of the volume', there is no record of his having considered collecting here the items in *Mark Twain's Merry Tales* which had not appeared in England. He had, however, planned to include 'Mental Telegraphy' and had had to withdraw it at the last moment when he remembered that it was in *The £1,000,000 Bank Note*.

By now there was growing confusion as to what was collected in England and what was not. Thus an innocent request from Mrs Clemens in Vienna in 1897 for a presentation copy of the volume 'which has in it the little farce "The Meisterschaft"' [256] put Chatto & Windus into a quandary. Only when they were unable to identify it (could it, they asked enterprisingly, be 'That Awful German Language' from *A Tramp Abroad* under another title?) did Clemens recall that it might not even have appeared in England [256a] One of the *Merry Tales* pieces, it was not in fact collected here until 1900 in *The Man That Corrupted Hadleyburg*.

Inevitably while Clemens was in London his demands on his publishers increased. When he heard that Besant's review of *Joan of Arc* had been 'copied in the St. Louis papers with large display headings' [200*] it was Chatto who was asked to trace the original (which he had missed in *The Queen*) and who, within three days, had obtained a copy from Besant himself.

The firm was also kept busy despatching complimentary copies of Mark Twain's books [210, 254]. A request to send sixteen early copies is jauntily signed 'Ihr ergebensterhochwohlgeborenergeehrterhochachtungsvoller S.L. Clemens' [251*]. Having inscribed some twenty-two for friends in India and elsewhere, he asks Chatto & Windus to 'send a cuss in a cab' to collect them from him for packing and despatch [216*]. At his request they sent a complimentary *Joan of Arc* to Mr Gladstone (perhaps Mark Twain felt that the *Sydney Telegraph's* two great benefactors of mankind should be in closer touch). When he wanted a copy of Barrie's *Margaret Ogilvie* or Olivia wanted Cassell's *Dictionary of Cookery* it was Chatto who supplied them at a 25% discount [214, 213,]. When the box-office attendant at a London theatre was discourteous to Clara and Jean, their father complained not to Chatto but to Bram Stoker, whose theatrical connections were stronger [202]. On every other domestic problem, however, it was to the publishers that reference was automatically made. Spalding, for example, advised the Clemenses that a good cook could be had for £35 including beer-money. (It was probably not the wages that led to them changing English cooks three times in as many months when, in Hartford, they had had fewer changes in eighteen years.)[1] He also made their rent payments on the Tedworth Square house [201] and looked after matters as trivial as arranging for the repair of two broken wine-glasses at a cost of eightpence [245]. He was frequently asked to re-direct letters [235a, 250], sometimes imperiously ('For goodness sake send me my mail. Clemens'

[234*]) and sometimes with requests not to disclose their address. [249]. On another occasion Olivia, who, during her husband's bankruptcy, handled their finances [258], deposited £500 with Chatto which he then transferred in £100 instalments on demand to her current account in the City Bank [211, 218, 222, 225].

The Chattos now lived in Cumberland Terrace, Regents Park, and in 1895 had appeared in the same 'Celebrities at Home' series in *The World* that, eleven years earlier in happier times, had featured the Clemenses' Hartford house. The first part of the article described the publisher in his office, and his pride in his authors (Mark Twain is named as 'one of Mr. Chatto's cordial friends'); the second part dwelt on the 'commodious abode' in Cumberland Terrace for which he had given up 'an out-of-town life with its tranquil delights of amateur gardening and agriculture'. It spoke of his library of fiction and African travels, his interest in science, his enjoyment of astronomy, his collection of paintings, and his skill as a cellist. Rather later than this, one of his granddaughters has told me, he formed a small family orchestra, as well as actively encouraging his grandchildren in painting, singing, and other arts. *The World* emphasises the cultured domesticity and family aura of his home, the elegance and comfort of the drawing-room presided over by Mrs Chatto, gracious and intelligent yet 'neither a typical blue-stocking nor a modern woman with a mandate'. The Clemenses must have felt very much at home in such an atmosphere; that there was also a billiard-room would have made it doubly attractive to Mark Twain. The two families certainly became very close at this time.

Like all young people, the Clemens girls liked to be in the fashion, and in 1896 the fashion was cycling. *The Queen,* the weekly arbiter of taste, was packed with advertisements for cycling skirts, cycling safety skirts, cycling corsets, even the 'cycling' style of curl fringe especially recommended for that form of exercise. Elliman's advertised their embrocation with a picture of a man falling from a cycle; the *St. James's Gazette* featured news almost daily of cycle mishaps, fatalities, and even, on one occasion, a duel fought on cycles (in Paris, naturally). *The Queen* had a weekly column of cycling news; they reviewed *A Guide Book for Lady Cyclists* and *Everybody's Cycling Law,* while Chapman & Hall were reported to be issuing a special series of novels for cyclists and *St. James's Gazette* had a lively cycling parody of Browning's 'How They Brought the Good News from Ghent to Aix'.

Clara and Jean wished to acquire bicycles, and Chatto was the obvious person to consult. He referred the matter to his youngest son, also an Andrew and now with the firm. To him Clemens wrote engagingly ('You know about bicycles & I and my daughters don't'), asking him to accompany them to Regent Street to buy two [201*]. (They would have found the price to be about £10 each.) Andrew recommended the 'Swift', and a letter to him from Clara settles on two of these 'if they can be had at once, if not, then two of the next best make' [206]. The purchase was duly made, and Clemens thanked Andrew Jr. effusively on behalf of the whole family for 'this great service' and 'the trouble you have taken for us about those bicycles'; the girls were 'charmed with the machines' he wrote [207*]. Jean in a separate letter reported 'one or two things out of order' on her bicycle and asked that a man be sent to 'fix it' [208]. This too was arranged, for Mrs Clemens, sending a cheque a week later, assured Chatto that her daughters found 'cycling quite another thing now that they have their own machines' [209].

The following May brought a new problem when the Clemenses' neighbour in Tedworth Square, a *Times* reporter, took exception to Clara's piano-playing: his newspaper work kept him up all night and he needed to sleep during the day. Clara's father showed the letter to a friend at the Athenaeum who counselled a compromise; this was not to Clemens's taste, so he went on to St Martin's Lane. Although on this occasion Chatto offered no opinion, Spalding recommended ignoring the letter, and his advice was gladly accepted.[2]

When the Clemenses moved to Vienna at the end of July their demands on the publishers, though more intermittent, continued. Now Olivia wrote almost as often as her husband, for business relationship and family friendship were becoming indistinguishable. When they forwarded his American mail, Clemens reproached them for re-stamping it ('Surely that must be an unnecessary expense? . . . a fully-paid foreign postage ought to chase a man all over the globe without extra cost') and urged them to re-direct it without extra stamps [246*]. Spalding explained that the Post Office had demanded the extra postage, but he nevertheless tried sending on four letters experimentally.

In November, deciding to put his 'In Memoriam' poem into print, Clemens naturally wrote to the dependable Spalding with meticulous instructions as to their requirements and the request that Spalding himself read and revise the proof [254]. Two weeks later the fifty copies were despatched: 'We thank you', wrote Olivia graciously, 'for the care and thought which gives us this result' [255].

In January 1898 Mrs Clemens asked them to investigate a report that *The Prince and the Pauper* was being staged at Crouch End in North London [260]. Within the week Chatto reported that Joseph Hatton was reviving the Beringer version, on which he had secured the rights in 1891, for a provincial tour. Enclosing a letter from Hatton promising royalty cheques weekly after 31 January, the publisher observed 'I do not feel so sanguine as Mr. Hatton does that he will recover his previous losses, although I agree with him that the play ought to help the sale of the book'. Chatto's guess was right, for there are no further references to Hatton's revival. It was, of course, this production to which Clemens referred in his letter of 20 January 1898 to H.H. Rogers [262]; annotating it, Lewis Leary (who did not know of Chatto's letter) finds no record of the staging of the play at this time. Olivia, replying from Vienna to Chatto, may have correctly divined one reason for the play's failure: she believed that the dramatisation could never succeed with an actress doubling the main parts; the most effective scenes in the book were the confrontations between the two boys and she was 'constantly hoping' to see the play performed in that way. Nevertheless, if it caused the book to be read more widely she would be pleased, 'for I think it is one of Mr Clemens best'. The Viennese bookshops, she added, 'all have More Tramps Abroad in the window. I should think Tauchnitz would do well with it' [261].

During the remainder of 1898 Chatto & Windus continued to perform for the Clemens family similar little tasks. They advised Olivia on how best to transfer to New York the royalty cheque they had paid her, and assured Clemens that, while they lived abroad and Mrs Clemens operated the family funds, cheques could be paid into his English account with no fear of the Inland Revenue authorities. They sent books to Olivia on their own initiative in case she wanted reading matter [271]; they despatched complimentaries when asked; they met Clemens's requests for *Aesop's Fables* and Hallam Tennyson's life of his father [278, 278a], as well as Clara's request for Green's *Short History of the English People* and Kipling's *Second Jungle Book* [276]. In reply to enquires from Clemens in June [275] (though why he wanted the information is not clear), Andrew Chatto went to the British Museum to find out how many copyright deposit books they had received since 1 January; unfortunately the details were forwarded in a separate note from the Museum which has not survived, but Chatto also furnished particulars of the firm's own publications – in 1897, 50 new titles and 106 new editions, and in the first half of 1898 33 new titles and 45 new editions.

II

Since *More Tramps Abroad*, however, they had had nothing new from Mark Twain, though a week after the book was issued a new proposal from him had startled them. Writing from Vienna, he produced the latest of the many schemes for making some more money that his fertile mind and impecunious condition were proliferating. So convinced was he of the merits of the scheme and the sympathy of his publishers that he began the letter almost as though he were in formal partnership with them:

Dear C & W:
    I think we should issue, with dispatch, a compilation of translations (with introduction by myself), on a 25% royalty (after expenses connected with gathering & translating the matter shall

have been taken out). Or on half-profit basis if you prefer that complication.*

The book, about which strictest secrecy was enjoined, was to deal with the Dreyfus case:

> My idea is this: that you send to Paris & gather up and translate the insanest of the newspaper articles that have appeared there . . . I shall want rough galley-proofs as fast as the book goes into type, from which to build my introduction . . . Six translators could do the work in a week, ten could do it quicker. One of you would have to go to Paris & superintend; & select the matter to be used. [253*]

Chatto and Spalding may well have had personal or business plans that precluded the Paris trip foisted on them thus imperiously; Clemens's gleeful promise that the book would 'make a showy exhibition of the French backside' may have reminded them of his feud with Paul Bourget and 'Max O'Rell' and convinced them that the new project owed more to his Francophobia than to his literary judgement. In any case Chatto thought it 'a game scarcely worth the candle'. He also assured Clemens that

> the feelings of the British public are not sufficiently stirred by the Dreyfus affair to make it likely that a booklet exposing the insanities of the French newspapers in connection with it would have any very great "boom". I fancy that there is here a prevalent idea that insanity is chronic in all French journalism – the exhibition of it in intense form in the present case would therefore lack novelty to us who do not take sides in the controversy . . . Finally and more to the point than any individual opinion of my own, comes the danger of distracting public attention which is now on the eve of being directed to your new book *More Tramps Abroad* which makes its appearance this week. To engender a "boom" in this book I consider is of much greater importance than diverting any energy on a new subject. Regretting that my surroundings as a Londoner have prevented my sharing the interest which you take in the Dreyfus Affair – but not doubting that you appreciate the devotion to your interests which prompts my counsel in a different line from your own view . . .

The forthrightness of this letter, tinged as it is with humour, is an index not only to Chatto's commercial shrewdness but also to the mutual confidence between the two men that Clemens's stay in London, otherwise so unhappy, had undoubtedly strengthened. 'The first real-life romance since Tichborne' was how Mark Twain had described the Dreyfus case in his letter to Chatto, and his interest in the Tichborne affair had been evident enough in *More Tramps Abroad*. He probably also saw Dreyfus as a modern parallel to Joan of Arc, a martyr like her to the injustice of a country that Clemens strongly disliked. That both cases had, however, ultimately led to strong popular feeling and assertions of the national conscience would have appealed to his democratic instincts and revived at least temporarily his old conviction that no country was so supine as to be beyond redemption. His hostility to Paul Bourget, however, would have been intensified by the knowledge that Bourget was a convinced anti-Dreyfusard.

When in 1898 Emile Zola published *J'Accuse* in defence of Dreyfus, another aspect of the Joan of Arc association became explicit in Clemens's reported observation, 'It takes five centuries to produce a Joan of Arc or a Zola'.[3] On 8 February he sent to his London publishers perhaps the most genuinely reproachful letter he ever wrote them. That he followed his usual custom, when complaining, of beginning the letter 'Dear C & W' is especially significant here, for he knew it was Andrew Chatto who had turned down the proposal. Bliss or Webster in such a situation would have been roundly castigated in person, but his respect for Chatto had grown with the years. Indeed, one of the striking features of this letter is the finality with which, he claims, he accepted the November decision even though he disagreed with it:

> When you declined my proposed Dreyfus book I was stupefied with astonishment, for the like of that opportunity couldn't come again in five centuries. The book would be in print, now, & on the market, if I had stuck to my projects. It never once occurred to me that Harpers had a house in London; *no* way occurred to me to get the file-searching & translating done; & so I laid my MS away unfinished & dropped the matter out of my mind. Sho! It would have been a most killingly readable book. The first chapter — the only one finished — fits into today's news as snugly as if it had been written since breakfast this morning.
>
> I'm trying hard not to cry over the spilt milk, but I *am* crying over it just the same; for I knew, at the time, that we were wasting the opportunity of the century, & of course I know it all the better, now. Oh, dear, that book died that the Tramps Abroad might live — what irony it is!
>
> Tell me it isn't *so*. I shouldn't believe it; still it might comfort me, & comfort is what I'm after. [264*]

Chatto's reply offered a little comfort but rather equivocally: 'The responsibility of killing a book of yours is so terrible, that it requires to support it a greater emulation of the character of Brutus than I possess'. He 'did not recognise your offspring in the proposed bulky compilation of the insanities of the French newspapers'. He would like to foster, as 'a much more promising project', 'a killingly readable book of your own writing, with only a moderate proportion of illustrative quotations' and pledged himself to secrecy if he could be allowed a sight of the completed chapter. On the other hand, 'Does not the experience of M. Zola justify the counsel of your devoted publisher! and "give you pause", and also perhaps supply some comfort?' Perhaps it did, for Mark Twain abandoned the project in that form without further discussion. Instead he diverted his attention to the larger issues of 'Concerning the Jews' (published in *Harper's Monthly* in 1899) in which he criticised incidentally the absence of Jewish support for Dreyfus. The retaliatory criticism – that Mark Twain had taken no public stand on Dreyfus either – would at least have been avoided had he accepted Chatto's somewhat belated encouragement.

The insularity of Chatto's letter rejecting the original suggestion is uncharacteristic. Translations of French novels had long been a feature of the house's lists. By that date they had already published at least five of Zola's, as well as R.H. Sherard's biography of him. In the March 1898 catalogue the number had risen to twelve (Chatto had sent Clemens a copy of *Paris* in February); a thirteenth was to follow 'shortly', as was also *With Zola in England* by Ernest A. Vizetelly, who had done most of the translating. Vizetelly recalled as a turning point in his own career Chatto's acceptance of his 'translation of Zola's "Downfall" after it had been refused by every other house of repute in London'.[4] Once again Chatto had backed his own judgement boldly and successfully, and his apparently Francophobic stance in the letter to Clemens was probably adopted as a tactic for jollying him out of a project that Chatto thought was misconceived.

Clemens's adumbration of it had not been felicitous: it sounds too much like an opportunist exercise in book-making and prejudice. It may be, too, that Chatto was not sufficiently persuaded by Mark Twain's use of reprint matter in *More Tramps Abroad* to be confident that his Introduction to the Dreyfus articles would be 'killingly readable'. There is, moreover, a demonstrable discrepancy between Mark Twain's initial description of the book as a collection of translated articles with an Introduction by him, and his February reference to having written only the first chapter. Chatto may be forgiven for not having recognised Clemens's intention earlier (indeed, it is by no means certain that Clemens himself had). Two things, however, are certain. Mark Twain's 'devoted publisher' was always more interested in the author's own creative writing than in his editorial projects; he would have been much readier to consider a book by Mark Twain on Dreyfus than the 'bulky compilation', the effectiveness of which he was probably justified in doubting. He was also genuinely determined 'to engender a "boom" ' in *More Tramps Abroad;* to have brought out the Dreyfus anthology with the promptness that Clemens and topicality required might well have prejudiced his undoubted success with the promotion of the travel book. On the other hand Mark Twain's disparaging allusion to *More Tramps Abroad* in February is as reliable an index to his view of the book as his plea for 'comfort' is to his state of mind in his Austrian exile.

Early in 1898 he told Howells that he could not get along without work, eight or nine consecutive hours sometimes, seven days a week: 'It isn't all for print, by any means, for much of it fails to suit me' [263]. In May, he sent two pieces to Chatto and then cabled him for their instant return. One of these was a letter to the *Daily Chronicle* called 'A Whisper to Distressed Exiles' on the withdrawal of which Chatto urged him to change his mind: it was 'so admirable a view of the United States position' that the *Daily Chronicle* 'would jump at the chance of printing it. It would do a great deal of good'. The other piece was entitled 'A Fable, for private circulation'. 'I agree, however', Chatto told him, 'with what I take to be your second thoughts about The Fable. This seems to me to be superfluous'; he recommended removing the reference to it in 'A Whisper . . .' before submitting that for publication. 'A Whisper . . .', Chatto's advice about which Mark Twain does not seem to have taken, was almost certainly a manifestation of that enthusiastic support for the Spanish-American War which has embarrassed some recent Mark Twain scholars. 'A Fable' in all probability was a version of one of the pieces subsequently published either by Bernard De Voto in *Letters from the Earth* or by John S. Tuckey in *Mark Twain's Fables of Man.* Chatto would have advised against the publication of such pieces in the same spirit that had led him to encourage the removal of some of the blacker passages in the manuscript of *More Tramps Abroad,* probably believing that they would disconcert many of Mark Twain's regular readers.

Some of Clemens's other projects at this time were theatrical; he collaborated with one Austrian playwright, Sigmund Schlesinger, in a comedy *Der Gegencandidat, or Woman in Politics* [262] and translated *Bartel Turaser* by another Austrian, Philipp Langmann. Bram Stoker was to be his London dramatic agent, but it was Chatto who was asked, in July, to find out what had happened to the scripts of *Bartel Turaser* and another piece called *The Purgatory* [269, 270]. The former, he discovered, had been submitted to Beerbohm Tree and returned by him to Lt. Col. J.B. Bowyer-Lane; a letter from this gentleman which Chatto forwarded to Clemens has not survived but was presumably a rejection. The impresario Charles Frohman (brother of Daniel Frohman who had dramatised *The Prince and the Pauper*) read *The Purgatory* and returned it to Stoker who, Chatto told Clemens, had written direct to him about it in the previous week.

Frustrated as a dramatist, Mark Twain wrote 'About Play-Acting' at this time, adding to it as an afterthought an oblique reference to the Dreyfus case in the sentence about 'this same tough civilization saving its honour by condemning an innocent man to death' [277]. Similarly in 'From the "London Times" of 1904', (also written at about this time) the extent to which Dreyfus preoccupied him is also apparent. By September 1899, when Dreyfus was released, Clemens and his

family had become devotees of the London osteopath Heinrick Kellgren, and Clemens sent a long letter to Chatto asking him to recommend to Mrs Dreyfus, through Zola, that Kellgren would successfully
restore her husband's broken health (he was also to recommend Kellgren to William James in 1899) [318, 319]. He assured Chatto that
Mrs Clemens ('& you know that she is not a flighty person') would
vouch for the accuracy of this letter ('the one I wrote last night she
edited into the fire'). A jaunty postcript (signed, unusually, 'Mark
Twain') added

> The Prince of Wales wished to call Kellgren when he hurt his
> knee in Rothschild's house — the doctors defeated it. The Princess
> of Wales called him once — the Queen defeated that (I think she
> is a Conservative). [311*]

Retaining the reference to the Prince but omitting those to other members of the Royal Family, Chatto duly sent to Zola a transcript of the
letter from 'our highly esteemed friend Mr Samuel L. Clemens, the
distinguished author, whose writings under the name of Mark Twain,
enjoy a world wide celebrity'.

III

Mark Twain continued to discuss with Chatto his literary projects
and Chatto was usually encouraging. A stranger, referring to Chapter
XVIII of *More Tramps Abroad*, suggested in an 'irreverently chaffy'
letter that the Buckley story was Mark Twain's way of preparing for a
publicity-stunt in which he would purport to have discovered such a
castaway and 'unload him onto the magazines' [279]. One magazine
founded in 1898, *The Wide World*, was in fact running a very similar
story: 'The Adventures of Louis de Rougemont. Being a Narrative of
the Most Amazing Experiences a Man Ever Lived to Tell'. De Rougemont, a 54-year-old Frenchman, was giving a first-person account of
being shipwrecked and, as a castaway, acquiring 'thirty years experience
as cannibal chief in the wilds of unexplored Australia'. He would
shortly, readers were told, be addressing the British Association on the
subject. The series began in August but the fifth instalment, in December, carried a shamefaced admission by *The Wide World* that what they
had accepted in good faith as fact was now seen to be very much open
to question; they would continue the series rather than disappoint their
readers, who were now urged to see de Rougemont as a 'master of
fiction who has had no equal in our language since Defoe'. (This did
not, however, prevent them from publishing in 1899 a piece by 'Baron
Corvo' on his experience of being buried alive.)

Telling Chatto of the Buckley accusation, Clemens light-heartedly
suggested claiming to be de Rougemont's sponsor and manager; 'but
unless he shows up better than he is doing now I am not going to risk

it, for I have a family on my hands' [279*]. Chatto immediately took this 'capital idea about Buckley' a step further; 'Why not yourself write his adventures with the savages, you could do it much better than Buckley himself could have done, & quite cut out de Rougemont?' He followed this up by sending Clemens the *Wide World* articles, but later drily expressed his doubts as to whether the publishers had found a great sale for de Rougemont's story. Meanwhile (20 October 1898) he encouraged another of Mark Twain's plans: 'It is a happy thought of yours to write a burlesque Narrative of the Adventures of your "döppelganger". The very idea of it raises a "grin" '.

Next month a communication from Mark Twain must even more assuredly have raised a grin, and it adds yet another dimension to his relations with his English publisher. On 13 November 1898 from Vienna he sent a letter marked 'Confidential' to 'Dear C & W'. He enclosed two newspaper clippings relating to the *Rubaiyat* of Omar Khayyam as a justification for the letter's assertion that 'Confound it, this seems to be the right time to privately publish my *"Omar's Old Age"*, written two or three months ago, but I've only written about 50 quatrains & am not ready'. A sample of sixteen quatrains, numbered between 1 and 46 was enclosed: twice the letter enjoined the burning of them when read, no one was to be shown or told about them, and in correspondence they were to be identified as 'ABC' [283*]. The reasons for this secrecy would become quickly apparent to Chatto, for what begins innocuously as a lament for the enfeeblements of old age becomes, in the third, fourth and fifth stanzas, a complaint at the depredations of germs, bacilli, and dental caries, and then, for nine uninhibited quatrains, a bawdy admission of an old man's failing sexual prowess and diminished control of bodily functions; then an abrupt transition takes it to two unexceptionable but sentimental quatrains envisaging reunion after death with 'Voices lost'.

In *McClure's Magazine* of January 1900, and in 'My Boyhood Dreams', under the title 'To the Above Old People', he published a serious twenty-stanza version of this.[5] The opening two stanzas of both are identical; the third, fourth and fifth stanzas of the version sent to Chatto are retained as the ninth, tenth and eleventh of this; the final two 'Chatto' stanzas become the antepenultimate and penultimate stanzas of the published version. The nine 'Chatto' stanzas omitted from the *McClure's* text explain his urgent instruction to Chatto to destroy the manuscript, though no rugby club would be in the least troubled by them. One comprises the single line 'Behold — The Penis mightier than the Sword' followed by the parenthesis '(The rest of this quatrain is indelicate)'.* It suggests that the whole thing was intended as a joke, especially as a completed version of that quatrain in a manuscript now at Yale is milder than several others. Even if it was a 'leg-pull', of course, Clemens must have been very sure that the recipient would not take umbrage at this sort of humour, but the covering letter opens up another possibility. In it he speaks of having been encouraged by an American friend to try bringing out a limited edition of a collectors' item, '500 copies at $50 a copy, or 30 copies at $1,000 a copy'; the friend, he claims, has undertaken himself to buy one of the $1,000 copies and to place five others. 'Come,' he asks Chatto ' – is it a wild and vicious scheme?' [283*].

Unsurprised, perhaps, by any fund-raising idea of Clemens's at this time, Chatto treated it seriously enough to reply in these terms:

> As a scathing satire on the crazy literary taste of today I consider the ABC a work of great genius – But in all my experience I have never known a case in which the writer of words of like inspiration did not at some time in after life regret the printing of them.
>
> It would be an easy matter of course for us at a moderate expense to have such a *brochure* set up in an *Edition de Luxe* for private circulation amongst a select few limited to say 30 copies which number I think could be distributed amongst collectors at perhaps £10, to £20 each, but I fancy that $1000 or £200 would only be paid by those friends who wish to raise a subscription to the author. The worst of the matter is that all the press men would expect free copies!

Clemens immediately replied on a postcard 'I agree to the unwisdom of it – in fact, in any form or at any figure' [284*]. That Chatto did not, as requested, burn the manuscript indicates that he was certainly neither shocked nor offended by it; his retention of it in the firm's safe suggests that he and Spalding enjoyed the joke, thought it too good to destroy, and then forgot it. The incident does, of course, raise the possibility that 'A Fable – for private circulation' may have been something in similar vein, and Chatto's guarded, terse comment on that might support the idea.

In *On the Poetry of Mark Twain,* Arthur L. Scott briefly traces Clemens's interest in the *Rubaiyat* back to the late 1870s. To his evidence it may be added that Clemens ordered a copy of the book from Webster in 1884,[6] and his notebooks of the '80s contain several references to and quotations from it. In 1892, in Rome, he transcribed four stanzas in a notebook; in 1894 F.D. Millett inscribed a copy of the Riverside Press edition to him, which Mark Twain annotated, drawing parallels between Omar Khayyam and Tom Paine.[7] When Fitzgerald comments on the poet's 'Having failed (however mistakenly) of finding any providence but Destiny . . .' Clemens scores through the parenthesis in ink. He preserved a *Hartford Daily Courant* cutting about the book, and in April 1899, from Vienna, ordered from Chatto a half-crown copy of it [287], while another notebook entry of 1897 suggests informing Sir Douglas Straight or J.M. Barrie 'that *I* am the Omar Khayyam Club of America'. Another Missourian who a few years later would have joined such a club was T.S. Eliot who, in *The Use of Poetry and the Use of Criticism,* recalls as 'like a sudden conversion' his discovery of the poem in about 1902; whether it gave Clemens also 'the almost overwhelming introduction to a new world of feeling' that Eliot describes is debatable, but it undeniably meant much to him and to many of his contemporaries, English and American. Baetzhold finds Mark Twain returning to it again in *The Mysterious Stranger.*[8]

The more scabrous aspects of Mark Twain's work like *1601* (1876) and the 1879 address to the Stomach Club in Paris would give little offence today, any more than would the 'Mammoth Cod' poem which probably also dates from the 1890s. The Omar Khayyam parody that he sent to Chatto is of less interest in itself than in the somewhat unexpected context in which it has survived, but it is a reminder, as are some of the items in the Scott volume, that as a poet Twain is often more effective when parody provides him with a mould into which his material can be poured. His satiric version of 'The Battle Hymn of the Republic', for example, written about 1901, is particularly successful; and the Chatto verses, though plainly less polished than that, do in their serious moments and even in some of the more ribald, arouse echoes of the tone and cadence of the *Rubaiyat.* To discuss it as a poem, however, would be as pointless as to use it as a basis for Freudian speculation about its author's psyche: like Yeats, though in a very different key, Mark Twain is raging against the manifestations of old age and sharing his feelings with a friend only five years his junior. A letter from Clemens to Osgood of 1881 was later annotated by his secretary, Miss Lyon, to the effect that the author 'liked to tease Osgood by sending him notes like this one' [81] : it too exhibits a similarly robust and coarse humour. That he would not have written in like bantering vein to either of the Blisses, to Webster, to Hall, or any of his other publishers substantiates the 'special relationship' with which this book is concerned, as does the tact with which Chatto turned down a manuscript over which his predecessor John Camden Hotten would have had no such scruples. Even in offering to print if Clemens insisted, Chatto was deliberately killing the scheme by suggesting that such an item would be bought only as an act of charity: Clemens's pride would, he knew, never allow that.

II

Clemens continued to be satisfied with Chatto commercially as well as personally. At the time discussions were going on as to the division of his American publications between Bliss and Harper; as a lever for raising above 12½% the royalty Harper proposed, Clemens reminded Rogers in October 1898 that Chatto now paid him 24% [280] . Five weeks later, he told Rogers that he had thought of finishing his *Autobiography* and letting 'Bliss and Chatto each make $15,000 out of it for me next fall (as they did with the Equator-book)' [282]; if he is accurate in his figures, it confirms my suggestion that *More Tramps Abroad* did relatively better in England than in the much larger American market.

In December 1898 Chatto & Windus declined Bliss's new popular uniform edition of Mark Twain's works, in order not to prejudice their own collected edition, but they agreed to seek subscribers for the Author's signed Edition de Luxe. The English price, they told Bliss, would be determined by them in consultation with Clemens, and it was Clemens who reopened the question with them in April 1899 [289]. Chatto, who had still received neither specimens nor prospectus, thought the American price of $200 'higher than the English public are accustomed to pay' and he suggested a figure of 12s. 6d. a volume, the price of their parallel edition of Robert Louis Stevenson. The retailer would take at least 12½%, Chatto & Windus would retain 10% as their share for a guaranteed sale, and Clemens would receive 9s. 6d.; out of this he would pay Bliss 2s. 6d. or 3s. to cover the cost of manufacture. The broad outlines of this seem to have been discussed in the two preceding years [233, 274].

In May 1899 the Clemenses decided to remove to London; they wished Clara to study music under Madame Blanche Marchesi, and it was of course Percy Spalding who again made all the preliminary arrangements for this and for their accommodation at the Prince of Wales Hotel. [290-296]. The dissatisfaction with this 'Hell of a Hotel' that Clemens later expressed to Rogers [304], finds no place in his letters to Chatto & Windus which are as cordial and as demanding as ever. One describes their abortive attempts to locate Spalding's home address for a social call [297]; another asks for information about the Royal Societies Club which Mark Twain is to address [302]; statements about the family's movements are sent to the publisher for release to the press and then countermanded [299, 300, 301]; appointments are arranged and rearranged [305, 313]; and the publisher is asked to obtain watches for Olivia and, of course, books [305, 307, 308, 308a].

When Clara's health seemed to require a change of air, they adjourned temporarily to the Kent coast at Broadstairs, 'where it costs a shilling to look at a cup of coffee, and two to drink it'. Chatto, he told Rogers, was 'vastly taken' with the de Luxe edition 'and wants to put 1000 on the English market for me' [298]. Andrew Chatto Jr was at this time in Australia representing the firm and his father promised him particulars of the edition in the hope that he would book some orders for it there. 'We have had a good deal of Mark Twain's company' he told him, adding that the purpose of the visit was to arrange publication of the edition. (Clemens himself had made a similar statement in a *Daily Chronicle* interview on 3 June.)

Second thoughts suggested that the figure of a thousand was over-optimistic; a letter from Chatto & Windus on 3 July to Bliss mentions, with Clemens's approval, the alternatives of '512 or 1012' – the odd dozen in each case being presumably complimentaries – and by 28 August the figure was fixed at 620. The twenty for presentation, review, and copyright libraries Bliss was asked to provide free, and he was asked to keep the price to Clemens at the 75c. a volume quoted for the larger number. Delivery was to be at regular intervals, beginning in November with two volumes. When Bliss replied that he would want 80c. a volume for a run of five hundred they passed the information on to Clemens with the assurance that they would adhere to Spalding's estimate of 9s. 6d. for him on every volume. By now the Clemenses were in Sweden for the summer, and it was Olivia who, on 7 September, acknowledged this letter, explaining that Mark Twain was *very* busy just now' and did 'not like to allow himself to get out of the spirit of his work into the irritations of business'. The supply of prospectuses they had sent, she told them, he could not possibly distribute 'as he could not have the face to . . . suggest to his friends to buy his books. It may be English but it is quite un-American to advertize oneself in this way'. The next sentence, however, suggests pique as the partial explanation of his attitude: 'Mr Clemens also feels that as the edition is so small you can surely have no difficulty in selling it' [309].

When Bliss began to raise doubts about the effect of English sales on American copyright, Clemens's first impulse, a note scribbled on the letter shows, was to stop the whole English edition rather than jeopardise copyright.[9] Wiser judgements prevailed, prompted by anger at the news that Harpers proposed charging him royalties on the English edition. 'What unspeakable sharks those Harpers are!' he exploded to Rogers, defining their proposal as 'robbery and fornication combined' [312]. The indefatigable Rogers reassured Bliss and dissuaded Harpers, but meanwhile Chatto had reduced his order to 235 numbered sets and fifteen unnumbered, while keeping open his option on the 620 run if required. In October Clemens, back in London (where, Bliss told him, 'it seems as if you were more within reach'), nevertheless autographed five hundred copies of the title sheet of Vol. I. These Bliss had presumably shipped before Chatto's final reduction of his order. In February 1900 Clemens told Bliss that 'A few weeks ago Chatto had marketed the most of his sets, but I don't believe he will need another 250 in these war times. Things have been very dead here this long time' [314*].

Certainly the indications are that this edition hung fire in England and Clemens's report to Bliss was probably over-optimistic. Between March and June 1900, for example, only twelve sets were ordered, and by October Clemens's earlier noble resolve against self-advertisement had weakened to the extent of promising to supply Chatto with a list of possible purchasers for the thirty-three sets he had on hand. His sensibilities were protected by Chatto's promise that 'We will of course take care not to post a circular to the addresses until after you have left these shores'. By January 1901, however, the promised list had not arrived, but they had sold a further four sets on their own. There is in fact no record of Clemens ever supplying this list: he is less likely to have been unable to think of potential British purchasers than either to have lost interest, or, more probably, to have been discouraged by Olivia from even this indirect canvass of his friends. One of those friends, J.Y.W. MacAlister, in July 1901 approached Chatto & Windus for three sets which he hoped to place with friends of his if the author would inscribe on the fly-leaf of Volume I of each a 'characteristic thought'. Even with this additional inducement, though, two of these three were still on Chatto's hands two years later, when a twenty-third volume was added to the original twenty-two. MacAlister, however, had two sets (nos. 15 and 169) and Clemens expressly asked Chatto to charge to his own account the new volume to complete both of these.[10] By 1906 eight sets were still in stock and these they offered to sell back to Bliss at £11. 5s. 0d. each (as against a published price of £14. 7s. 6d.), 'we paying the author for them which includes his royalty as hitherto'.

The inference to be drawn from all this is that Mark Twain's British public did not include bibliophilic collectors. When, in 1907, it was planned to add two more volumes to the series, it was not merely the increased price that made Chatto cautious in estimating his requirements. He would need, he explained, to consult the trade and previous subscribers, but he felt his needs could probably be met by one hundred copies on a sale or return basis. That he still had sixtyfive unsold copies of volume 23 makes it clear that by no means all purchasers of the original set had bothered to keep them up to date. The demand for Mark Twain's works was still very healthy in Britain but what was wanted were cheap, not de luxe, editions.

By 1900 Chatto & Windus were marketing their own Uniform Library Edition of twenty one titles (including *Mark Twain's Library of Humour*); of these, seven sold at 3s. 6d. each, ten at 3s. 6d. in cloth or 2s. in picture boards; one (*Mark Twain's Sketches*) at 2s. in boards only and three (*Joan of Arc, More Tramps Abroad,* and *The Man That Corrupted Hadleyburg*) at 6s. (cloth with gilt top). To expect people to pay 12s. 6d. for the same texts was plainly unrealistic. In 1901 they declined to import Bliss's new blue-cloth standard edition lest it interfere with sales of their own Uniform or the de Luxe; in 1903 they resisted, on the same grounds Harper's request to sell an American subscription edition in Britain and the colonies. Clemens, however, toyed with the idea of allowing Harmsworth to market the American set in Britain giving a ten or twelve per cent royalty which the author would divide with Chatto in a two to one ratio.[11] If this, said Chatto in November 1903, was what Clemens really wanted, he would consent to it or to an alternative they had tentatively discussed orally in 1900 whereby

Chatto & Windus should sell to Clemens their interest in all his British editions; it remained their belief, though, that his interests would be best served by maintaining the status quo. As six months later they had received no reply to that letter, it may be assumed that Clemens on reflection concurred as usual with their advice.

In 1907, in response to 'a pressing demand' from the trade and the public, they recommended bringing out a 3s. 6d. edition of *Joan of Arc*, *More Tramps Abroad*, and *The Man That Corrupted Hadleyburg*, paying Clemens 7d. per copy on all copies sold. They had also been 'constantly asked' for a much cheaper edition still of his books; a 6d. or 7d. edition 'would give an immense filip [sic] to their sale, at the same time substantially augmenting the royalty accounts which we have the pleasure of sending you half-yearly'. Some publishing houses were specialising in sevenpenny editions of copyright works in cloth bindings; they would grant a licence to one of these and at the same time reserve to themselves the right of issuing a sixpenny edition; titles would appear 'at judicious intervals' and Clemens would receive a half-penny on every copy sold. As this was the year in which Oxford conferred an honorary doctorate on Mark Twain the proposal was well-timed, and their assurance that they would do their very best to look after his interests was by now superfluous.

CHAPTER 11

FOREIGN RIGHTS AND
KINDRED MATTERS

I

By the first decade of this century Mark Twain's main books were
written, his reputation established internationally, and the American
publishing house to which he had been contracted since 1895, Harper
& Brothers, was the largest, most stable, and most business-like American
firm ever to handle his books. Had his American publication been
earlier in the hands of so experienced and reputable a house, the story
of his publication in England would have been much less interesting
and chequered, the role of Chatto & Windus in it much less significant.

That role, in any case, nearly came to an abrupt end in 1900 in
circumstances that cannot be fully documented because Clemens's
presence in London meant that the crucial negotiations were conducted
orally. Bliss, who was preparing volume 22 of the Autograph Edition,
had referred some textual queries to the author, only to receive a
reply, dated 30 March, empowering him to make any changes he liked:
'I cannot do it myself as I have neither of the stories by me. The proofs
are in the hands of the printers in Scotland' [316*]. The stories were
presumably two which were being collected for the first time in America
in the Autograph (Blanck identifies four such items in addition to the
poem on Susy); the proofs in Scotland, however, would have been for
the English edition of *The Man That Corrupted Hadleyburg and Other
Stories and Sketches* in which all four pieces were included. Asking
Bliss to send to him personally a proof of any such emendations for
incorporation in the English text, Clemens speaks of expecting a few
months' postponement of publication; he adds casually and parentheti-
cally '(I am changing English publishers)'.

How seriously this was taken by Chatto & Windus may be seen from
the survival of this memorandum dated 3 April 1900 and signed (unusually) by both Chatto and Spalding:

> Mr Clemens called today to ask whether our offer of £500 on
> account of 25 per cent royalty in advance on 6/- editions of his
> new volume of stories and Essays "The Man Who [sic] Corrupted
> Hadleyburg" &c. and 2d. in the 1/- royalty on editions at a lower
> price would stand good — when we said it would, and he said he
> would let us know in a day or two whether he would be able to
> accept it, as he was wishful of doing if possible. He then said,

when asked if he had signed the agreement as revised by him giving him the option of purchasing our interest in his other books – at the expiration of 5, 10, or 15 years, that he had come to the conclusion that he did not see any advantage to be gained by removing the books from our hands and that he therefore had decided not to disturb the present arrangement for the publication of his books by us.

The next day, confirming these arrangements to Clemens and promising a formal contract, they enclosed 'Messrs Blackie's cancelled agreement'. Unfortunately the house of Blackie has no record of any negotiations with Mark Twain, nor is there any obvious reason why he should have chosen that particular Glasgow firm. His reference to the proofs being 'in the hands of the printers in Scotland', however, is only explicable in those terms, for Chatto used Spottiswoode of London as the printer for the *Hadleyburg* volume. The emphasis on an advance on royalties – something he had never previously sought from Chatto – suggests that Clemens was experiencing what would now be called a cash flow problem. On the other hand, on the day before he called on Chatto, he had acknowledged a cheque from him for £1,019. 18s. 3d. from sales of the de luxe edition [317]; though a proportion of this had to go to Bliss, his own share was not negligible. Disappointment that Chatto had not done better with this edition may, of course, have strengthened the desire for change. There is no other reason for it apparent.

The breach once healed, however, relations were quickly back to normal. Social engagements in his notebook for 1900 include a number with Chatto, and the publisher seems to have been given considerable discretion over the contents of the *Hadleyburg* volume. 'On second thoughts', he told Clemens on 20 April, he had decided not to omit the 'In Memoriam' poem from the end of the volume, and to add 'The Captain's Story' and 'How I Dined with the Queen' which they had by them but had not previously collected. 'The Captain's Story' was one of the four *Merry Tales* pieces not hitherto collected in England; the text of the other three – 'Luck' 'Meisterschaft', and 'My Military Campaign' – Chatto told Clemens he was obtaining from Harper for inclusion as well. 'How I Dined with the Queen' is not readily identifiable. Two pieces collected in this volume for the first time anywhere were 'Christian Science and the Book of Mrs. Eddy' and 'Diplomatic Pay and Clothes', collected in America in 1907 and 1903 respectively. The importance of some of these English texts is attested to by letters from Clemens insisting that the only authentic text of 'Adam's Diary' is *as amended by me for the London* edition 3 or 4 years ago' [321*] and promising Bliss that Chatto would send him *Hadleyburg* so that he could include in the Uniform edition 'one or two things that I left out of the Harper edition' [320*].

When, in January 1902, the serialisation of *A Double-Barrelled*

Detective Story began in *Harper's Magazine* Chatto started collecting
the instalments in the hope that Mark Twain had enough other stories
on hand to make a six-shilling volume comparable to *The Man That
Corrupted Hadleyburg*. Finding that only the title story was available,
Chatto proposed a 3s. 6d. volume on which he offered the author the
usual royalty of sevenpence. This time, instead of having the book
re-set in England, he asked Harper to provide plates. 'Harpers ought
to have given you earlier notice' Clemens self-righteously told him on
19 April 1902 [326*]. The English edition appeared in June, the
British Library copy being accessioned on the 21st. The last new book
of Mark Twain's that Chatto & Windus issued in his lifetime, it is certainly one of the most elegant. The text, in unusually large type,
is set within a red-ruled frame in wide margins so that it is teased out
to book-length by having only about 120 words on each of its 179
pages. It was illustrated by Lucius Hitchcock and bound in blue cloth
with gilt lettering.

At the end of the year Clemens wrote to tell Spalding that he expected his book on Christian Science, with a rejoinder by 'the chief
writer of the cult', to appear at the end of March or in mid-April: 'So
you can tell the Harpers to send you early proofs' [328*]. Harpers'
London house had no information about the book when Chatto approached them and although they promised to refer to New York there
was silence for more than a year. In April 1904, in response to 'many
enquiries for the "Xtian Science" volume', Chatto again asked Clemens
for news of it. It was not in fact to appear until 1907, but by 1904
Harpers reached the understandable decision to distribute in England
their own editions of new Mark Twain titles, beginning with *Extracts
from Adam's Diary*. I find no record of this decision being communicated formally to Chatto, but it can hardly have surprised him. 'A Dog's
Tale' was reprinted in England from *Harper's Magazine* by the National
Anti-Vivisection Society before Harpers collected it in a new book with
other stories; and 'King Leopold's Soliloquy' was issued by Unwin.
The topicality and brevity of these pieces may explain why these
publishers rather than Chatto or Harper handled them. Similarly the
private and anonymous publication in America of *What Is Man?* (1906)
and Clemens's misgivings about that book sufficiently explain why it
was not issued in England in his lifetime. In the year of his death, however, it was brought out in London in an edition which identified the
author, but was published by Watts on behalf of the Rationalist Press
Association. In 1919 Chatto & Windus collected it as the title-piece
of a volume which contained fifteen of his other essays as well.

II

In November 1902 Clemens referred to Chatto & Windus an enquiry
about translation rights, as he had 'placed the sole authority over

translations in your firm's hands more than a quarter of a century ago, where it still remains with its authority unmodified' [327*]. For about the period he mentions, one of the important services that house had rendered him had indeed been the supervision of his translation and European publication rights: it is an aspect of their work that deserves mention.

In the brief autobiography he had prepared in about 1873 for Charles Dudley Warner, Mark Twain had noted

> Baron Tauchnitz proposes to isssue my books complete, on the Continent in English.
> And there's a chap going to issue them in Germany in the German language he says. Is now translating the Innocents.[1]*

Tauchnitz's paper-backed 'Collection of British and American Authors' in the English language, published in Leipzig and Paris for the continental market, was an important contribution to the cultural life of nine-teenth-century Europe, and the Baron's reputation for integrity stood unusually high. Bret Harte, in 1876, forwarded to Clemens a letter from Tauchnitz, who did not know how else to get in touch with him, seeking permission to publish *Tom Sawyer* and other books by Mark Twain. Harte's commendation ran thus:

> The Baron is a good fellow. Considering the fact that we have no copyright on the Continent, and that he *could* steal but *won't*, and that his editions are the perfection of letter-press, and that to be on his list is a kind of guarantee to the English-reading people there I'd advise you to accept his offer. He will send you from £50 to £100 according to the size of the book – as a gratuity. Of course as his books are contraband in England, it doesn't interfere with your rights *there*.[2]

By December 1876 Tauchnitz had *Tom Sawyer* in print and sent Clemens five hundred German marks for it. Exactly two years later he asked Mark Twain for copies of one or two others of his books for publication on similar terms.[3] In the spring of 1879 the two men met in Paris and Clemens reported to Howells in terms strikingly similar to Harte's:

> Tauchnitz called the other day – a mighty nice old gentleman. He paid me 425 francs for the Innocents – I think he paid me about 6 or 700 fr. for Tom Sawyer (it being new); he is going to print Roughing It by & by, & has engaged advanced sheets of my new book. Don't know what he will pay for the two latter – I leave that to him – one can't have the heart to dicker with a publisher who won't steal. [64]

Chatto was dealing on his own with Tauchnitz by about this time, for in 1880 he offered him Henry James's *Confidence* for £30 but accepted £20. Then in August 1881 Chatto was approached by Grädener & Richter of Hamburg with the request for continental rights to all Chatto & Windus novels. Chatto explained that this was impossible because many authors reserved those rights to themselves; he instanced, among others, Wilkie Collins, Walter Besant and Ouida, but did not specify Mark Twain. However, knowing *The Prince and the Pauper* to be in the press, Chatto enterprisingly wrote to Osgood and Clemens asking whether they were committed to Tauchnitz; if not, Chatto asked for authority to negotiate for a European edition of *The Prince and the Pauper* 'in the style of Tauchnitz' at a fee of £75. That he also enquired whether Tauchnitz pirated Mark Twain's earlier books suggests that this field was relatively unfamiliar to him. Having received the necessary authority [84], he wrote, with his usual business acumen, not to Grädener but to Tauchnitz, to say that the book should be available in December:

> The Author Mr Samuel L Clemens has received an advantageous offer for the issue of a continental edition of it, but before accepting it he writes to say that he would feel it a pleasant thing for you first to have an opportunity of making an offer for the book at a fair price, and desiring us to write to you in his interest in the matter. It would therefore afford us great satisfaction to arrange for the continental publication with yourself which we should be enabled to do by your offering for the new book a sum of not less than 100£.

The figure may have been chosen with the recollection that Tauchnitz had agreed only to two-thirds of the fee asked for *Confidence*; if so, the ploy succeeded, for Tauchnitz offered exactly the £75 that Chatto had promised the author. Explaining to Grädener that Mark Twain had decided in favour of Tauchnitz with whom his business relations had been 'of so cordial and friendly a nature', Chatto accepted the offer while reiterating to Tauchnitz that he was obtaining for goodwill what others would have paid £100 for. Clemens heartily approved Chatto's actions with the memorable phrase 'there is neither wisdom nor fairness in changing publishers except for good & palpable business reasons' [86]. Although, in reporting the transaction to Clemens, Tauchnitz's son was doubtful whether even now his European copyright was wholly secure, he was evidently satisfied, for he subsequently offered to break, for 'such an esteemed author of ours, as yourself', his rule never to supply specially-bound copies for clients. It is a measure of the Tauchnitz operation that in December 1881 he sent Chatto a presentation copy of the two thousandth title in their series.

In July 1882 he paid Clemens five hundred marks for *The Stolen White Elephant* and promised him a copy in a special red binding. Confusion could easily have arisen from Tauchnitz's dealing with the author direct, as Chatto pointed out to Clemens in November 1881. It did arise in another case that caused Chatto some embarrassment in 1882. Robert Buchanan sold to Tauchnitz the rights in his *God and Man* which Chatto, to whom Buchanan's contract had explicitly assigned all rights, had disposed of to Grädener. This problem was resolved by Chatto's agreeing to relieve Tauchnitz of the copies already printed and to find a market for them. Nevertheless, when *Life on the Mississippi* was announced, Tauchnitz still wrote first to Clemens.[4] Chatto again took up the bargaining, again asked for £100, and again accepted a lower figure, this time of £85. Tauchnitz's reasons were that much of it had already been published, and that 'as there is no protection for us in America, none is for the Americans here' so that his payment would not buy him complete safety from rival firms.[5] Chatto now began the practice of sending proofs of the text in batches to Tauchnitz and 'simultaning' with him to give the copyright as much force as he could. At the same time Tauchnitz gave Clemens four hundred marks for a volume of *Sketches,* determining the figure by reference to the three hundred marks each that he had earlier paid for *The Innocents Abroad* and *Roughing It.* Clemens would not, however, agree to his publishing *The Gilded Age,* perhaps for fear of complications with Routledge.[6]

For *Huckleberry Finn,* which the author requested him in advance to negotiate with Tauchnitz, Chatto again asked £100, predicting that it would prove so much more popular than any of its predecessors that a larger sum could have been asked. Orders were flowing in, other continental publishers were being 'discouraged in your favour . . . and we have so high an opinion of the merit of this volume that we were hoping that you would think it cheap at this price'. Again Tauchnitz stuck at £85, this time because of 'the very limited sale of English Literature, in general, on the Continent' just now. Probably Clemens's diagnosis of the German reaction quoted in Chapter 6 was fully justified. In January 1888 Chatto began to prepare Tauchnitz for the *Library of Humor;* in April he was forecasting 'a still greater sale of this volume than for the previous one', but despite this and its larger size, he asked only £85. Perhaps he foresaw the problems the book would create for Tauchnitz who decided that only one third of it was publishable in Germany, though for that portion he offered £40. Many of the contents, he thought, 'though certainly received with the greatest sympathies in America, are in consideration of the political and social views in this country, perhaps not so well adapted for publication in our series'. Clemens consented to this drastic curtailment of the anthology [126], but I have often wondered whether a confused recollection of this could be a partial explanation of that remarkable outburst in the following year at the liberties taken to fit his books for the English public. Was he erroneously attributing to Chatto and the English public the sensitivities of Tauchnitz and the Germans? The even greater difficulties that the *Yankee* created for the Baron were discussed in

Chapter 7: on that book he beat Chatto down from £85 to £60, because 'I do not believe that this book will be successful in my Continental Series'.

If Chatto wanted an opportunity to get continental prices back to their former level, he saw one in March 1891. Bram Stoker had joined Heinemann & Balestier as a director and had approached Clemens about acquiring his continental rights. Clemens automatically referred him to 'my friend Chatto, 214 Piccadilly', explaining 'Years & years ago, I gave in to his hands, without restriction, all my continental business, & he has always conducted it to my satisfaction' [415*]. Any arrangement Stoker could make with Chatto, Clemens added, would be acceptable to him. He wrote on the same day to Chatto, asking 'Do you know my friend Bram Stoker, Irving's manager?' and authorising Chatto to use his 'plenary powers' to come to any arrangement he liked. That the letter, dated 29 March, ends 'Merry Xmas!' is indicative of the relief Clemens felt at being able to transfer the responsibility for a decision [144*]. Writing to Howells about it, he again expressed his appreciation of the 'whole world of bother & letter-writing' Chatto had saved him by handling such matters. Stoker, he continued, had offered him 12% '& if I had been attending to the matter myself instead of referring it to Chatto, I should have vaguely and roundaboutedly asked him how he thought the enterprise was going to be able to stand that' [146]. Chatto also decided that Heinemann's capital of £20,000 was 'rather small for so ambitious an undertaking', but he thought their offer might 'have at least done some good in making the "Baron" *sit up* and if as he says, he means to pay higher prices if you secure more favourable offers from the rival company, I am inclined to counsel giving him the preference'. He reassured Tauchnitz that he would still be given the first offer, and then waited almost a year to put it to the test.

In February 1892 he offered Tauchnitz two books. One was Ambrose Bierce's *In the Midst of Life* for which he asked the 'very modest price' of £25 even though 'a distinguished journalist' had written 'if that book isn't the literary sensation of the season, I'm no judge'. The second was *The American Claimant* for which, with much less boosting, he coolly asked £400 because of 'a very favourable proposal from another house'. The Baron sat up with a jolt. *In the Midst of Life* he accepted as offered, 'Though Mr Bierce is an author still quite unknown on the Continent'; but '£400 for *one* volume is so entirely out of proportion to the sale on the Continent that you will, I have no doubt, reconsider the matter'. None of Mark Twain's last three or four books had sold more than four thousand copies, he said, and it would need a sale of twentyfive thousand to cover an advance of £400; he was 'sure that your & Mr Clemens's sense of justice will not permit of *our* loss being too heavy & disproportionate'.[7] Affecting surprise at the suggestion that a new Mark Twain novel would not sell twentyfive thousand copies in Europe, Chatto acknowledged that Tauchnitz's 'frank statement of the actual sales throws a new light on the subject'. With a flourish of magnanimity, but in the knowledge that Stoker had offered £100 as an advance on a 10% royalty, (not the 12% he had originally proposed), Chatto agreed to the same sum from Tauchnitz 'to retain the cordial relations already existing'. It was, however, to be regarded as an advance on a royalty of 20%.

In the event the percentage mattered little for Tauchnitz's estimate of the market was sound. After Clemens's death Chatto & Windus had to tell Paine that £32. 19s. 8d. of the advance was still unearned. Not surprisingly when Chatto suggested similar terms for *The £1,000,000 Bank Note* in April 1893, Tauchnitz again referred to exaggerated expectations of sales, and an outright payment of £60 was agreed. A year later the same sum was paid for *Tom Sawyer Abroad* and again, in November 1894, for *Pudd'nhead Wilson*. For *Joan of Arc*, perhaps because its subject seemed more promising, Tauchnitz gave £100, but in November 1896 he quoted disappointing sales on that as a reason for paying no more than £50 for *Tom Sawyer, Detective*. For *More Tramps Abroad* the price agreed was £120, to be increased if it proved 'an unexpected success'. On 17 March 1900 Tauchnitz assured Clemens that it would always give him 'the greatest pleasure to include your fine books into my Continental Series'; though short stories did less well than novels, 'I am yet ready to pay you the highest price I ever have given for your books i.e. Sixty Pounds a volume'. Tauchnitz reckoned 75,000 words to a volume, and Clemens's note on the envelope implies that he told Tauchnitz that *Hadleyburg* would not run to two volumes.[8] For some reason that was not negotiated through Chatto, but that practice was resumed with *A Double-Barrelled Detective Story* (£50). In March 1907, however, Spalding authorised Harpers to deal direct with Tauchnitz over *The $30,000 Bequest* collection as it contained 'stories which have not come our way'.

The elder Tauchnitz had died in August 1895, and Chatto had sent a letter of condolence to the son who now ran the business. Mark Twain's feelings were summarised in a piece of dictation towards the end of his life:

> This father and this son have one prodigious distinction which I believe no other publishers have ever enjoyed — to whit, that they were never thieves. I have known a great many publishers, and have cordially liked them and have not been above associating with them, but with the exception of these two, I have never known one who was not a thief.[9]

The context makes it clear that this encomium related to Tauchnitz's reputation for paying royalties even after the expiration of copyright. As none of Mark Twain's works were in that category it was an altruistic tribute, more an impromptu indicative of his feelings about 'a mighty nice old gentleman' and his son than a considered judgement on the profession as a whole.

III

Translation rights were first discussed with Chatto in 1882 when Robert Lutz of Stuttgart applied for permission to translate *The Prince and the Pauper* into German. Chatto told Clemens that he had authorised this 'for the very modest sum of 15£. It ought to be worth more but we find it very difficult to make translators pay at all and we consider on the other hand that translations of a book advertise the original'. Clemens was sceptical: 'It you ever hear from that translator again, you will have better luck than I have ever had. I believe I have never heard from any one of them the second time, from any corner of Europe' [90*]. He was unnecessarily pessimistic. Despite Chatto's fear that 'his knowledge of English will very likely cause him to draw upon his imagination before he gets through with the job', Herr Lutz would become a regular client.

At the end of the year Chatto was able to tell Osgood that Mark Twain's interests were now protected in Scandinavia, even though no international copyright law applied there. J.H. Schubothes, a Copenhagen publisher, was paying '21/- per sheet for the authorisation of a translation of the "Mississippi Sketches" '. Osgood was asked to assure Clemens that 'this gentleman is the only real "Simon Pure" for those countries, in case any rivals should make direct application'. Clemens duly ratified the agreement [94], and Chatto became engaged in correspondence with C. With at Schubothes Boghandel about translating *Life on the Mississippi* into Danish and Norwegian for £17. A Swedish enquiry had gone direct to Clemens who referred it to Chatto for a decision: 'If it's the King, you want to be a little circumspect in your language, you know; but if it's some mere common body, just let into him right & left, & call him anything you want to, & I'll back you' [97]. It was not the King, Chatto assured him, but they had got the same £17 fee that they had 'extracted' from the Danes. Chatto's practice seems to have been to specify a price per printed sheet of the translation but to settle for a lump sum. For 10s. per sheet With was offered such portions as he pleased of the Tauchnitz volume of *Sketches;* and in 1893 *The £1,000,000 Bank Note* and *The American Claimant*. Whether With accepted the *Yankee* when it was offered is not clear.

An Italian, Signor E. Fongi, paid £10 in May 1892 for the Italian rights to *The Prince and the Pauper,* only to have it refunded in June 1893 when Chatto found that the rights had already been disposed of; to whom is not recorded. He also acquired the Italian rights to *Tom Sawyer,* in October 1892, for the same amount.

The French had entered the field in November 1884. A. Hennuyer of Paris offered 750 francs for the right to translate *Tom Sawyer* and *Huckleberry Finn*. Less than two months later Chatto sent a copy of the *Tom Sawyer* translation to Clemens who replied delightedly 'I think that this is the first French money I have corraled' [107*]. It was to be some time before he was to corral any more, for Chatto & Windus appear to have had no further French applications until 1900 when they sold to M. Jussaud for £10 the rights to *The Man That Corrupted Hadleyburg*. Then in 1901 Clemens forwarded an application for H. Motheré of Finisterre to publish a translation of *Roughing It*: 'I have told him you control my foreign business & will arrange with him' [323*]. Chatto settled for 'the extremely moderate sum of Twenty Pounds'. In 1903 Mme la Baronne Jean de Gail of St Germain-en-Laye paid £10 for the rights in *Tom Sawyer, Detective*, but for an unspecified reason Chatto regretted that *A Double-Barrelled Detective Story* and 'Two Little Tales' could not be included in the transaction. In February 1899 Chatto had listed for Clemens the titles of books for French translations of which he had given no permission. If the list was accurate and if we ignore the other titles just mentioned, there was at this time no French language version of *The £1,000,000 Bank Note*, *Pudd'nhead Wilson*, *Tom Sawyer Abroad*, *More Tramps Abroad*, or, perhaps most surprisingly, *Joan of Arc*.

If the number of translations is any criterion Mark Twain was distinctly more popular in Germany. In 1886, reminding Chatto that 'All authority over translations of my books in Europe is vested in your firm' [110*], he referred to him an enquiry from F. Siemens von Ostermann of Dresden who wanted to translate *A Tramp Abroad*, *Life on the Mississippi* and *The Prince and the Pauper* 'which I have just finished to read'. Perhaps responding to his enthusiasm ('Many times I must laugh heartily, when I think of your remarks considering our language, it is too good!'), Chatto left to his discretion 'such payment on behalf of the author . . . as you may consider fair'. Four days later he returned to Robert Lutz a cheque for £3. 15s. 0d. which he had sent to cover a German translation of a selection of Mark Twain's humour. Lutz was invited to re-submit it if he would agree not to describe it as an 'authorised' edition. To Clemens Chatto explained that 'we had already suggested to Herr F Siemens . . . that he should make you a more substantial offering for the little word "authorised".' In fact their letter to Siemens Ostermann had specified no figure and had apparently ignored their earlier permission to Lutz in respect of *The Prince and the Pauper;* the inconsistencies are unusual, but Clemens did not notice them in his grateful surge of goodwill:

It was a blessed day that I struck the idea of heaving the translators on to your shoulders. You know how to sugar-coat them +

make them feel good. Keep on doing it, & God reward you. I
shall continue to refer them to you. [111*]

A letter from Austria dated 18 December 1889 was re-directed with the
autograph note added 'Respectfully submitted to you, Chatto' but in
1891 Clemens changed his tactics. *McClure's Magazine* had American
serial rights for *The American Claimant* and wanted to acquire the
European serial and book rights for a German-language version. 'This,'
Clemens told Fred Hall, 'is better than bothering Chatto — & fully as
profitable'. Reminding Chatto that this could not affect arrangements
he might make with Tauchnitz for an English-language continental
edition, he asked him to relinquish his German-language rights in this
instance to McClure; this Chatto obligingly did [147-149, 151, 152].

As early as May 1893 the Deutsches Verlag Anstalt of Stuttgart
(with whom Robert Lutz was connected) applied for the German-
language rights to the title story of *The £1,000,000 Bank Note* and paid
£2. 8s. 6d. for it; in October they asked for *Pudd'nhead Wilson*. In
1896 Chatto offered them *Joan of Arc* for £50; and in August 1897
they asked for advance sheets of *More Tramps Abroad*. By 20 October
Lutz had decided that he would have to omit some chapters for reasons
that are unexplained, and a price of 1,200 marks was agreed in view of
this. Lutz's translations, however, did not please Professor Roeth of
Bochum, who complained to Chatto in 1897 that they were 'paraphrases
of the original text which the translator contracts and retrenches at
pleasure'; moreover, he 'has not always accommodated his language to
the genius of the original'. On what terms, Roeth asked, might he be
allowed to translate some of the principal works, or at least to adapt
'the charming work entitled 'Adventures of Tom Sawyer' for the use
of young German readers'? Chatto asked £15, provided that Roeth
could establish that no German translation existed.

A random enquiry for the translation rights of 'From the London
Times of 1904' must have especially pleased Clemens in 1899. The
applicant, Mrs Adolfine Frühauf, wanted, she said, 'to bring this splendid
satire on the Dreyfus case to the notice of the German people'. Before
forwarding her letter Clemens, predictably, wrote on it that he had 'no
objection to her using the article' [286]. Chatto asked two guineas for
a single newspaper publication.

When in February 1899 he summarised for Clemens the titles not
translated into French, Chatto told him that of these titles Lutz had
translated into German *The £1,000,000 Bank Note, Pudd'nhead
Wilson, More Tramps Abroad* and *Tom Sawyer, Detective*. In respect of
the last, however, a complication arose two months later, when Jacobs
of Berlin issued an unauthorised translation before Lutz's was on the
market. Chatto sent to Clemens in Vienna a form to be signed before a
commissioner to establish ownership of copyright, advising him to have

the form endorsed in German 'any proceedings are to be at Herr Lutz's expense'. Evidently this stratagem was not successful, for as late as May 1909 Chatto expressed his surprise to Lutz that, notwithstanding the Berne Convention, a German Court of Appeal had ruled that the rights of *Tom Sawyer, Detective* had not been protected; no other details survive, however. In 1902 Lutz paid £4 for 'Concerning the Jews' and £1. 18s. 10d. for 'Christian Science and the Book of Mrs Eddy', both from the *Hadleyburg* volume; and Clemens urged Chatto to offer him *A Double-Barrelled Detective Story* [326]. Chatto asked £20 but Lutz seems not to have taken the option.

Five years later Harpers sought to clarify the position regarding translations and Chatto spoke of Lutz's having translated twelve volumes. There was no possibility of compiling an authoritative list, he explained, because some permissions might have been given before Chatto became Clemens's agent or by his American publishers before Harper. In any case, the Berne Convention allowed the translation without permission of any book not translated within ten years of its first publication. Somewhat stiffly he added 'We should like Messrs Harpers to remember that sole authority for all translations has been vested in ourselves by the author, and we should regret any change in arrangements which have been in existence for more than a quarter of a century'. If they were satisfied, Mark Twain certainly had every reason to be.

IV

Too complex for full discussion here, and relevant to my subject only insofar as Chatto was involved, are the questions of colonial rights and Mark Twain's long interest in and campaign for international copyright. Correspondence with Osgood in 1881 shows that, for each of *A Tramp Abroad* and *The Prince and the Pauper,* Chatto paid Clemens £20 for the Australian rights; but in no other instances was a separate payment made for these. Canada, however, was another matter.

In the absence of legislation copyright lore flourished. The British Imperial Act of 1842 had guaranteed copyright to any book first published in the British dominions provided that the author, whatever his nationality, was at the date of publication resident in the dominions. An imperfect understanding of this led Clemens in 1870 to ask Routledge's New York representative whether a copyright for *The Innocents Abroad* could be obtained by the author's paying a visit to Canada [1]; having been first published in America, the book could claim no British or Imperial protection. 'There seems to be no convenient way to beat these Canadian re-publishers anyway' [3], he told Bliss rather prematurely at about this time. By 1873, however, when *The Gilded Age* was in preparation and Clemens was in London, the date of American publication was fixed so as to allow Routledge to publish on the same day or the day before, and the author planned to secure his position by remaining in England after that date. One wonders whether the strict letter of the law would not also have required the presence in England of the co-author, Charles Dudley Warner, for the copyright to be fully effective. Routledge also stipulated that the Canadian market was to be supplied by a two-shilling edition imported from England. Clemens wrote to his wife: 'The Routledges would not yield up Canada to Bliss — which is very well for Warner and me, because high-price books don't extend one's reputation fast or far enough' [29*]. There does not seem to have been any Canadian piracy problem with that novel, but it had not the attractiveness of *Tom Sawyer,* which is where the trouble began.

Mark Twain tried to forestall this by seeking the advice of the Librarian of Congress, A.R. Spofford, who told him that 'the first publication in England is essential to copyright there but previous entry here will secure you in the United States'.[10] Had Clemens asked specifically about Canada he might have learnt that that country had passed an Act in 1875 which gave copyright, in respect only of books printed and published in Canada, to an author who could establish either that he was a Canadian citizen or a *bona-fide* resident in Canada at the time of issue. A principle of reciprocity also obtained, but as the United States had no corresponding provision that was of no benefit to him. In November 1876 he became aware that 'Belford Bros., Canadian thieves are flooding America with a cheap pirated edition of Tom Sawyer' [50]. The one thing that emerges with complete clarity from the subsequent flurry of correspondence between Chatto, Conway and Clemens is that no one had any sure idea of how far English copyright protected against piracy in Canada a book published in England by an American author. Belford told Chatto with blunt truculence: 'We know Americans are in the habit of taking out copyright in England, but we doubt if it would hold there: we are well advised that it gives no right in Canada'. Believing that Conway held the English copyright and as 'Commercially speaking, Toronto is twice as far from Hartford as it is from London', Clemens urged Conway and Chatto to 'go to work & prosecute Belford and collect that royalty' [53*].

By the end of January 1877, however, Chatto had confirmed that English copyright on first publication extended to all the colonies, but that some, including Canada, had the right to import foreign reprints of English copyright books: he guessed that Belford might be observing the strict letter of the law by printing copies on American soil and then 'importing' them into Canada. Whether the subsequent distribution of such copies in America was an offence against American copyright law he did not know; the author was the only person who could test this by legal action. Clemens meanwhile was persuaded by

Bliss that Canadian law allowed copyright in Canada only to such books as were registered in Canada within sixty days after English publication [51]. Conway, whom Clemens was inclined to accuse of negligence over this, was able to cite cases where this rule had certainly not obtained. On another occasion the understandably confused Clemens quoted the law as requiring Canadian registration within sixty day *before* English publication [55]; and desperate but inconclusive discussions were held as to whether reassignment of the English copyright to either Conway or Chatto would affect the issue. Meanwhile Belford continued marketing *Tom Sawyer.*

When *A Tramp Abroad* was in the making the possibility was considered of registering it either at the English Custom House or at the Department of Agriculture, (which was, surprisingly, at that time the appropriate Government Department) to prevent copies being sent into Canada from America. On 11 November 1879, however, Chatto reported that that could be done only if an actual copy could be deposited; as Mark Twain was still writing it this was out of the question, and then, as has been seen, the premature American publication seriously jeopardised the English and colonial copyright.

When *The Prince and the Pauper* was ready in 1881 Osgood recognised that a separate edition had to be produced in Canada to secure copyright there, and this he arranged with the Montreal publisher Samuel Dawson. Dawson pointed out that, in addition, the author had to be resident in Canada on the day of publication, so Clemens agreed to pay a short visit to the Dominion [83, 87]. This attracted enough publicity for Thomas Nast to make it the subject of a cartoon; that it was the Department of Agriculture with whom registration had to be effected increased the joke.[11] Legal action against any Canadian infringement, Osgood advised, would have to be initiated in England and he therefore recommended a nominal transfer of the English copyright to Chatto. This was also done with *Life on the Mississippi,* of which Dawson issued a Canadian edition (as he later did of *Huckleberry Finn*) and Clemens wrote to Chatto making himself responsible for any legal expenses Chatto might incur in protecting the Canadian rights [96]. By 1889 Canadian public opinion was hardening against Americans being allowed copyright there, and Dawson spoke of having 'had to fight a very cautious and unpopular fight over those books of Clemens'. For the *Yankee,* Dawson re-emphasised the importance of actually printing in Canada: the importing of sheets would not suffice. No longer in business himself, he recommended Daniel Rose, whom Clemens had earlier described as a scoundrel [85]. Hall persuaded Rose to publish it, with Clemens again in temporary residence, as he proved by sending his visiting card to Chatto from a hotel at Niagara Falls: 'A true date, duly set down' he notes against 6 December 1889 [137*]. On the same day Chatto sent him a letter about Canadian rights, on the envelope of which Clemens wrote 'Keep as evidence in case of infringement'.[12]

Dawson predicted the radical change in copyright law that came in 1891. It was in anticipation of this that Hall made his proposal (discussed at p. 154) for Webster & Co. to publish Chatto & Windus titles, but the discussion of this concentrated rather on Anglo-American than on Canadian implications. Chatto felt that 'simultaning' guaranteed the American author's security in Britain, but was less confident of the advantages for the English author in America. He proposed that they should try, as a test case, selling to Webster for American publication Herbert Ward's *My Life with Stanley's Rearguard* and one or two other titles, but there is no clear indication of the outcome.

V

The International Copyright agreement of 1891 had been long desired and campaigned for by many authors and publishers, Mark Twain among them. In 1872, the year when he protested in the London press about Hotten's piracies, the Library Committee of Congress was considering a scheme prepared by New York publishers. *The Athenaeum,* on 9 March, saw many drawbacks to it, but regretted that there was no parallel movement in Britain: 'What is wanted is a measure that the friends of copyright on both sides of the Atlantic can urge upon their respective Governments at the same time'. Authors with international reputations having most to gain from such a measure, it was from them that the impetus came. When in 1873 Mark Twain was invited to speak at the Lord Mayor of London's Banquet he thought of ending the speech with a reference to the subject [29]. By 1875 Charles Reade had become sufficiently concerned about the problem to publish a series of pieces in the *Pall Mall Gazette* which was reprinted in the New York *Tribune*. Howells invited Mark Twain to comment on these in the *Atlantic* but Clemens preferred a more direct approach to Congress at that time.[13] He was evidently in touch with Reade later on the subject, for Reade, in a letter probably written in 1883 or 1884 and probably addressed to Walter Besant, enclosed a note from Mark Twain and recommended his enrolment in the Society of Authors.[14] This body was set up under Besant's chairmanship early in 1884 with the establishment of international copyright as one of its primary objectives. Besant extended an invitation to Clemens in November (Reade had died in April) to become a Foreign and Honorary Fellow, and asked him to suggest courses of action if he wished.[15]

Just how much Mark Twain had learnt about international copyright from his own experience becomes apparent in the controversy between himself and his compatriot Brander Matthews in the *Princeton Review* in 1887-8. The ease with which he can show up Matthews's misunderstanding of the law makes lively reading, but it shows also how muddled and unsatisfactory the whole system was. Clemens was always inclined to argue too much from his own experience: the London *Daily News* welcomed his admiration for the British system of allowing copyright to any work published for the first time in this country but pointed out that an American author of lesser standing who could not persuade a British publisher to anticipate his American appearance was still as vulnerable here as every British writer was in the United States.

Interviewed by 'R.D.' for the *Pall Mall Gazette* in 1889, Clemens was asked to comment on E.C. Stedman's opinion that 'American literature doesn't now require protection, that it has survived and overcome pirated editions, and is now on its own legs'. He agreed that America needed a national literature, but argued that copyright was essential to prevent publishers neglecting the home-grown product because the pirating of English books was economically more advantageous. He then turned the discussion into an attack on the English writers whose uncomplimentary views on the United States gained, under the prevailing system, too wide and too harmful a circulation there. Though he is not named, Matthew Arnold was clearly still rankling in Clemens's memory; the facility with which phrases from the 'thin-skinned Englishmen' letter of July 1889 [130] recur in this interview suggests that that letter, though addressed to Chatto, was really directed at Arnold. In any event, Clemens's motives for supporting International Copyright in principle, though strong, were certainly mixed. He found it difficult also to agree with the views of others on how it might be implemented. R. Pearsall Smith's views put forward in the late '80s got short shrift from him, as did Augustine Birrell's a decade later.

Whether, as has been argued, the passage of the International Copyright Act in 1891 put an end to cheap book publishing in the United States may be debated, but it did not put an end to piracy. On 18 November 1896 the *Daily Chronicle* published an interview with Dr William Robertson Nicoll on his visit to the United States with James Barrie. It included a reference to the pirating of Barrie in the United States, and Clemens, who was living in London at the time, at once composed a reply. He stated categorically that 'There is copyright in America for the writings of all English authors. If Barrie's books have been debauched there by the pirate it is no one's fault but Mr Barrie's'. This letter he sent to Chatto for onward transmission to the *Chronicle*: 'Can you shove this in without letting them know who wrote it?' [204*]. Chatto replied that he had forwarded it after having it transcribed lest the handwriting were recognised: he had signed it 'An American' rather than ' "London Publisher" or something' as Clemens had suggested. The *Chronicle* did not publish it, but Chatto told Clemens in advance that if they did it would be likely to be accompanied by an editorial reminder that only established authors could afford the simultaning that would

Mark Twain that not every author had been so well protected by his publisher as he.

The subject continued to preoccupy Clemens. In 1899 he offered John Kendrick Bangs, editor of *Harper's Weekly,* an article on copyright but asked him not to use it for the present as without the statistics that he would supply later 'the article is a eunuch' [285] (the sexual imagery of this letter and its allusions to flatulence recall, on a smaller scale, his Omar Khayyam parody). In 1900 he testified (presumably in more sober terms) to the House of Lords Select Committee on Copyright, and received a letter of congratulation from the publisher Maurice Macmillan on his 'most interesting & important statement'.[16] Macmillan endorsed the view that there was no copyright in ideas, only in the literary composition that embodied the idea; and that, unlike a patent, a copyright should be granted in perpetuity. He doubted, however, whether the noble Lords on the committee were receptive to concepts of such novelty. It was probably these sentiments that led to the two men meeting socially over the ensuing months about as frequently, if Clemens's notebook is reliable, as he and Chatto did. It was also to his notebooks, a few years later, that he confided two aphorisms: one to the effect that the only thing impossible to the Almighty was to find any sense in copyright laws, and the other, perhaps with the Select Committee in mind, 'Whenever a copyright law is to be made or altered, then the idiots assemble'.

CHAPTER 12

CONCLUSION

I

Had it not sounded so aggressively proprietary, especially in the Bicentennial year in which this book was completed, I had planned to call it 'England's Mark Twain'. In the last twelve years of his life, however, he became 'England's Mark Twain' in a very real sense. That he was listened to with respect by a Select Committee of the House of Lords, invited to a royal garden party at Windsor, and given an honorary doctorate at Oxford is a measure of his public reputation. His position as a writer was, despite a few voices raised in disagreement, also firmly established, but it was as a writer, no longer merely as a humorist. In the summer of 1906, looking back on *Mark Twain's Library of Humor,* he decided 'This book is a cemetery', because the authors represented therein 'were merely humorists. Humorists of the "mere" sort cannot survive'. His reputation in England may have strengthened his assertion 'I have always preached. That is the reason that I have lasted thirty years'.[1]

The statement has a Shavian ring to it, and it is not surprising that when, in the following year, Shaw and Mark Twain met for the first time they immediately took to each other. Clemens was also delighted to discover from Shaw that William Morris had been one of his admirers as well; he recalled Morris being pointed out to him on the street during his 1873 visit to England, but had never met him [322]. The widening circle of his British literary acquaintance in the first decade of this century, however, is well-known. Kipling, who was honoured with him in the Oxford ceremony in 1907, was an old friend; reports of his illness in 1898 had very much worried Clemens in Vienna [268]. In 1905 Kipling and twenty-seven other British writers signed a cable to Clemens on the occasion of his seventieth birthday. When in the previous year Clemens had asked nostalgically 'Who is it I *haven't* known?'[2] he was not referring specifically to his British contemporaries, but he might well have done, especially by 1907. Kipling, Shaw, Barrie, Max Beerbohm, Conan Doyle, James Bryce the historian, Anthony Hope, Marie Corelli, Frances Hodgson Burnett, Elinor Glyn, even a young man with a reputation for his Boer War reporting called Winston Churchill, — these and many more he had met and known on his visits to England since 1899 at least.

Names perhaps less well remembered now might usefully be added as evidence of the range of his appeal. In the closing years of the nineteenth century, for example, the *Pall Mall Magazine* contained two tributes to him. In one, Carlyle Smythe, who had met Clemens in India, tried to define 'The Real 'Mark Twain''.[3] His assurance that the author of *A Connecticut Yankee* is not 'somewhat cantankerously disposed towards England' implies the survival of some doubts on that score. He quotes Matthew Arnold asking, after a visit to Hartford, 'Is Mark Twain never serious?' Smythe's answer to this is quite unambiguous: for him Mark Twain is certainly not a mere humorist, and he instances the *Yankee* and *Pudd'nhead Wilson* as containing 'abundant proofs that the writer has quite as firm a grasp of some of the profoundest problems of the day as many of the specialists have'. Smythe's awareness of the importance attached to heredity in Mark Twain's thinking in the *Yankee* is also discriminating. He sees him as an uneven writer, but an important one, original, direct and dedicated to his craft. The book on which he bestows especial praise was, a few issues later, to be eulogized by another *Pall Mall* contributor: 'if a work of incontestable genius has been issued in the English language during the past quarter of a century, it is that brilliant romance of the great rivers, *The Adventures of Huckleberry Finn*'.[4] This was William Archer, drama critic and translator of Ibsen, to whom in the following year Percy Spalding was instructed by Mark Twain to send at his expense a complete set of the edition de luxe.

Smythe's respect for *Joan of Arc* was similarly paralleled in authoritative quarters. In October 1899 Basil Wilberforce wrote to Clemens from the House of Commons and again in April 1900 asking him to speak on her to private gatherings (ninety people is the figure given in April);[5] 'I have read *everything* that has been written about Joan of Arc', Wilberforce assured him, 'and nothing can approach your book upon her for power, vividness and appreciation of her character'. In July 1900 Spalding sent a letter from his cousin asking about the dramatic rights of *Joan of Arc* but Clemens was apparently reluctant to relinquish them. Whether there was any connection between this and a letter from Andrew Chatto nine years later is not clear: it enclosed for Clemens 'an early copy of a drama on "Joan of Arc" which I hope may be of interest to you. It is written by a young friend of mine and I think it has merit'. In 1909 too Chatto told him of an enquiry from Captain Basil Hood 'the well-known playwright' about dramatising 'The £1,000,000 Bank Note'.

Sir Walter Besant, who had praised *Joan of Arc* so highly when it first appeared, incurred a further enthusiastic expression of gratitude from Clemens by an article in *Munsey's Magazine* of February 1898. It prompted Clemens to the realisation that 'we often see in pictures & books things which artist & author did not themselves know they had put there' and, conversely, how often a query from a printer's reader may reveal that a passage 'doesn't say what you thought it did; the gas-fixtures are there, but you didn't light the jets'. Besant had also, he told him, stirred in him 'again the longing to go back to the seclusion of Jackson's island & give up the futilities of life. I suppose we all have a Jackson's island somewhere, & dream of it when we are tired' [266*]. Clemens must have dreamed of Jackson's Island again a year later when he had accepted Besant's *The Pen and the Book* from Harper's for review and discovered that 'there was no way of doing a review that wouldn't cut into [Besant's] feelings . . . The book is not reviewable by any but a sworn enemy of his, for so far as I can see, there isn't a rational page in it' [285]. Friendship was too strong: lacking the heart to go on with it, he abandoned the review.

At about the same time a British writer notorious for the enemies he made by his reviews – 'I am not as you know usually reverent or even affectionate to my contemporaries' – wrote almost fulsomely to Clemens in Vienna to say how delighted he was that words of his had given pleasure to the Mark Twain about whom he had 'never had any doubt or hesitation'. This was the usually censorious Robert Buchanan, who added 'I cannot count the hours of delight which I owe you' and who again struck the by now inevitable note: he envied Mark Twain his sense of humour, 'but to be wise & just also, as well as sunny & glad, is something more – in that you are doubly blest, & a double source of blessing to your readers'.[6] If the meeting that the two men promised each other ever took place, I know of no record of it, but so often the things of which records survive are the least important. Of a visit to Bryce, for instance, we know only that Clemens went home in the wrong overcoat, and then wrote to assure his host 'I did not do it intentionally, it was only habit' [315*]. Through Bryce he met William Knight, Professor of Moral Philosophy at the University of St. Andrews, who invited the Clemenses to his home in Scotland; a visit to Sweden for Clara's health prevented their accepting [303], and there is no further information about what the professional and the amateur moral philosophers thought of each other.

More Tramps Abroad also increased interestingly Clemens's range of acquaintance. There was, for example, Francis Henry Skrine who, in 1897, had retired to England after a distinguished career of nearly thirty years in the Indian Civil Service. It may well have been in India that they first met, for in November 1897 a complimentary copy of *More Tramps Abroad* was ordered to be sent to Mrs Skrine on publication [252]. Then in 1899 an engaging letter to Skrine from Sweden thanks him for the promise to present Clemens with an inscribed copy of a book, probably *The Heart of Asia* which Skrine published that year in collaboration with Sir E.D. Ross. Clemens also refers to the 'great & interesting surprise' that it is to him to learn the correct pronunciation of 'trait'. (Three years earlier he had confided to his notebook his fascination with the mysteries of 'Kirkcudbrightshire' and the decision to pronounce no British place-name until he had heard a native say it).[7] The easy candour with which he continues says as much for his unassuming modesty at the height of his career as it does for his friendship with Skrine:

> I am now reminded that there are half a dozen common (I mean much-used) words in our language which have never been orally used in my presence, & which I have often uttered with my pen but never with my mouth — I didn't & don't know how to pronounce them & was & am & ever shall remain too lazy to look in the dictionary & find out. When they rise to my lips in conversation I swallow them & substitute a word which I am not afraid of. Other lazy people have this way, no doubt. [310*]

In 1902, sending New Year greetings to 'those well-beloved Skrines', he expressed amazement at the idea of Kipling calling for conscription and launched ebulliently into a parody of the refrain of 'The Absent-Minded Beggar' [325].

Kipling and *More Tramps Abroad* brought him another unexpected correspondent in the person of Sir Martin Conway, a man of many parts with a reputation as a mountain-climber and explorer as well as an art historian (he was shortly to become Slade Professor at Cambridge). He had twice been Chairman of the Society of Authors but though Mark Twain was a member they had not met in that context. It was in January 1899 that Conway, on a sea voyage, decided to pass the time by correcting some of Mark Twain's errors for him. 'A queer letter', Clemens wrote on it, noting that he had left it unanswered and that Conway was a stranger to him.[8] Mark Twain's views on the Taj Mahal in *More Tramps Abroad* and, in *The Innocents Abroad,* on the Sphinx are challenged, with the gratuitous addition of the assertion 'You yourself I think are inclined to accept popular opinion too easily'; there is a brief discussion of the relation between perfection and true beauty in art, agreement with 'much of your S African criticism', and then a reminder of facts that 'are not often remembered by critics of S African blunders': had it not been for British intervention, 'at a cost to us of 5 millions', the Boers would have been exterminated by the Zulus, but as soon as the Zulu threat was removed the Boers ungratefully demanded their freedom. Conway then digresses into quoting two stanzas of a poem by an unidentified 'young Artillery officer' as the true original of Kipling's 'Gunga Din', contrasts shovel-board as described in *More Tramps Abroad* with shovel-board as played on the ship on which Conway is travelling, and breaks off only when it has become too hot to remember the other points he wanted to raise. For all its relaxed and rambling inconsequentiality — and it gives an impression of Conway's intellectual ability that is probably less than fair — the letter is an interesting example of the response Mark Twain aroused in British readers, of their readiness to engage in long-distance conversation with him, and of the seriousness with which they treated his views.

Six months later Conway was to meet Clemens and his family at a dinner party: 'Had a long talk with him & found him most entertaining & interesting but with a clearly marked bohemian background. His lecture tour reminiscences were delightful'.[9] During the rest of the year Conway called regularly on the Clemenses, sent him some tobacco which, Clemens assured him, 'justifies its reputation. Many many thanks' [306*], and — a gesture which his guest would have appreciated even more — took Clemens to dinner at the Athenaeum.

II

Clemens's wellknown fondness for London clubs had originated in the 1870s and continued undiminished. He was able to indulge it frequently after 1900, especially in the company of J.Y.W. MacAlister. MacAlister (1856-1925) had given up a career in medicine because of ill-health and had turned to librarianship, founding *The Library* in 1889. He served on various public and international committees on culture as well as on hygiene and medicine, and was knighted in 1919. When Clemens was engaged in promoting the health food Plasmon, Mac-Alister was naturally one of the friends he sought to involve in the enterprise; in August 1901, for example, Spalding offered to supply MacAlister with more information if necessary and in November 1904 Clemens sent his agent Ralph Ashcroft to MacAlister with a letter of introduction to 'the officers of our London Plasmon Companies' [329]. It was, however, on clubbability and a sense of humour that their friendship was based, and in the congenial atmosphere of the Savage Club that it prospered. On 9 June 1899 MacAlister was in the chair when Clemens was elected an honorary life member.[10] MacAlister's speech on this occasion facetiously attacked him as a humorist but praised his work as a pioneer in 'bringing the English and Americans into closer sympathy'. (Three days later Clemens was to take up this cue in his address to the Authors' Club when he spoke of leaving 'to posterity if we cannot leave anything else, a friendship between England and America that will count for much' and produced the celebrated epigram 'Since England and America have been joined together in Kipling, may they not be severed in Twain').[11]

The Savage Club dinner was commemorated in an impromptu sketch by Phil May, the well-known humorous artist, of himself, Mark Twain, MacAlister and a fourth. For at least two years May illustrated MacAlister's Christmas cards,[12] and the three men obviously found more in common than merely a sense of humour. They were together again at the Savage on 7 July 1900 when it was Clemens's turn to take the chair at the six-course dinner, and this time Bram

Stoker joined them in autographing the menu.[13] It is possible that May was responsible for the line-drawing that headed the menu too. MacAlister's attempts to promote the edition de luxe of Mark Twain's works were mentioned in Chapter 10; it was at his instigation that Clemens, in 1907, was to commit to paper the recollections of his first visit to London quoted in Chapter 3; and after Clemens's death MacAlister was to provide Paine, at Spalding's request, with a quantity of letters he had received from the humorist over the years. Again, it was a family friendship, for MacAlister's second son, Ian, who was in his early twenties at the turn of the century, addressed the English Speaking Union in 1938 on his personal reminiscences of Mark Twain.[14]

By 1900 Clemens had also become friendly with Anthony Hope Hawkins, author (under the name of Anthony Hope) of several best-sellers, most notably the Ruritanian romance *The Prisoner of Zenda*. Seeing the two men lunching together at the Savoy in June gave Rupert D'Oyley Carte the happy idea of inviting Mark Twain ('although I have not the honour of knowing you personally') to the dinner he was giving to welcome Sir Henry Irving back from his American tour.[15] It is only surprising that the invitation had not already been made at the suggestion of Bram Stoker who had been Irving's manager. Clemens was still in touch too with W.T. Stead who regularly sent him the *Review of Reviews*, anthologised Mark Twain's work, and kept in touch with him after his return to New York in the autumn of 1900 [322]. Clemens had been away from America for almost a decade when he went back this time.

His last visit to England was the short but climactic one to receive the honorary Litt. D. at Oxford. How many engagements he crammed into that time it is impossible to say. The ceremony was on 23 June and there were many public appearances in London, Oxford and elsewhere in conjunction with that. The highlights of one later week, however, are a convenient epitome of his interests. On 4 July he addressed the American Society in London at its Independence Day Banquet at the Hotel Cecil: as was customary with him on such occasions, a humorous and anecdotal speech modulated into a peroration of tribute and gratitude to 'Old England, this great-hearted venerable old mother of the race . . . the Protector of Anglo-Saxon Freedom' whose ties with America were so long-standing and durable.[16] Two days later he was dining at the Savage Club among old friends, with Sir James Linton R.I. in the chair.[17] Two days after that he was honoured at the *Punch* dinner and presented with the original of the cartoon in the 26 June issue where Mr Punch drinks to Mark Twain's health, happiness, and perpetual youth.[18] Two days later again, at the Lord Mayor's Banquet in Liverpool, he took the opportunity once more to express his affection for England in his last major public appearance in this country [331].

Oxford had honoured him as a man of letters: the four engagements just summarised displayed him in the four other roles that he was now fulfilling — spokesman to Americans for Anglo-American friendship, the darling after-dinner speaker of clubland, the professional humorist, and unofficial American ambassador to the people of Britain. A tribute to his British reputation that must have pleased him by its simple spontaneity was the letter from a Mrs Edith Draper of Ormskirk, Lancashire, in 1906. She asked for a photograph of Mark Twain for her husband, a £1-a-week railway clerk, to whom she gave one of Mark Twain's books every Christmas and birthday. 'He is never tired of reading them and they keep him at home many a time when he would be out at night'. Family pressure alone, she explained, had prevented them from naming their baby after Mark Twain; the only other cause of regret to her was that 'you aren't an Englishman & more espically [sic] a Lancashire man'.[19] In its own way, this is as indicative of the esteem in which he was held as was the letter from Arthur Conan Doyle in 1909 congratulating him on *King Leopold's Soliloquy*, sending him his own *The Crime of the Congo,* and expressing his pleasure that this 'great American' was helping to bring 'the two great English-speaking nations shoulder to shoulder in protecting the helpless'.[20]

III

The making of new friendships did not prevent the reviving of old. With Moncure Conway he seems to have had little contact over a number of years. In 1882 he had thanked Conway heartily for an essay on Tennyson 'as beautiful as music' [88] . Conway gave up the South Place ministry in 1884 and returned to America; in the following year he and his daughter visited the Clemenses, and in 1886 he tried to place his novel, *Pine and Palm,* with Charles Webster & Co.[21] In 1893 he agreed to return to South Place, but although he remained there until 1897 and was thus in residence while the Clemenses were living at Tedworth Square, the death of Susy and the pressures of writing *More Tramps Abroad* made them reluctant to see even old friends. In March 1897 Clemens declined an invitation from a Mr. Burgess because 'the hurt of my bereavement is still with me, & I do not go out or see any one. Some day this will change; but until then I must continue my hermit life, & get such contentment out of it as I may' [221*] . On similar grounds he declined an invitation to the Lord Mayor's banquet [217] .

By the end of 1900, however, Mark Twain was attracting in America attention and some notoriety for the attacks on imperialism and imperialistic wars already discussed. Moncure Conway wrote to the New York *Times* (the letter was printed on 11 January 1901) deftly linking Mark Twain, in this respect, to the great liberal tradition of nineteenth-century American literature and expressing the hope that 'the bugle call of Samuel Clemens will be the signal for an uprising of intellectual forces in America' similar to that which the Dreyfus case had generated in France. Whether he knew of his old friend's obsession with the Dreyfus case or had private information about 'To the Person Sitting in Darkness' which Mark Twain published a few weeks later does not emerge. With the understandable pride of a prophet vindicated he allows himself the justifiable comment 'I have these many years recognised that Mark Twain's humor is apt to feather a very serious arrow'.

This letter, although Clemens does not say so, was doubtless one reason for the post card he sent Conway on 10 March, care of Harpers:

I have lost your address. I hunted for you yesterday, for some time, & sampled three doorbells unsuccessfully: they said you didn't live there. I wanted to say I have seen your article on Illusions of Philanthropy, & I think that even *you* have never done anything with a pen that is more beautiful than that, or deeper and richer.

Mark   [324*]

The warmth and generosity of this must have pleased its recipient and within a week the two men were dining together at the Century Club. Probably they resumed their old rivalry on the billiard table. A few weeks earlier, also at the Century, Moncure had beaten another dinner guest of his at the game. This was Martin Conway, who claimed a distant kinship with Moncure, and whose wife was American. As Martin had twice visited the Clemenses since his arrival in New York and 'had a good time' it is likely that he and Moncure talked of Mark Twain and that Martin spoke of having played billiards with him in London eighteen months earlier until two in the morning. He may also have mentioned being recently taken to Gilder's by Clemens and having met 'Mr Fairchild who was Secy. of the Treasury under Cleveland'.[22] Another friend that Clemens and Moncure Conway may have discovered they now had in common was Professor William Knight whom Conway had known since the 1870s and whom Clemens had more recently met.

When, in June 1904, Moncure Conway read in the press of Olivia Clemens's death, he wrote at once to Clemens, apostrophizing him as 'Old comrade of happy years, comrade now in bereavement' (Ellen Conway had died in 1897). These were not, he assured him, 'words of formal sympathy':

I knew the woman, – saw the soul in her clear deep eyes thirty years ago in her Hartford Paradise, beside the Avon, and elsewhere as the years came with their troubles and sorrows, – beheld her simply at intervals, but always to feel how happy it was for us all that beside you was that lovely lady with her fine artistic instinct. Never did I witness more blending of tact, graciousness, and insight than in those evenings at Normandie Hotel when you read us bits of what you were working on.[23]

This was, surely, precisely the right note to strike for Clemens, but its genuineness is shown by its unconscious echoing of phrases and images that Conway had used of Olivia in the '70s and '80s. His final recollection of her in the Paris hotel may well be more just to her true influence on Mark Twain's work than are those critics who present her as a humourless Mrs Grundy cramping his genius by her expurgations.

In a postscript Conway mentioned that his *Autobiography* was to appear in the autumn. It was in due course reviewed in the New York *Times Saturday Review of Books* and at the top of his copy Clemens scribbled 'This is a good notice. Dr Conway ought to see it. I have ordered the book, & I know I shall enjoy it'. That this survives among Conway's papers indicates that he knew of his old friend's interest: could he have seen the marginalia with which Clemens adorned his copy of the *Autobiography* he would have been even prouder. Reference has already been made to some of these; most of them indicate approbation of Conway's comments, even identification of Clemens's own position with Conway's, as well as nostalgia for times past ('I seem to have met the most of the people mentioned in this book') and his own recollections of people and incidents occurring in the narrative.

When Mark Twain's seventieth birthday was celebrated by the banquet at Delmonico's on 5 December 1905 Conway was, as he ruefully wrote to Clemens, 'not thought worthy to be included among those who gathered around you last night'. The omission is a strange one, for he was, as he added with dignity, 'in my humble way your old friend — among the oldest'. The recent appearance of his two-volume *Autobiography*, and the attention it had attracted, makes it even more surprising that he was overlooked. It did not, however, prevent his ending his note to Clemens with an expression of his pleasure 'at the good evidences that you lose no fibre of mind and heart with advancing years';[24] nor did it prevent his inviting Clemens to dinner at the Century Club three months later. They met again in 1906 at Andrew Carnegie's and Conway told Clemens how much the Conway sons, who had known him in London in the '70s, would like to meet him again. Clemens agreed to a lunch engagement rather than an evening, and Conway later proposed 12 January 1907 'at the Lafayette restaurant, corner of 9th St. and University Place'.[25] There is no record of their meeting again, and in November 1907 Conway died in Paris. His son Eustace duly invited Clemens to the funeral service in New York on 14 December. On the letter Clemens wrote simply 'I'll go to it'.[26] It is his last comment on a friendship of more than thirty years which, although not one of the most influential in Mark Twain's career, certainly meant more to him than has hitherto been recognised by his biographers.

IV

What Clemens had called, in 1897, the hurt of his bereavement never left him: it was instead intensified by other losses. Whatever public honours and banquets still awaited him, one side of his life was to become increasingly hermit-like and lonely.

The illness of Olivia in 1902 threatened him as nothing had since Susy's death. To Chatto's expression of sympathy he responded with a note, the optimism of which does not belie his loneliness:

> Mrs Clemens has now been in her bed more than three months, and we have several times been greatly alarmed about her, but you will be glad to know that in these latter days she is making all visible progress towards recovery, and that we feel quite confident that within a few months she will be on her feet again, and as well as she was before this attack of nervous prostration befell her.
>
> If she knew I was writing she would send warm messages to both families [sc. Chatto's and Spalding's], but as she is not allowed to know anything that is going on I send them myself.
>
> It is about two months since I have seen her [;] no one is allowed in the sick room except Clara and the physician and the trained nurse. [327*]

Spalding replied at once to say how 'much concerned & grieved' Chatto and he were. 'We have many pleasant recollections of your last visit to England, and are looking forward to again seeing you both with your daughters amongst us'. When in July 1903 they read in the press of his projected trip to Florence with Livy they repeated their hopes of a visit, but it was not to be, and Olivia's death in 1904 evoked the following simple but moving letter:

> My dear Clemens,
>   Your great sorrow echoes sympathetically through my heart —
> Oh, the pity of it.
>   My wife and daughters join in heartfelt condolence with yourself and daughters.
>
>   Ever faithfully yours
>   Andrew Chatto

Its idiom, formal and yet emotional, belongs to a by-gone age; yet in the context of the whole body of correspondence between those two men it has its own eloquence. Little things are significant: 'My dear Clemens' rather than the usual 'Dear Mr. Clemens', and the 'Ever faithfully yours' which is almost effusive by Chatto's usual standards. In that respect the letter conveniently sums up much of what I have tried to say about their relationship: from the evidence that survives, formal and necessarily incomplete as it is, it is not unreasonable to infer a sympathy, warmth and fellow-feeling that went far beyond the normal publisher-author relationship and became a friendship that was important to both. If it is a matter of inference rather than of incontrovertible proof it is because, in such friendships, what survives on paper for posterity is often the least important of its aspects for the participants. Thus there is no mention in this correspondence of the death in October 1905 of Andrew Chatto's wife Katherine, yet it is most unlikely that Clemens did not know of it or express his condolences. (In 1901, for example, Spalding had told him 'Mrs Chatto has been (& still is) very ill for several months past'.)

The correspondence in the remaining years of Clemens's life was largely a routine transmission of royalty cheques and cordial expressions of hope that he would re-visit England. When he did so in 1907 for the Oxford ceremony the tightness of his schedule meant that Spalding had to write twice to Ralph Ashcroft before a meeting was arranged, but at the end of his visit, on 11 July, Clemens went to Spalding's home in Harley Gardens to discuss the re-issue of his books in a sixpenny or sevenpenny edition and to arrange, now that Harpers had taken over the edition de luxe from Bliss, for the English publication of volumes 24 and 25. Though it seems improbable that he did not see Chatto on this trip, there is no conclusive proof that he did. Nor can one be sure when he gave Spalding the silver brandy flask, engraved with the signature 'Mark Twain', that still survives.

With the royalty cheque in January 1908 went Spalding's expressed hope 'of again seeing you on this side during the Spring or Summer'. On the reverse of the letter Clemens wrote 'Yes, thank him & say I'm grown too old to travel but I'm hoping to see them on *this* side'.[27] Evidently this was no empty courtesy but was obviously repeated more formally, for on 8 July 1909 Spalding wrote to regret that he and Mrs Spalding could not accept Clemens's invitation to America:

> Mr Chatto and his son desire me to say that it would also give them much pleasure to do so, so don't think that we are "too unsociable": we will all come some day, and I believe that you will soon have had enough of us! Meanwhile, do come over and see us! We all often look back with the greatest pleasure to your visits to England, and only wish they were more frequent.

Three weeks later they were commiserating with him on his ill-health:

> We are indeed sorry to hear that you are not well, and have unfortunately to stay in the house throughout the Summer. This would not be such a hardship were you in England, for we have had immense quantities of rain, reminding one of what we are told did happen in the days of Noah: however, one of our Partners a few days ago was consoled with the sight of a rainbow!

For Clemens life had few consolations left. Unwell himself, he was to see his daughter Jean die of epilepsy at Christmas 1909. By now Clara, the only surviving member of his family, was married. A trip to Bermuda failing to improve his health, he returned home to the appropriately named Stormfield at Redding, Connecticut, where, on 21 April 1910, he died.

Andrew Chatto outlived him by only three years, dying at the age of 72 on 15 March 1913 at his home in Radlett, Hertfordshire. 'A distinguished and lovable figure', the *Book Monthly* called him, 'a publisher of genuine literary taste'. The reminiscence with which that obituary ended makes a fitting conclusion to this narrative:

> He was a delightful man to meet socially as well as in business, and nobody who was present will forget the lunch which he gave to Mark Twain in the dining-room over the firm's offices in St. Martin's Lane, when the American humorist paid one of his last visits to England. Mark Twain was easily the first person of the company; and Andrew Chatto, sitting at the top of the table, with that look of quiet humour in his eye, full of story and re- miniscence, was as easily second.

V

Among the commemorative notices published after Mark Twain's death was one in the *North American Review* signed 'Britannicus'; The writer claimed to have been 'with him frequently in those memorable weeks' of 1907 when the Oxford degree was conferred on him, and asserted that Mark Twain was as popular in England as in the United States. Sir Ian MacAlister, in his 1938 speech to the English Speaking Union, went further: American intellectuals, he argued, had always under-rated Mark Twain but in England, in addition to enjoyment of his humour, there was 'an appreciation of him as a really serious and important literary figure as well'. In 1889 a Willesden lady had assured Clemens that 'we English have the greatest admiration and appreciation of your writings'.[28] Such comments, as well as all the evidence pro- duced in this book, put in a strange light William Faulkner's 1922 dis- missal of Mark Twain as 'a hack writer who would not have been con- sidered fourth rate in Europe'.[29]

To try to quantify reputation is idle. However, some impression may be gained by counting the number of copies published, and in Appendix I this information is given for the titles issued during Mark Twain's life- time by Hotten and by Chatto & Windus. The total comes to more than 910,000. Routledge's print orders are complicated by the issuing of *The Innocents Abroad* and *Roughing It* in two-volume editions; in both cases more copies of one volume than of the other were printed. Ignor- ing this finer distinction and regarding the two titles as though they were a single volume each, we can approximate the sales of *The Inno- cents Abroad* at 152,000 between 1872 and 1902; in the same period *Roughing It* sold 77,000. *The Gilded Age,* between the first print order of December 1873 and the sale of the title to Chatto in 1892, totalled only 10,500. Thus Routledge, Hotten and Chatto issued at least 1,150,000 copies of Mark Twain's books in his lifetime; to this should be added the figure for Routledge's *Jumping Frog* and *Sketches* (which I do not have), and the incalculable number of copies pirated by firms such as Ward, Lock & Tyler.

Of the titles issued exclusively by Chatto & Windus – the only ones for which reliable total figures are available – *A Tramp Abroad* comes easily at the top with 174,250 copies. *The Prince and the Pauper* comes next with 99,250 – more than nine times as many as *Joan of Arc*. Surprisingly *Tom Sawyer* is almost 100,000 behind *A Tramp Abroad,* reaching only 76,000; but more unexpected still is *Huckleberry Finn* whose total of 43,500 is 2,500 lower than *Life on the Mississippi. A Yankee at the Court of King Arthur* comes sixth with 40,000 while *Pudd'nhead Wilson* (12,000) is only 1,000 ahead of *Joan of Arc.* Clemens's 'gaudy' English income (to use his own word) from Chatto & Windus during his lifetime was upwards of £20,500.

Mark Twain's standing, on both sides of the Atlantic, derived from his own genius as a writer and from the perspicacity of readers with catholic tastes. In focusing attention on the details and circumstances of his English publication I have sought to show that, in their different ways, the Routledges, Hotten and Chatto served him remarkably well, and that he was fortunate in friends such as Moncure Daniel Conway. I am not claiming for his English publishers, able as they were, any exceptional promotional skill. Andrew Chatto was a good business man, but as the *Book Monthly* said of him:

> He thought of the quality of the book he was going to issue, as well as of its possible success. If you talked with him, he would point you to its ability, to its freshness, to the charm of its style, and he was content to let it take care of itself in a commercial sense. He was, in fact, an old-fashioned publisher, and that, perhaps, had a good deal to do with his success.

What Chatto contributed to Samuel Clemens's income is impressive and capable of definition. What he contributed to Mark Twain's development as a writer can only be conjectured. The hours that the two men spent in each other's company and with each other's family, the easy relationship that a shared sense of humour gave them, and the respect that each developed for the other's abilities must have had their influence on both. At the very least, Chatto and his house were important factors in ensuring that England and America were 'not severed in Twain'.

APPENDIX I

PRINTINGS OF MARK TWAIN'S BOOKS BY HOTTEN AND CHATTO & WINDUS 1870–1910

The information given below is summarised from the Chatto & Windus ledger books; it relates to the forty years between John Camden Hotten's piracy of *The Jumping Frog* in 1870 and Mark Twain's death in 1910. Items 1–3 inclusive and 5–10 inclusive were originally issued under the John Camden Hotten imprint, the remainder under the Chatto & Windus imprint. Titles are listed in the chronological order of their original publication.

Entries are tabulated as follows:

Short title, followed by the serial number in Jacob Blanck's *Bibliography of American Literature* vol.2.

    (a) date and size of first print order

    (b) date(s) and size of reprint orders within the first twelve months of publication

    (c) first and last dates of subsequent reprintings, the number of such reprintings (in words), and the total number of copies ordered

    (d) similar information for cheap editions (where identifiable)

    (e) total number of copies of the title issued over the period

1. *The Jumping Frog* (3587)

(a)	12 April 1870	2,000
(b)	–	
(c)	6 July 1871 – 7 July 1873 (six)	12,000
(d)	3 November 1873 (1s.0d)	2,000
(e)		16,000

2. *The Innocents Abroad* (3590)

a)	May 1870	8,000
b)	October 1870	6,000
c)	1871 – 1873 (three)	34,000
d)	–	
e)		48,000

3. *The New Pilgrim's Progress* (3591)
   a) 2 August 1870   8,000
   b) 29 October 1870   5,000
   c) 1871 – November 1873 (four)   31,700
   d) –
   e)   44,700

4. *The Innocents Abroad* (Chatto & Windus)
   This edition, not separately identified by Blanck, brings together (2)
   and (3) above in one volume, sold at 7s. 6d.
   a) 1 July 1881   5,000
   b) 27 October 1881   5,000
   c) –
   d) 6 October 1893 (3s.6d.)   2,000
      20 July 1897 – 22 April 1910 (eight)   16,000
   e)   28,000

5. *Mark Twain's Pleasure Trip* (3597,3602)
   N.B. The ledgers do not differentiate between the two editions
        separately identified by Blanck and, as will be seen, there is
        no reference to the 1873 printing that is assumed at entry 3602.

   a) 5 May 1871   2,000
   b) –
   c) 8 June 1875 – 30 May 1882 (four)   8,000
   d) 26 May 1885 (2s.0d.)   1,500
      7 May 1887 – 22 April 1910 (eight)   12,000
   e)   23,500

6. *Mark Twain's (Burlesque) Autobiography* (3329)
      May 1871   5,000

7. *Eye-Openers* (3331)
   a) 6 May 1871   6,000
   b) 12 September 1871   5,000
   c) 1 March 1872, 7 October 1872 (two)   10,000
   d) –
   e)   21,000

8. *Screamers* (3333)
   a) 1871   11,000
   b) –
   c) 1872   8,000
   d) –
   e)   19,000

9. *Practical Jokes* (3342)

a) 11 June 1872	8,000
b) 11 September 1872	6,000
c) 27 September 1873	3,000
d) –	
e)	17,000

10. *Choice Humorous Works* (3351)

a) 19 August 1872	2,000
b) –	
c) 12 November 1873 – 20 September 1876 (three)	6,000
d) –	
e)	8,000

    See also 12 below.

11. *Adventures of Tom Sawyer* (3367)

a) 29 April 1876	2,000
b) 6 October 1876 (illustrated)	2,000
c) 5 February 1885 – 13 October 1894 (three: 7s.6d.)	5,000
d) 7 September 1877 (2s.0d.)	6,000
15 November 1877 – 14 September 1909 (twenty-one)	40,500
24 June 1897 (3s.6d.)	1,500
7 December 1898 – 25 February 1910 (seven)	14,000
12 November 1907 (6d.)	5,000
e)	76,000

12. *Choice Humorous Works* (revised and corrected by the Author) (3613, 3656)

    See 10 above

a) 5 February 1878	2,000
b) –	
c) 12 September 1879 – 11 May 1892 (eight)	14,000
d) 21 May 1897 (3s.6d.)	1,500
22 September 1899 – 6 August 1907 (three)	5,500
e)	23,000

13. *An Idle Excursion* (3615)

a) 13 February 1878	6,000
b) –	
c) 25 April 1881, 7 August 1883 (two)	3,500
d) –	
e)	9,500

14. *A Tramp Abroad* (3386)

   a) 1 April 1880: vol.I   ) of 2-vol. 10*s*.6*d*.
      26 April 1880: vol.II) unillustrated ed.   500

   b) 26 April 1880   2,500

      7 May − 14 July 1880 (five)   6,750

      August 1880: 1-vol. illustrated 7*s*.6*d*.   5,000

      September 1880 − 29 July 1881 (Seven in the first
      twelve months after issue of 7*s*.6*d*. one-volume edition)   29,000

   c) 27 October 1881 − 14 January 1891 (five)   13,500

   d) 13 March 1884 (2*s*.0*d*.)   10,000

      1 July 1884 − 15 March 1910 (fifteen)   36,000

      21 September 1896 (3*s*.6*d*.)   3,000

      6 August 1897 − 5 April 1909 (seven)   18,000

      23 July 1907 (6*d*.)   50,000

   e)   174,250

15. *The Prince and the Pauper* (3396)

   a) 24 September 1881   5,000

   b) 3 and 30 November 1881 (two)   10,000

   c) 13 October 1891   3,000

   d) 30 November 1881 (2*s*.0*d*.)   4,000

      24 January 1888 − 27 April 1909 (eight)   16,250

      28 October 1897 (3*s*.6*d*.)   1,500

      6 September 1899 − 19 November 1909 (five)   9,500

      12 November 1907 (6*d*.)   50,000

   e)   99,250

16. *The Stolen White Elephant* (3403)

   a) 25 May 1882   3,000

   b) 13 June 1882 − 4 January 1883 (three)   6,000

   c) −

   d) 25 January 1884 (2*s*.0*d*.)   8,000

      18 September 1888 − 5 August 1893 (three)   6,000

      3 December 1896 (3*s*.6*d*.)   1,000

      13 October 1897 − 27 April 1909 (five)   5,000

   e)   29,000

17. *Life on the Mississippi* (3410)
   a) 12 February 1883   12,000
   b) 9 May 1883   4,000
   c) 16 November 1894 – 3 July 1899 (two)   4,000
   d) 1 February 1887 (2*s*.0*d*.)   10,000
      21 October 1887 – 27 April 1909 (seven)   12,000
      16 February 1904, 26 April 1909 (3*s*.6*d*.) (two)   4,000
   e)   46,000

18. *Adventures of Huckleberry Finn* (3414)
   a) 16 October 1884   10,000
   b) 8 December 1884   3,000
   c) 12 January 1885, 26 March 1888 (two)   4,500
   d) 10 October 1889 (2*s*.0*d*.)   2,000
      26 August 1890 – 7 January 1910 (seven)   12,000
      12 April 1897 (3*s*.6*d*.)   1,500
      22 April 1898 – 6 June 1906 (six)   11,000
   e)   43,500

19. *Mark Twain's Library of Humor* (not listed in *BAL*)
   a) 19 March 1888   10,000
   b) –
   c) –
   d) 21 April 1890 (3*s*.6*d*.)   2,000
      30 October 1902, 2 August 1906 (two)   4,000
   e)   16,000

20. *A Yankee at the Court of King Arthur* (3429)
   a) 24 September 1889   10,000
   b) 17 March 1890   5,000
   c) –
   d) 15 March 1893 (2*s*.0*d*.)   10,000
      1 August 1894 – 27 April 1909 (five)   6,000
      11 October 1897 (3*s*.6*d*.)   1,500
      9 November 1899 – 5 August 1908 (four)   7,500
   e)   40,000

21. *Roughing It* (not listed in *BAL*)
   a) 27 December 1889   2,000
   b) –
   c) 25 January 1897 – 14 December 1905 (four)   7,000
   d) –
   e)   9,000

22. *The Gilded Age* (not listed in *BAL*)

a) 9 March 1892 (2s.0d.)	3,000
b) 29 April 1892	2,000
c) 9 March 1899 − 28 September 1909 (four)	4,500
d) −	
e)	9,500

(N.B. excluded from the above are copies ordered in October 1885 made up from sheets purchased from Routledge and quoted only in quires)

23. *Sketches* (3657 only)

a) 9 March 1892	3,000
b) 19 May 1892	2,000
c) 1 December 1896 − 9 March 1908 (five)	7,750
d) −	
e)	12,750

24. *The American Claimant* (3434)

a) 23 June 1892	10,000
b) −	
c) 1 August 1902	1,500
d) −	
e)	11,500

25. *The £1,000,000 Bank-Note* (3436)

a) 30 March 1893	10,000
b) −	
c) −	
d) 14 February and 27 August 1895 (2s.0d.)	7,000
e)	17,000

26. *Tom Sawyer Abroad* (3440)

a) 28 February 1894	10,000
b) −	
c) 9 September 1901 − 25 January 1908 (three)	4,500
d) −	
e)	14,500

27. *Pudd'nhead Wilson* (3441)
    a) 12 April 1894   10,000
    b) –
    c) –
    d) 5 October 1905 (3s.6d.)   1,000
       10 March 1908   1,000
    e)   12,000

28. *Joan of Arc* (3446)
    a) 25 March 1896   6,000
    b) –
    c) 9 April 1902   2,000
    d) 7 August 1907 (3s.6d.)   3,000
    e)   11,000

29. *Tom Sawyer, Detective* (3448)
    a) 3 November 1896   5,000
    b) 24 May 1897   750
    c) 14 September 1898 – 19 October 1909 (five)   5,000
    d) –
    e)   10,750

30. *More Tramps Abroad* (3453)
    a) 12 August 1897   5,000
    b) 10 November (5,000), 25 November (3,000),
       22 December 1897 (5,000), 8 March 1898 (5,000)   18,000
    c) –
    d) 11 October 1900 (6s.0d.)   2,000
       7 August 1907   5,000
    e)   30,000

31. *The Man That Corrupted Hadleyburg* (3460)
    a) 30 May 1900   6,000
    b) 13 September, 8 November 1900 (2,000 each)   4,000
    c) –
    d) 7 August 1907 (3s.6d.)   2,000
    e)   12,000

32. *A Double-Barrelled Detective Story* (3471)
    a) 31 May 1902   6,000
    b) c) d) –
    e)   6,000

APPENDIX II

A CALENDAR OF LETTERS
BY MARK TWAIN AND MEMBERS OF HIS
FAMILY

This Appendix lists in chronological order all letters by Mark Twain and members of his family on which I have drawn in the writing of this book. A few have been quoted in full, some in extract, and many have been cited only as authority for statements made in the text. I have listed every surviving letter to Chatto & Windus known to me, including telegrams, memoranda etc., though a few of them have not been important enough for citation or reference.

Key to the Calendar:

(a) serial numbers correspond to the figures in square brackets in the text by which the references are identified.

(b) where possible undated letters have been assigned a date by other evidence; such dates are printed in square brackets. A question mark in the date column means that the letter is believed to belong to this period in the sequence but no date more precise can be assigned to it. A name in round brackets following the date indicates that the writer was Mrs Clemens (OLC) or one of their daughters. All other letters are, of course, by Mark Twain.

(c) the following abbreviations have been used to indicate addressees:

AC	Andrew Chatto
C & W	Chatto & Windus
CLW	Charles L. Webster & Co.
EB	Elisha Bliss (American Publishing Co.)
FB	Frank Bliss (son of EB)
FJH	Fred J. Hall (Charles L. Webster & Co.)
HHR	Henry Huttleston Rogers
JRO	James R. Osgood
JYWM	J.Y.W. MacAlister
MDC	Moncure Daniel Conway
OLC	Olivia Langdon Clemens
PS	Percy Spalding (Chatto & Windus)
WDH	William Dean Howells

(d) the fourth column identifies, wherever possible, the owner of the manuscript. Where a copy has been used instead of the original this is indicated by (ts) for typescript and (photo) for photocopy. The following abbreviations have been used to identify owners:

AC	Mr Andrew Chatto
Berg	The Berg Collection, New York Public Library
BL	The British Library
Bodleian	The Bodleian Library, Oxford
Buffalo	The Lockwood Collection, University of Buffalo
C & W	Chatto & Windus
Cambridge	Cambridge University Library
Columbia	The Conway Collection, The Columbia University Libraries, New York.
Congress	The Library of Congress
Detroit	Detroit Public Library
Folger	The Folger Library, Washington D.C.
Hannibal	The Mark Twain Museum, Hannibal, Mo.
Hartford	The Mark Twain Memorial, Hartford, Ct.
Harvard	Rogers Theater Collection, Harvard University
Houghton	The Houghton Library, Harvard University
Huntington	Henry E. Huntington Library, San Marino, Cal.
Morgan	Pierpont Morgan Library, New York.
MTP	The Mark Twain Papers, University of California Library, Berkeley.
N.L. of S	The National Library of Scotland
Reed	Reed College, Oregon.
Routledge	Routledge & Kegan Paul, London.
Salm	The Collection of Peter A. Salm, New York City.
St. John's	The Doheny Collection, St. John's Seminary.
Shrine	The Mark Twain Birthplace Memorial Shrine, Florida, Mo.
Va.	The Clifton Waller Barrett Library, University of Virginia.
Yale	The Beinecke Library, Yale University.

(e) the final column indicates previous publication in *full* of the letter referred to; no attempt has been made to identify previous quotation from or partial reproduction of letters. The following abbreviations have been used:

Am.Lit. XI	William Bryan Gates, 'Mark Twain to his English Publishers', *American Literature* vol. XI, 1939, pp. 78-80.
CEAANL	*CEAA Newsletter*, an occasional publication of the Center for Editions of American Authors.

CHHR	Mark Twain's Correspondence with Henry Huttleston Rogers 1893-1909, ed. Lewis Leary (The Mark Twain Papers series), 1969.		
LLJCH	Julia Collier Harris, *The Life and Letters of Joel Chandler Harris*, 1918.		
LLMT	*The Love Letters of Mark Twain*, ed. Dixon Wecter, 1949.		
MTHL	*Mark Twain – Howells Letters: the Correspondence of Samuel L. Clemens and William Dean Howells* (2 vols.), ed. Henry Nash Smith and William M. Gibson, 1960.		
MTLP	*Mark Twain's Letters to his Publishers 1867-1894*, ed. Hamlin Hill (The Mark Twain Papers series), 1967.		
MTLW	*Mark Twain the Letter Writer,* ed. Cyril Clemens, 1932.		
MT to Mrs F.	*Mark Twain to Mrs. Fairbanks*, ed. Dixon Wecter, 1949.		
P & A	*Portraits and Autographs: an Album for the People*, ed. W.T. Stead, 1890.		
Paine	*Mark Twain's Letters,* 2 vols., ed. Albert Bigelow Paine, 1917.		
RCN	*Reed College Notes* VIII, April 1946.		

	DATE	ADDRESSEE	OWNED BY	PUBLISHED
	1870			
1.	3 March	EB	MTP (ts)	
2.	11 March	EB	Berg	
	1871			
3.	June	EB	MTP	MTLP no. 47
4.	23 ?	Blamire	Va.	
	1872			
5.		JRO	MTP (ts)	MTLP no. 52
6.	21 [June]	Blamire	Va.	
7.	10 July	Blamire	Routledge	
8.	21 July	Blamire	Va.	
9.	7 August	EB	Yale	MTLP no. 53
10.	11 August	Orion Clemens	MTP	Paine pp.196-7
11.	25 September	OLC	MTP	
12.	6 October	MDC	Columbia	
13.	25 October	OLC	MTP	
14.	2 November	Mrs Fairbanks		MT to Mrs F p.168

15.	3 November	James Redpath	Hartford (ts)	
16.	6 November	Mrs Jane Clemens	MTP	Paine pp.201-2
17.	8 November	*Telegraph*	Va.	
18.	?	MDC	Columbia	

1873

19.	21 April	A.R. Spofford	Congress	
20.	1 July	MDC	Columbia	
21.	14 July	Charles Flower	Folger	
22.	16 July	EB	Yale	MTLP no.57
23.	16 July	Charles Dudley Warner	Yale	MTLP no.58
24.	27 July	T.B. Pugh	Yale	MTLP no.59
25.	?	*Punch*	Morgan	
26.	3 December	OLC	MTP	
27.	9 December	OLC	MTP	
28.	12 December	Robert Routledge	Routledge	
29.	13 December	OLC	MTP	
30.	23 December	OLC	MTP	
31.	25 December	OLC	MTP	

1874

32.	13 February	Charles Kingsley	Va.	
33.	28 February	John Brown	Yale	Paine pp.214-6
34.	26 April	L.J. Jennings	Folger	
35.	27 October	Charles Flower	Folger	

1875

36.	5 July	WDH	Berg	MTHL no.82
37.	5 November	EB	MTP (ts)	MTLP no.72
38.	23 November	WDH	Berg	MTHL no.99
39.	16 December	MDC	Shrine	

1876

40.	5 January	MDC	Shrine	
41.	11 January	WDH	Berg	MTHL no.101
42.	18 January	WDH	Berg	MTHL no.103
43.	9 April	MDC	Columbia	MTLP no.76
44.	16 April	MDC	Columbia	MTLP no.77
45.	24 [July]	MDC	Columbia	
46.	1 August	MDC	Shrine	MTLP no.80
47.	14 August	Eustace Conway	Shrine	
48.	23 August	WDH	Berg	MTHL no.127
49.	28 October	Mrs Conway	Columbia	
50.	2 November	MDC	Columbia	MTLP no.82
51.	13 December	MDC	Columbia	MTLP no.83
52.	29 December	MDC	Columbia	

	1877			
53.	10 January	MDC	Columbia	
54.	6 August	MDC	Columbia	
55.	[August]	EB	MTP	
56.	15 September	Richard Bentley	Va.	
57.	7 November	AC	Va.	
58.	8 November	MDC	Shrine	
59.	10 December	AC	Berg	
	1878			
60.	21 January	MDC	Columbia	
61.	15 March	WDH	Houghton	MTHL no. 185
62.	27 June	WDH	Houghton	MTHL no.192
	1879			
63.	30 January	WDH	Houghton	MTHL no.196
64.	15 April	WDH	Houghton	MTHL no.199
65.	25 April	AC	MTP (ts)	
66.	29 May	AC	Berg	
67.	19 August	AC	Berg	
68.	26 September	A.R. Spofford	Congress	
69.	[November]	General Noyes	Huntington	
	1880			
70.	19 January	MDC	Columbia	MTLP no.95
71.	27 March	C & W	C & W	
72.	20 April	MDC	Berg and Columbia	MTLP no.97
72a.	[April]	C & W	Berg	MTLP p.124
73.	23 April	WDH	Houghton	MTHL no.229
74.	25 April	C & W	C & W	
75.	29 April	WDH	Houghton	MTHL no.231
76.	1 May	C & W	C & W	
77.	1 May	MDC	Columbia	
78.	[May]	FB	MTP	
79.	8 October	MDC	Columbia	
80.	1 December	C & W	MTP (photo)	MTLP No.99
	1881			
81.	30 March	JRO	Berg	MTLP no.104
82.	25 August	C & W	C & W	
83.	2 October	JRO	MTP (ts)	MTLP no.111
84.	7 October	C & W	BL	Am. Lit. XI
85.	1 November	JRO	Harvard	MTLP no.115
86.	11 November	AC	Berg	
87.	27 November	C & W	C & W	

1882

88.	5 February	MDC	MTP (ts)	
89.	23 February	E.H. House	Va.	
90.	3 March	AC	Yale	
91.	29 May	C & W	C & W	
92.	10 June	C & W ?	Berg	
93.	27 October	C & W	Berg	

1883

94.	28 February	C & W	C & W (copy)	
95.	17 May	FB ? or C & W ?	Yale	
96.	11 June	C & W	C & W	
97.	1 September	AC	BL	Am. Lit. XI
98.	12 November	AC	C & W	
99.	21 December	JRO	Harvard	MTLP no.134
100.	?	C & W	C & W	

1884

101.	20 January	CLW	MTP (ts)	
102.	28 February	A.R. Spofford	Congress	
103.	3 March	AC	Va.	
104.	1 April	AC	MTP (ts)	
105.	5 November	C & W ?	Va.	
106.	December	AC		MTLW p.24

1885

107.	11 March	AC	C & W	
108.	8 September	C & W	C & W	
109.	[November]	Joel Chandler Harris		LLJCH p.566

1886

110.	2 June	AC	C & W	
111.	12 July	C & W	C & W	
112.	15 July	E.O. Somerville	Houghton	
113.	14 September	AC	C & W	

1887

114.	19 February	AC	C & W	
115.	1 March	CLW		MTLP no.175
116.	3 August	CLW	Berg	MTLP no.182
117.	15 August	FJH & CLW	Berg	MTLP no.183
118.	19 September	AC	C & W	
119.	19 September	C & W	C & W	
120.	5 December	C & W	MTP	Paine p.493

1888

121.	8 January	C & W	C & W	

122.	16 January	C & W	C & W	
123.	14 February	AC	MTP (photo)	
124.	7 March	AC	C & W	
125.	[March]	C & W	C & W	
126.	6 June	AC	C & W	
127.	15 July	CLW	Berg	MTLP no.199
128.	15 July	AC	Va.	
129.	17 September	AC	BL	Am. Lit. XI

1889

130.	16 July	AC	C & W	Paine pp.524-5 (variant)
131.	24 July	FJH	Congress	MTLP no.204
132.	20 August	FJH	Va.	MTLP no.205
133.	21 August	C & W	C & W	
134.	28 August	Dan Beard	Congress	
135.	5 September	FJH	Berg	MTLP no.206
136.	11 November	Dan Beard	Congress	
137.	6 December	C & W	C & W	
138.	20 December	?	Congress	
139.	[December]	C & W	C & W	

1890

140.	27 February	Daniel Whitford	MTP	
141.	17 March	W.T. Stead		P & A p.63
142.	15 December	FJH	Berg	

1891

143.	28 February	WDH	Berg	MTHL no.506
144.	29 March	AC	C & W	
145.	29 March	Bram Stoker	Berg	
146.	4 April	WDH	Berg	MTHL no.511
147.	13 May	FJH	Berg	MTLP no.224
148.	20 May	FJH	Berg	MTLP no.226
149.	12 July	AC	C & W	
150.	18 July	AC	C & W	
151.	25 July	AC	C & W	
152.	26 July	FJH	Berg	MTLP no.229
153.	15 August	AC	C & W	
154.	7 October	C & W	Va.	
155.	9 October	C & W	Berg	
156.	20 October	FJH	Berg	MTLP no.234
157.	27 October	FJH	Huntington	MTLP no.235
158.	28 October	FJH	Huntington	MTLP no.236
159.	22 November	C & W	MTP (ts)	
160.	20 December (OLC)	C & W	Berg	

161.	22 December	C & W	C & W	
162.	27 December (OLC)	C & W	Berg	
	1892			
163.	12 January	FJH ?	Berg	
164.	27 January	C & W	BL	Am. Lit. XI
165.	2 February	FJH	Berg	MTLP no.247
166.	27 March	C & W	MTP (ts)	
167.	24 April	FJH	Berg	MTLP no.252
168.	13 October	FJH	Berg	MTLP no.261
169.	10 November	C & W	Berg	
170.	24 November	FJH	Berg	MTLP no.264
	1893			
171.	30 April (OLC)	C & W	Berg	
172.	23 May	C & W	Va.	
173.	12 June	C & W	MTP (ts)	
174.	5 August	C & W	MTP (photo)	
175.	14 August	FJH	Berg	MTLP no.289
176.	18 August	C & W	MTP (ts)	
	1894			
177.	17 June	C & W	C & W	
178.	2 July	C & W	Yale	
179.	4 July	AC	Berg	
180.	6 July (OLC)	C & W	C & W	
181.	2 September	HHR	Congress	CHHR no.35
	1895			
182.	3 January	HHR	Congress	CHHR no.62
183.	21 January	HHR	Salm	CHHR no.64
184.	8 February	HHR	Congress	CHHR no.68
185.	4 April	C & W	Va.	
186.	7 May	AC	C & W	
187.	June (OLC)	C & W	C & W	
188.	11 June	HHR	MTP	CHHR no.82
189.	13 June	FB	Hartford (ts)	
	1896			
190.	10 March (OLC)	C & W	Berg	
191.	31 July	C & W	Berg	
192.	7 August (Clara)	C & W	Berg	
193.	[August] (Clara)	C & W	Berg	
194.	14 August	C & W	Berg	

195.	16 August	OLC	MTP (ts)	LLMT pp.317-9
196.	19 August	C & W ?	Berg	
197.	10 September	HHR	Salm	CHHR no.136
198.	20 September	HHR	Salm	CHHR no.137
199.	6 October	HHR	Salm	CHHR no.139
200.	29 October	C & W	Va.	
201.	31 October	C & W	Va.	
202.	2 November	Bram Stoker	Berg	
203.	13 November	C & W	Berg	
204.	[18 November]	C & W	Huntington	
205.	[13 ? November]	AC jr.	AC	
206.	[16/17 ? November] (Clara)	AC jr.	AC	
207.	22 November	AC jr.	AC	
208.	23 November (Jean)	AC jr.	AC	
209.	30 November (OLC)	AC jr.	AC	
210.	18 December (OLC)	C & W	Berg	
211.	23 December (OLC)	C & W	Berg	
212.	24 December	C & W	Berg	
213.	December (OLC)	C & W	Berg	
214.	? (Clara)	C & W	Berg	
	1897			
215.	19 January	FB	Berg	
216.	1 February	C & W	Berg	
217.	2 February	Lord Mayor	Houghton	
218.	3 February (OLC)	C & W	Berg	
219.	23 February	WDH	Berg	MTHL no.526
220.	26 February	HHR	Salm	CHHR no.157
221.	3 March	- Burgess	Detroit	
222.	9 March (OLC)	C & W	Berg	
223.	19 March	FB	Berg	
224.	26 March	FB	Yale	
225.	1 April (OLC)	C & W	Berg	
226.	14 April	C & W	Berg	
227.	14 April	JYWM	Berg	
228.	16 April	C & W	Berg	
229.	24 April	C & W	Berg	
230.	26-28 April	HHR	Salm	CHHR no.164
231.	3 May	FB	Berg	

232.	7 May	C & W	Berg	
232a.	18 May	HHR	Salm	CHHR no.165
233.	3 June	HHR	Salm	CHHR no.166
234.	15 June	C & W	Berg	
235.	22 June	PS	Berg	
235a.	?	C & W	Berg	
236.	[26 ? June]	C & W	Va.	
237.	?	C & W	Va.	
238.	2 July	FB ?	MTP (ts)	
239.	19 July	C & W	Berg	
240.	22 July	C & W	MTP	CEAANL no. 3
241.	23 July	C & W	MTP (photo)	
242.	24 July	C & W	MTP (photo)	
243.	25 July	C & W	Va.	CEAANL no. 1
244.	27 July	FB	Berg	
245.	30 July	AC	Buffalo	
246.	31 July	C & W	Berg	
247.	9 August	C & W	Berg	
248.	[c.16 August]	C & W	Va.	CHHR p.295
249.	29 September	C & W	Va.	
250.	2 October (Clara)	C & W	Berg	
251.	23 October	C & W	MTP (ts)	
252.	11 November	C & W	Berg	
253.	19 November*	C & W	Berg	
254.	20 November	PS	Yale	
255.	? (OLC)	C & W	Berg	
256.	2 December (OLC)	C & W	Berg	
256a.	9 December (OLC)	C & W	Berg	
257.	16 December	FB	Reed	RCN
258.	23 December	C & W	C & W	
	1898			
259.	10 January (OLC)	C & W	C & W	
260.	12 January (OLC)	C & W	Berg	
261.	19 January (OLC)	C & W	Berg	
262.	20 January	HHR	Salm	CHHR no.189
263.	22 January	WDH	Houghton	MTHL no.528
264.	8 February	C & W	Va.	
265.	11 February	FB	Reed	RCN

266.	22 February	Walter Besant	Berg	
267.	26 February	C & W	Va.	
268.	3 March	James M. Tuohy	St. John's	
269.	15 March	HHR	Salm	CHHR no.196
270.	22 March	HHR	Salm	CHHR no.198
271.	21 April (OLC)	C & W	Berg	

*The date '1895' on this letter is an obvious error. Cf. CHHR p. 287 fn.1

272.	7 May	Richard Gilder	Yale	
273.	17 May	C & W	Berg	
274.	10 June	HHR	Salm	CHHR no.206
275.	29 June	C & W	Berg	
276.	[August]			
	(Clara)	C & W	Berg	
277.	11 August	?	Va.	
278.	13 September			
	(OLC)	C & W	Berg	
278a.	24 September			
	(OLC)	C & W	Berg	
279.	26 September	C & W	Berg	
280.	1 October	HHR	Salm	CHHR no.215
281.	12 October	C & W	Berg	
282.	6-7 November	HHR	Salm	CHHR no.218
283.	13 November	C & W	C & W	
284.	19 November	C & W	C & W	
	1899			
285.	1-11 March	J.K.Bangs		MTLW
286.	2 April	C & W	Berg	
287.	10 April	C & W	Berg	
288.	2-13 April	WDH	Berg	MTHL no.535
289.	25 April	C & W	Berg	
290.	4 May	C & W	Berg	
291.	10 May	PS	MTP (ts)	
292.	23 May	C & W	Berg	
293.	24 May	PS	MTP (ts)	
294.	25 May	C & W	Berg	
295.	31 May	C & W	Berg	
296.	1 June (OLC)	AC	Berg	
297.	4 June	C & W	Va.	
298.	6 June	HHR	Salm	CHHR no.230
299.	7 June	PS	Berg	
300.	9 June	C & W	Berg	
301.	June	C & W	Berg	
302.	[18 June]	C & W	Berg	
303.	24 June	Wm. Knight ?	Morgan	

304.	25 June	HHR	Salm	CHHR no.231
305.	30 June (OLC)	AC	Berg	
306.	5 July	Martin Conway	Cambridge	
307.	6 July	PS	Berg	
308.	20 August (Clara)	C & W	Berg	
308a.	23 August (Clara)	C & W	Berg	
309.	7 September (OLC)	C & W	C & W	
310.	15 September	F.H. Skrine	Yale	
311.	24 September	AC	Berg	
312.	4 October	HHR	Salm	CHHR no.237
313.	17 October	PS	Berg	

1900

314.	22 February	FB	Yale
315.	21 March	James Bryce	Bodleian
316.	30 March	FB	MTP (ts)
317.	2 April	C & W	C & W
318.	17 April	William James	Houghton
319.	23 April	William James	Houghton
320.	18 September	FB	Hartford

1901

321.	1 January	Irving Underhill	Berg
322.	21 January	W.T. Stead	Va.
323.	25 January	C & W	C & W
324.	10 March	MDC	Columbia

1902

325.	7 January	F.H. Skrine	N.L. of S.
326.	19 April	C & W	C & W
327.	22 November	C & W	C & W
328.	15 December	PS	Va.

1904

329.	22 November	JYWM	Detroit

1907

330.	21 February	JYWM	Berg
331.	30 June	Jean Clemens	Hannibal
332.	4 July	George Bernard Shaw	Va.

1910

333.	12 March	Clara Gabrilowitsch (née Clemens)	Hannibal

NOTES

Chapter I

1. See p. 25 below.
2. *Mark Twain's Speeches* ed. A.B. Paine (1929) p.186.
3. Dewey Ganzel, 'Samuel Clemens and John Camden Hotten', *The Library*, Fifth Series, XX, September 1965, 230-242.
4. A copy of this letter, dated 21 May 1872, is in the Mark Twain Papers at the University of California, Berkeley, (cited hereafter as 'MTP').
5. Autograph note on the fly-leaf of the copy of *The Piccadilly Annual* (1870) owned by the Lilly Library, Indiana University, Bloomington.
6. Margaret Duckett, *Mark Twain and Bret Harte* (1964) p.84.
7. Dennis Welland, 'John Camden Hotten and Emerson's Uncollected Essays', *Yearbook of English Studies,* 6, 1976, 156-175.
8. 'Dod Grile' was Ambrose Bierce. See M.E. Grenander, 'Ambrose Bierce, John Camden Hotten, *The Fiend's Delight*, and *Nuggets and Dust'*. *Huntington Library Quarterly,* XXVIII, 1964/5, 353-371.
9. Clyde K. Hyder, *Swinburne's Literary Career and Fame* (1933) p.43.
10. The anecdote was told to me by Ian Parsons when he was Chairman of Chatto & Windus.
11. Manuscript in the Pierpont Morgan Library, New York.

Chapter 2

1. *Mark Twain's Letters to His Publishers 1867-1894,* ed. Hamlin Hill (1967) pp. 54, 83-85, (cited hereafter as *MTLP*).
2. MTP.
3. Original in the Clifton Waller Barrett Collection, University of Virginia Library.
4. Clifton Waller Barrett Collection, University of Virginia Library.
5. Henry Nash Smith, ' "That Hideous Mistake of Poor Clemens's" ', *Harvard Library Bulletin*, 9, 1955, 145-180.
6. Arthur L. Scott, 'Mark Twain's Revisions of *The Innocents Abroad* for the British Edition of 1872', *American Literature*, 25, 1953, 43-61.
7. Contract in the Beinecke Library, Yale University.

8. *The Bookseller,* 1 September 1870 p.761; *The Athenaeum,* 24 September pp. 395-396; *The Saturday Review,* 8 October pp. 467-468.

9. Dennis Welland, 'Mark Twain the Great Victorian', *Chicago Review,* 9, 1955, 101-109. Eliot's essay on Tennyson formed the Introduction to a selection of his poems in 1936 and was collected in *Selected Essays* (1951). His essay on *Huckleberry Finn* formed the Introduction to Cresset Press edition in 1950.

10. The letter from Bliss is owned by Chatto & Windus; it is dated 25 March 1881.

11. See Guinevere L. Griest, *Mudie's Circulating Library and the Victorian Novel* (1970), especially pp 179-180 and 199-201.

12. The letter, dated 21 January 1874, is in MTP.

13. Van Wyck Brooks, *The Ordeal of Mark Twain* (1920).

14. The reviews of *The Gilded Age* referred to will be found in *The Standard,* 29 December 1873 and *The Athenaeum* 10 January 1874; those of *Democracy* in *Blackwood's Edinburgh Magazine* May 1882, *The Athenaeum* 24 June 1882, *The Fortnightly Review* 1 July 1882, *The Edinburgh Review* July 1882, *The Westminster Review* October 1882.

Chapter 3

1. Blamire's letters (dated 26 July, 6,9, and 15 August 1872) are in MTP. Clemens's side of this correspondence after 21 July has not survived but can be inferred from Blamire's replies.

2. See Aaron Watson, *The Savage Club* (1907) Chapter XII, pp. 131-135.

3. This notebook recorded impressions of England for Livy's benefit. My quotations are taken from a typescript in MTP.

4. It was published under the title 'British Benevolence' on 27 January 1873.

5. See Moncure Daniel Conway, *Autobiography: Memoirs and Experiences of Moncure Daniel Conway,* 2 vols., (1904) (cited hereafter as 'MDC Autobiog.'); and Mary Elizabeth Burtis, *Moncure Conway,* 1832-1907 (1952).

6. MTP.

7. Clemens's copy of the *Autobiography,* to which subsequent references will also be made, was shown to me at Perry, Missouri, in 1968, by Chester L. Davis, editor of *The Twainian.* He had published descriptions of it and some of Clemens's marginalia in *The Twainian* for September/October 1953, November/December 1953, and January/February 1954.

8. The letter, dated 6 December 1876, is in the Folger Library, Washington, D.C.

9. *Lectures and Essays by the late William Kingdon Clifford*, ed. Leslie Stephen and Frederick Pollock (1879).

10. See *The Autobiography of Mark Twain*, ed. Charles Neider (1961) Chapter 38, (cited hereafter as 'Neider').

11. Edith Colgate Salsbury, *Susy and Mark Twain: Family Dialogues* (1965) p.23.

12. Fred W. Lorch, *The Trouble Begins at Eight: Mark Twain's Lecture Tours* (1966); Charles Warren Stoddard, *Exits and Entrances* (1903).

13. Both letters are in MTP. Smalley's is dated 9 December.

14. H.R. Haweis, *American Humorists* (1882) pp. 172-173.

15. MTP.

16. Howard G. Baetzhold, *Mark Twain and John Bull: The British Connection* (1970) p.370, (cited hereafter as 'Baetzhold').

17. Quoted in *The Adventures of Colonel Sellers*, ed. Charles Neider (1965) p. xxix. Baetzhold (p.327) identifies this as the piece referred to in Shirley Brooks's letter of 14 December mentioned above.

18. MTP.

19. MTP.

20. *The Twainian* January/February 1954.

21. Aaron Watson, *The Savage Club* (1907).

22. 'After-Dinner Speech', in *Sketches New and Old* (vol. xix of the Author's National Edition of Mark Twain's works) pp. 234-7. The manuscript, in the Beinecke Library of Yale University, is attributed to 1872 but 1873 seems more likely. In the penultimate sentence the manuscript refers correctly to Charles II (the printed source has 'Charles I') and I have followed this in my quotation.

Chapter 4

1. The information in these two paragraphs is based primarily on Salsbury, *Susy and Mark Twain*, pp. 28-36 and the quotations are also taken from there.

2. This and all other communications from Conway to Clemens cited in this chapter are in MTP unless otherwise stated.

3. MDC Autobiog.

4. *Ibid.*

5. *Ibid.* I pp. 257-258.

6. Howells to Clemens, 21 November 1875, in *Mark Twain – Howells Letters* ed. Henry Nash Smith and William M. Gibson, (2 vols. 1960) I p. 110 (cited hereafter as MTHL).

7. This letter is at the Mark Twain Memorial Shrine, Florida, Missouri.

8. MDC Autobiog. II p.132.

9. MTHL *loc. cit.*

10. 24 March 1876. MTP.

11. Letter of 24 March 1876. MTP.

12. Letter of 24 March 1876. MTP.

13. I first called attention to this in 'A Note on Some Early Reviews of *Tom Sawyer*', *Journal of American Studies* I, 1967, 99-103.

14. Letters of 6 May and 10 August 1876.

15. MDC letter of 10 August 1876.

16. See p. 80 above. It appeared in the issue of 19 December.

17. See *The Twainian* July/August 1947.

Chapter 5

1. The sources on which I have drawn in this book are, in addition to the firm's letter-books, Oliver Warner's introduction to their centenary volume, *A Century of Writers 1855-1955*; Frank Swinnerton's recollections in *Swinnerton: An Autobiography* (1937), *Background with Chorus* (1956), and a letter to me; 'Celebrities at Home: No. DCCCLXXIX: Mr Andrew Chatto at Piccadilly and at Cumberland Terrace, Regent's Park' in *The World* 17 April 1895; 'The Great Publishing Houses: VI: Chatto & Windus' in *T.P.'s Weekly* 11 October 1912; obituaries in the press at the time of his death; and recollections of members of his family, by whom my attention was drawn to the last three items listed here.

2. Such information about Windus as comes from sources not listed in the preceding note will be found in obituary notices in *The Times*, 9 and 10 June 1910.

3. The letter dated 27 September [1879] and another dated 26 February [1880] are still in the firm's possession.

4. The firm does not have Gissing's letter but only Chatto's reply. Bentley's comment is quoted in R.A. Gettman, *A Victorian Publisher* (1960) p.220.

5. The originals of these ten letters to Chatto are in the Huntington Library: the text will be found in Cecil Y. Lang (ed), *The Swinburne Letters* (1959). See also Jean Overton Fuller, *Swinburne* (1968) pp. 201-6, 279, 292 etc.

6. *The Swinburne Letters* vol. 4, p.78.

7. The letter, dated 15 December 1876, is in MTP, as are those dated 16 and 28 November 1876 mentioned in my next paragraphs.

8. The letters, dated 1 and 4 January 1878, are in MTP.

9. Routledge to Clemens, 26 April 1876, in MTP.

10. *MTLP* pp.112-113.

11. *Mark Twain's Notebooks and Journals* ed. Frederick Anderson *et al.* (1976) vol. II, 1877-1883, pp.333-339, (cited hereafter as *Notebooks*).

12. This letter is owned by Chatto & Windus. It is not mentioned by Hamlin Hill in *MTLP* or in *Mark Twain and Elisha Bliss*, so presumably no copy was kept by Bliss.

13. Dated April 1880 and, like the letter mentioned in fn. 12, owned by Chatto & Windus.

14. Like other letters in this sequence, this is also in the possession of Chatto & Windus.

15. 15 December 1880, in the Berg Collection, New York Public Library.

16. 20 December 1880, MTP.

17. *MTLP* p.104. It must be emphasised that the key letters owned by Chatto & Windus and described or quoted in the present chapter had not been seen by Hill.

18. MTP.

Chapter 6

1. MTP owns a press cutting from the *Cincinnati Enquirer* which gives this information on the authority of an interview with Mark Twain. Place of publication and the emphasis on this method of issuing books suggest Conway as a possible author of it.

2. See R.A. Gettman, *A Victorian Publisher*, pp.108-109 and Asa Briggs, ed., *Essays in the History of Publishing* (1974) p.147.

3. Neider, Chap. 44.

4. A fragment of a letter attributed to Henley (Huntington Library, HM 722) claims the authorship of this 'crackling review', as I first pointed out in a footnote to 'A Note on Some Early Reviews of *Tom Sawyer*' (*Journal of American Studies* 1, 1967, 100).

5. Both letters (4 May and 20 December 1880) are in MTP.

6. MTP.

7. MTP.

8. Her letters to him are in MTP.

9. *MTHL* I p.434.

10. Bellows's letter of 24 April 1883 which is thus annotated, and his letter of thanks dated 6th June, are in MTP.

11. Letter dated 5 August 1884. MTP.

12. Original in MTP.

13. Letter dated 21 March 1884. MTP.

14. Webster's letter of 5 April 1884 is owned by Chatto & Windus, as are his letters of 20 June and 19 September cited in my next paragraph.

15. This letter, also dated 22 August, is in MTP.

16. MTP has references to a letter of 15 April 1888 in which Clemens

expressed his satisfaction at Stevenson's views; the letter from the Scottish Society of Literature and Art of 27 September 1886 is in MTP.

17. *Notebooks* II, p.68.

18. Justin Kaplan, *Mr Clemens and Mark Twain* (1966) Chapter XI, section III. The meeting with James and Whistler is referred to in the same place.

19. *Notebooks* II, p.335.

20. *Notebooks* II, pp.293-339.

21. A limited edition of 100 copies of this address was privately printed in 1952.

22. The letter is in MTP. See also Baetzhold p.72.

23. *Notebooks* II, p.64.

24. Notebook for 24 October 1890 – 14 June 1891 (not yet published). MTP.

25. Notebook for May 1883 – September 1884 (not yet published). MTP.

26. Notebook for 4 April – 8 August 1885 (not yet published). MTP.

27. *Notebooks* II, p.461.

28. *Notebooks* II, p.163.

29. MDC *Autobiog.* II, p.146.

30. Arlin Turner, *Mark Twain and George W. Cable: the Record of a Literary Friendship* (1960), pp.43-114.

Chapter 7

1. The letter, undated but postmarked 25 May, is in MTP.

2. The Dickens letters are in MTP.

3. Letter of 12 August 1886 from George Standing, printer and publisher, to Clemens in MTP.

4. A.B. Paine, *Mark Twain. A Biography* (1912), vol. II, pp.887-888.

5. Letter of 14 October 1890 from C.M. Dally of New York to Clemens in MTP.

6. A.B. Paine, ed., *Mark Twain's Letters* (1917) vol. II pp. 523-525.

7. *MTHL* II, p.612.

8. The letter is owned by Chatto & Windus.

9. Marginal note on letter from Hall dated 29 July 1889 in MTP.

10. Marginal note on letter from Hall dated 16 October 1889 in MTP.

11. Baetzhold, Chapter 7.

12. Letter dated 1 February 1890 – MTP.

Chapter 8

1. Baetzhold, pp.280-283. The reference to Byron is quoted by Van Wyck Brooks in *The Ordeal of Mark Twain*, Chapter I.
2. *A Connecticut Yankee in King Arthur's Court*, Chapter XVIII.
3. Letter dated 25 June 1888. MTP.
4. Neider, Chap. 51.
5. Clemens's side of this correspondence has not survived.
6. Letter dated 17 January 1890. MTP.
7. Paul Fatout, 'Mark Twain, Litigant', *American Literature* 31, 1959, 30-45.
8. Letter dated 12 April 1890. MTP.

Chapter 9

1. Notebook for 21 September – 3 December 1896 (not yet published). MTP.
2. Dennis Welland, 'Mark Twain's Last Travel Book', *Bulletin of the New York Public Library*, 69, 1965, 31-48. This article treats the subject in closer bibliographical detail than the present chapter, which, however, adds one or two minor pieces of information not available to me in 1965.
3. Paul J. Carter Jr., 'Olivia Clemens Edits *Following the Equator*', *American Literature* 30, 1958, 194-209.
4. The manuscript is owned by the Berg Collection of the New York Public Library, as is the typescript copy which was prepared for the American publisher (not for the British, as Carter conjectures in the article cited in fn. 3). It will be seen from Appendix II that much of the relevant correspondence is also in the Berg Collection.
5. The letter is owned by Chatto & Windus; that it is not mentioned by Lewis Leary in *Mark Twain's Correspondence with Henry Huttleston Rogers* suggests that no copy was retained by Bliss.
6. Letter dated 6 July 1897 in the Beinecke Library, Yale University.
7. Chatto to Clemens 2 August 1898; Clemens's letter containing the suggestion does not seem to have survived.

Chapter 10

1. Notebook for January 1897, (not yet published). MTP.
2. Notebook entry dated 24 May 1897, (not yet published). MTP.
3. Justin Kaplan, *Mr Clemens and Mark Twain*, Chapter 16, section III.

4. In a letter dated 21 April 1913 to Andrew Chatto Jr. on the death of his father, still in the possession of the family.

5. It is reprinted in Arthur L. Scott, *On the Poetry of Mark Twain* (1966), pp. 123-125.

6. Webster debited Clemens's account 67c. in respect of this on 27 May 1884 (accounts in MTP).

7. The book is in MTP.

8. Baetzhold, p. 238.

9. Letter dated 15 September 1899. MTP.

10. This arrangement is confirmed in Chatto's letter to Clemens dated 27 November 1903; Clemens's letter authorising it does not seem to have survived.

11. Notebook entry dated 14 November 1903, (not yet published). MTP.

Chapter 11

1. Manuscript in the Pierpont Morgan Library, New York.

2. Letter dated 5 September 1876 in MTP. Printed in Margaret Duckett, *Bret Harte and Mark Twain* p.99.

3. Letters dated 6 December 1876 and 28 December 1878. MTP.

4. Letter dated 26 September 1882. MTP.

5. Letter dated 21 February 1883 owned by Chatto & Windus, as are all Tauchnitz letters quoted, unless otherwise stated.

6. Letters from Tauchnitz to Clemens dated 31 March and 7 May 1883. MTP.

7. This letter from Tauchnitz, dated 29th February 1892, is in the Houghton Library, Harvard University.

8. Letter in MTP.

9. Dictation of 25 October 1907. MTP.

10. Telegram dated 17 April 1876. MTP.

11. Reproduced in Milton Meltzer, ed. *Mark Twain Himself: a Pictorial Biography* (1960) p. 153.

12. Letter dated 6 December 1889. MTP.

13. *MTHL* I, pp.97 ff.

14. Letter dated 13 March [   ] in Library of Congress.

15. Letter dated 5 November 1884. MTP.

16. Letter dated 5 April 1900. MTP.

Chapter 12

1. Neider, Chap. 55.
2. Kaplan, *Mr Clemens and Mark Twain*, chapter 17, section III.
3. *Pall Mall Magazine*, 16, 1898, 28-36.
4. William Archer, 'America and the English Language', *Pall Mall Magazine*, 16, 1899, 231-235.
5. Letters dated 16 October 1899 and 16 April 1900. MTP.
6. Letter dated 19 May 1899. MTP
7. A notebook entry in 1896, (not yet published). MTP.
8. Letter dated 20 January 1899, tipped into a copy of *Following the Equator* presented by Clemens to Twichell and now in the Beinecke Library, Yale University.
9. Entry for 17 June 1899 in a diary now owned by the University Library, Cambridge.
10. Aaron Watson, *The Savage Club*, Chapter XI.
11. *Kiplingiana* (New York, 1899) pp. 115-116.
12. Copies of those for 1898 and 1899 are owned by the Victoria and Albert Museum, London.
13. Owned by the Detroit Public Library, Michigan.
14. 'Mark Twain, Some Personal Reminiscences', *The Landmark*, 20, 1938, 141-147.
15. Letter dated 2 June 1900. MTP.
16. From a booklet reprinting the speeches, in the Beinecke Library, Yale University.
17. The menu is in the Mark Twain Museum, Hannibal, Missouri.
18. Reproduced in Baetzhold, p.249.
19. Letter dated 29 December 1906. MTP.
20. Letter dated 9 October 1909. MTP.
21. Letter dated 21 June 1886. MTP.
22. Information from entries in the Martin Conway diary at Cambridge University Library.
23. Letter undated, postmarked 7 June 1904. MTP.
24. Letter dated 6 December 1905. MTP.
25. Letter dated 9 January 1907. MTP.
26. Letter, undated. MTP.
27. Letter from Spalding dated 9 January 1908.
28. Letter from Mary E. Cheesewright, dated 21 October 1889. MTP.
29. In *The Mississippian*, 17 March 1922. Quoted in Joseph Blotner, *Faulkner: A Biography*, 1974, vol. I, p. 333.

INDEX

N.B.   Titles of newspapers and periodicals referred to are listed alphabetically under 'Periodicals' and not individually in the body of the Index.